What Others Are Saying about Ana Tampanna's message...

"This book strikes a universal chord in the psyche of American women. We relate to Ana's struggles as she searches for approval in a culture obsessed with thinness, and we applaud her as she learns to define beauty in her own terms. Ana, thank you for offering your wit and wisdom to all of us who are overstressed!"

—HELEN NAPLES AND LOIS GARDNER, OWNERS,
WOMEN'S WELLNESS & FITNESS CENTERS,
INTERNATIONAL AWARD WINNERS AND
EXPERTS ON WOMEN'S HEALTH AND FITNESS

"Ana has captured the true spirit of sisterhood with wit and wisdom. Through her willingness to share she has validated all women who seek to heal the world."

—DELORES "D" SMITH, ED.D,
PRESIDENT/CEO OF THE
WINSTON-SALEM URBAN LEAGUE

"Delightful book encouraging women-to-women networking and activation of your wisdom! The author's insights will empower you."

—PRISCILLA V. MAROTTA, PH.D.,
AUTHOR OF *POWER AND WISDOM:
THE NEW PATH FOR WOMEN*

"Ana Tampanna is one of the World's most creative people. Her unique ability to teach while we laugh is almost unmatched."

—PATRICIA FRIPP CSP, CPAE
AUTHOR, KEYNOTER, EXECUTIVE SPEECH COACH
AUTHOR OF *GET WHAT YOU WANT*

"Ana Tampanna ignites the inner drive to experience all life has to offer, while inspiring us to nurture the inner self. She delights her audiences and makes the meeting planner look good."

—PATRICIA CHIVERS
FLORIDA LOBBYIST

"I crave stories of how other women are "doing" it—how we are each crafting a life of meaning and beauty. Ana Tampanna offers her story with verve and honesty. What a treat!"

—JENNIFER LOUDEN, AUTHOR OF
THE WOMAN'S RETREAT BOOK AND
THE COMFORT QUEEN'S GUIDE TO LIFE

"Ana's presentation was motivating, refreshing, and FUN. Her ability to involve the audience through practical exercises was outstanding. Her discussion of what individuals need to work effectively in an organization was on target. This was a professionally motivating presentation."

—DONNA BENNINGER
EXECUTIVE DIRECTOR OF MEMBERSHIP
WINSTON-SALEM CHAMBER OF COMMERCE

"Ana has a wonderful style of teaching life's lessons from which we can all benefit in a most illustrative, entertaining, funny, light-hearted, heart-warming, and sensitive fashion."

—SHARY GARD
TALLAHASSEE, FL

"Our women's retreat was life changing. Ana was both entertaining and educational. We couldn't have had a more inspirational weekend. Many Anaisms continue to affect my life in a positive way a year later!"

—JEAN WHITEHEAD, BSN,RN
REGISTERED NURSE

The Womanly Art of
Alligator
Wrestling

Inspirational Stories
for Outrageous Women
Who Survive by Their Wisdom and Wit

Ana Tampanna

Silsby Publishing Company
WINSTON-SALEM, NORTH CAROLINA

Although the author and publisher have made every effort to ensure the accuracy and completeness of information contained in this book, we assume no responsibility for errors, inaccuracies, omissions, or any inconsistency herein. Any slights of people, places, or organizations are unintentional. The poem entitled "A Woman's Place" is printed by permission of the author, RaVonda Dalton-Rann.

First printing 2002
Second printing 2002

ISBN 0-9710321-4-9

LCCN 2001126044

ATTENTION CORPORATIONS, UNIVERSITIES, COLLEGES, AND PROFESSIONAL ORGANIZATIONS: Quantity discounts are available on bulk purchases of this book for educational, gift purposes, or as premiums for increasing magazine subscriptions or renewals. Special books or book excerpts can also be created to fit specific needs. For information, please contact Silsby Publishing Company, P.O.Box 5243, Winston-Salem, NC 27113-5243; ph 336-794-0065.

To EJ Burgay,
A Champion Alligator Wrestler

ACKNOWLEDGMENTS

As a teller of life stories, I have been inspired and encouraged by particular role models I have met through the National Speakers Association. Glenna Salsbury, CSP,CPAE; Patricia Fripp, CSP, CPAE; Nancy Coey; Kay Johnson, CSP, Emery Austin, CSP,CPAE; Aldonna Ambler, CSP, Nan Leaptrott, and Ernie Wendell are all incredible speakers and trainers who openly share their knowledge and wisdom with others. Because of them, I felt encouraged to tell my stories, both spoken and written.

I tested my writing first on my inner circle of family and friends who never tired of listening. Jana Curran, David Scruggs, and Allison Brandy have been a patient and receptive audience and have given me permission to share parts of their lives in this book. Ann Tyndall, Ph.D. not only listened but affirmed me endlessly. Cynthia Curtis shared with me her perspective as an African American while we connected as mothers and Girl Scout leaders.

My mother, Margaret Scruggs, taught me basics of writing and lovingly edited and re-edited my first efforts. She is my number one cheerleader and my creative partner in circuses, costumed productions, parties, and business ventures.

My very special thanks to the lay readers who read my first draft of this book, giving me their honest reactions, suggestions, and corrections. They are: Connie Mann, Nan Leaptrott, Mary Jamis, Rebecca Terry, Bambi Stoll, Karen Binkley, Allison Brandy, Lynn Reister, Martha Jones, Laura Graban, Debra James, and Jan Sawyer. Pat Speaks tweaked the final copy. Patricia Poe, my editor, then wove her magic touch throughout and provided the wonderful editing that brought professional polish to the final copy.

My devoted husband, Robert, and my children, Simone and John, have loved and supported me, listened to my stories, and adapted to a tighter budget when I left my business to write. Robert not only cleans the house, but also holds a vision of success for this book. My father, Richard Scruggs, brings sweetness to life in his later years that communicate his unconditional love with or without words.

I thank Joan Wilkins, Ph.D. for her deep wisdom and Patricia Chivers and Sara Roberts who invested in me as employers and touched me deeply as friends.

Jamina Johnson and my goddaughter, Jeanne Elizabeth Bond, are young women who wrestle alligators of their own with determination and talent. They are the new breed of independent, assertive women, rooted in their faith, who have supported me as well.

Organizations have nurtured my growth and strengthened my wrestling muscle. First Presbyterian Church of Tallahassee as well as Unity of Tallahassee and Parkway United Church of Christ in Winston-Salem have provided me with loving church communities. World Wide Marriage Encounter with our Couples Circles in Tallahassee and Winston-Salem helped my husband and me to wrestle alligators of enormous proportions. The Girl Scouts of the United States of America empower girls and provide women with incredible leadership opportunities. The YWCA of Winton-Salem and the Winston-Salem Urban League fight racism while enabling women to connect on a heart to heart level. All have opened my eyes to new possibilities, and to the loving energy of people on a spiritual path. And finally, the Women's Wellness and Fitness Centers helped me keep my sanity throughout this project.

TABLE OF CONTENTS

Dinner Parties for Sharing Wisdom and Outrageous Stories

*There was no way for me to understand it
at the time, but the talk that filled the kitchen
those afternoons was highly functional. It served as
therapy, the cheapest kind available to my mother and
her friends…But more than therapy, that freewheeling,
wide-ranging, exuberant talk functioned as an outlet
for the tremendous creative energy they possessed.*

—PAULA MARSHALL, *THE MAKING OF A WRITER:
FROM THE POETS IN THE KITCHEN*

This is a book for women on a quest to find their personal mission and the creative expression of their hearts' delight. Women in harmony on a similar journey strengthen each other as we each share our unique blend of wit, wisdom, and resourcefulness, which is the essence of women.

This book is also for women who seek freedom from the cultural binds that confine us to a frantic gallop, going nowhere, like hamsters on a running wheel. We blindly pursue mythical promises of beauty, security, and success, yet few of us feel as if we ever achieve those goals.

As I struggled on my own quest, I became aware of the need for validation. My neediness appalled me at first until I came to terms with it. After reading Ann Wilson Schaef's book, *Women's Reality*, I understand in a much clearer light how that need is a normal reaction to living in a world controlled by a white male system. Women are just now learning about the courage, wit, and wisdom of their female ancestors who historians neglected to include in our textbooks. Our support, input, and contributions have not been validated for centuries. Yes, we have made progress, but this is the exception and not the rule. As I listen to other women, I hear their need for validation as well. Brilliant, creative, extraordinary women are craving validation from a society that values money, power, sex, and male athletics—is it any wonder we continue to feel needy?

Ann Wilson Schaef celebrates with us the emerging "female system," a system where women of different backgrounds and different races connect with each other. This female system fosters loving relationships, facilitative leadership, personal growth, and peace. This system can, indeed, bring harmony and balance to the white male system that controls our economy and our nation's decision making. But first, women need to connect with each other on a heartfelt, spiritual level. This connection can release us from self-limiting judgment, and empower us as we validate each other.

Connection happens naturally when women have the opportunity. Such connection happens by storytelling, through sharing with each other our journeys of pain, our lessons of love and forgiveness, our ability to laugh at our naiveté, our courage to take risks, and our willingness to fight for our children. Through this sharing process, we are motivated into action by our applause for each other and by our shared laughter and tears, which nurture a profound sense of relief, encouragement, and support.

Each time one of these connections occurs for me, I feel as if I have received a present. I received a gift when the nurse sat on my bed at three in the morning to comfort my fear of being childless at the age of twenty-two after surgery for an ovarian tumor. Another gift came when a hairdresser sat on the porch steps with me as I pondered my futile search for beauty, love, and self-worth, and again, when a straightforward widow coached me on how to make marital sex exciting. It also happened when my professional mentor recounted the story of her own diminishment by her mother, and when my Thai manicurist shared the story of locating the American father who abandoned her. Each woman shared stories from her life, and each one spoke directly to my heart.

This book is a collection of my own life stories, written as connecting points for you to ponder. The true stories are grouped by issues we women face rather than by chronological order. If you can recognize some of your own battles and your struggles with yourself, if you can laugh at my mistakes and fondly remember your own, if you can remember your past with new insight and appreciation for what you have survived, then we have forged a special connection as women—a validation for us both.

Women in our culture are stretched like rubber bands. We have little time to connect, much less to nurture each other. We work, chauffeur children, manage our businesses, and attend professional meetings and PTA, limiting our encounters with each other to brief chats on the run. Like the fast food we consume now rather than the home-cooked family meals of our past, our encounters with each other are limited to quick exchanges of pleasantries and logistical information.

An old woman, tiny from osteoporosis yet still spry and happy, yearned for the fellowship of the quilting circle she enjoyed in the early 1930s.

"We solved a lot of problems, we did," she reminisced, her eyes sparkling. "We saved marriages, counseled each other on child-rearing, and healed a lot of physical maladies."

Despite our busy lives, we don't have to feel isolated. Throw a dinner party just for women, gatherings of two or more, all ages and backgrounds. Invite women with positive, upbeat personalities, women you want to know better, or women whose energy seems warm and caring. Invite women who laugh. I know it takes energy to organize a dinner party at first, so ask everyone to bring a dish, share a babysitter, and keep the work to a minimum. Take these stories of mine as a starting point. Read aloud, then stop. Someone will say, "That reminds me of the time when…" Another story launched, another heart connection. Universal validation. The story read at another dinner party will elicit a different reaction. These women's dinner parties can provide not only delights for the palate but also food for souls.

Before I begin sharing my own stories with you, I must recognize two women authors whose works inspired me to write my stories. Sarah Ban Breathnach, a writer who teaches us how to delve in to our pasts as archeologists, digging up relics of our authenticity, and SARK, an artist who encourages women to play, write, paint, and bathe in the moon-light. These are both women connecting with women from the heart, birthing new ideas, facilitating positive change, and finally, encouraging the emergence of a Sister, ready to take flight into self-awareness.

Why Alligators?
Eat or Be Eaten!

Stress is an ignorant state.
It believes that everything
is an emergency.

— NATALIE GOLDBERG, *WILD MIND*

Every year around May, Florida newspapers feature stories about a local resident surprised to discover an alligator lounging in the bottom of the family pool or sunning himself in the backyard. Or blocking traffic on a community road, his nine-foot body stretched across the pavement in no hurry to cross to the other side. Mating season causes alligators to grow restless, and they venture into new territory in hopes of finding a mate. The local sheriff hastens to the location where the reptile lies immobile, ignoring the growing crowd, his strong legs and powerful tail ready for battle as a noose suspended from a pole encircles his neck, hoping to lead, lift, or direct the scaly amphibian off the road and into a truck. Throughout the years that I lived in Florida, these stories elicited a small prayer from me, thankful that I did not meet up with a lustful alligator on my back porch.

The fear of a gator attack, though, haunted me. It is no wonder that I had nightmares of something big and terrible totally out of my control devouring my child or me. These prehistoric flesh-eaters lurk in the natural bodies of water throughout Florida. Ponds, lakes, streams, and rivers carried legends of alligators eating dogs, geese, and yes, even people. These bad dreams weren't confined to the night, either. I worried about

1

alligators any time I was close to water in Florida. A romantic canoe ride with my husband on the Ocala River suddenly developed into a potentially close encounter when Robert accidentally tipped our canoe over.

"Why on earth did you stand up?" I had cried, flailing in the warm river water near our overturned boat. I nervously scanned the water for long, dark shadows approaching me.

Luckily, we escaped the alligators that time. Robert laughs at this archival event, but I still shudder.

People in the south often quote the old country adage: "When you're up to your neck in alligators, find out who forgot to drain the swamp."

When things go wrong in real life, it seems to happen in multiples. Sometimes I feel completely consumed by challenges, or up to my neck in alligators. I know I'm not alone. As I write, my friend and neighbor, Jana who is featured in many of my stories, battles alligators of her own. A single mom, Jana has her own multiple alligators to do battle with, especially since she started a new job after fourteen years at home. The first week, Jana awoke at five in the morning to hear her new water heater pouring gallons of water into the basement bedrooms and all of her storage. Her son's mattress lay in three inches of water, a giant sponge weighing a ton. Another alligator appeared two days later. Jana received a call that her favorite sister-in-law collapsed on the way to her daughter's college, and lay dying in a strange hospital. After a nine-hour trip to the hospital, Jana found her hooked up to a multitude of tubes and machines, tears streaming down her face, her husband desperately e-mailing hospitals in Europe to find a new set of lungs. Dire situations like this consume our emotional and physical energy as much as if real alligators were feeding on us. No amount of swamp draining can prevent these crises.

Some of life's alligators can be violent, reaching up out of nowhere and dragging you down into the murky depths of depression and despair. But, they can also be persistent irritations that tear away at your self-esteem. Sometimes smaller things, like subtle, barbed comments from a relative or a jealous co-worker, the losing battle with weight, or your inability to provide for a child's needs can slowly but surely eat away at your self-esteem. These small alligators can be as vicious as the bigger ones. The reptiles, regardless of their size, actually drag their victims down into the water and drown them before eating them. How many times do you feel like you are being dragged down by life's circumstances and are drowning in mounting bills, frustrating relationships, and growing feelings of powerlessness? The roof leaks, the garage door won't open, your daughter needs braces, and your husband gets laid off.

A typical male wrestling with such problems physically grapples with sheer force, or swells up in angry intimidation, ranting and raving until everyone gives into him, with varying degrees of success. Women tend to wrestle with such problems in a very different manner, using more art than might. The womanly art employs finesse, not force. She tends to be soft but smart in her approach to the alligators around her neck. Her power comes more from passion and determination than brute strength, with more internal wrestling than external. How appropriate since the biggest alligator of all is not found in external situations, physical monsters, or even the act of drowning. The biggest alligator is fear. Connecting with her spiritual source, a woman can do anything. Through our stories and our talks with each other, we need to remind each other of that spiritual connection. Without a doubt, my weakest, most vulnerable, and loneliest times in life occurred when I left my circle of women friends.

As I contemplated the title for this book, I remembered the speech given by Janet Reno for a Girl Scout National Convention. Ms. Reno told stories about her mother. A diminutive journalist in South Florida, her mother shocked people with her outrageous individualism. She actually wrestled real alligators in the Everglades ! But providing a house for her family became her biggest metaphorical alligator of all. Janet Reno described how her mother observed construction workers, and then copied what she saw, digging first a foundation, then laying down the cinderblock. Each time she finished building part of the house, she returned to the professionals and asked how to do the next step. Although she received some help with the heavier aspects of the construction, she nearly built that house herself, permitting Janet to hammer shingles on the roof. When a powerful hurricane hit years later, Janet's elderly mother refused to leave her rocking chair, secure in the knowledge that she built a sturdy house.

Janet learned valuable lessons from her mother's determination to tackle such an untraditional goal for such a small, unskilled woman. In turn, I shared in this lesson learning because she imparted her story to me. We all can learn valuable lessons from each other, by sharing our own stories. Just as Janet learned from her mother, our daughters listen intently to our stories, and watch attentively as we wrestle our alligators. They learn from our attitudes, our faith, and our pride in our accomplishments. What could be more gratifying than to watch the next generation of women stand authenticated by their past and confident of their futures? I fantasize about them singing, dancing, and painting their success—validating themselves and the women before them.

I have discussed several issues that can occur in life that might be perceived as alligators lurking in the water, ready to leap up and consume you without warning. What are your alligators? Take time to list them:

The big, recurring themes that seem to hold you back;
The daily irritations that leave you feeling incompetent;
The crises that threaten to paralyze your life;
The current messes that have accumulated and drain your energy.

Outrageous Alligator Wrestling in My Youth:
Confessions from Kitchens I Have Known

*Cooking may be as much
a means of self-expression as
any of the arts.*

— FANNIE MERRITT FARMER, *THE BOSTON
COOKING-SCHOOL COOKBOOK*

Survival, for me, has always been about using my wit, especially when I lived my life in fear, before my faith became a source of wisdom for me. For many years, the biggest monster alligator of all was life itself. Succeeding in graduate school, living as a single woman, achieving recognition as an avant-garde artist, and operating a unique business all involved wit, risk taking, and my absolute determination to "go for it."

One example of how I used my wits for survival was through my cooking, which I frequently relied upon to please people. In the old days, I would resort to cooking whenever I needed approval. I depended on my culinary skills to boost my grades, regardless of the subject. I retreated to the kitchen to solve problems, resolve conflicts, make art, build a reputation, and find friends.

Today my kitchen fosters little alligators in the form of hungry children and demanding work vying for my time. I now dread the daily chore of routine cooking, whose sole purpose is to fill up empty bellies. Cooking has become a time drain, interrupting my work with no reward other than the quieting of grumbling children and husband, all

5

finicky eaters, messy snackers, and unappreciative creatures on the run waiting impatiently for me to throw something edible at them. But when I cook for women friends with adventurous palates, my kitchen once again becomes a happy place, a playful venue of pleasure.

It makes sense to me for a woman to rely on such familiar skills as she confronts life. Many of us are at home in the kitchen, not just as a place to prepare a meal but because it has always been the heart of the house to us. Intimate conversations with our mothers occurred over vegetable chopping. At parties, people always congregate in the kitchen. At family gatherings, secrets are exchanged in the kitchen—the inner sanctum of the family home. As women have entered the workplace, however, this kitchen aura has changed. Many women today rarely set foot in the kitchen, only using the space to microwave a meal or two. How do you view your own kitchen? Does it support you or does it overwhelm you, or do you avoid it altogether, delegating the distasteful chore to another member of the family or simply eating in restaurants? I know one woman who keeps an arrangement of dried flowers on her stove, as a reminder to the family that she does not, will not, and never will, cook!

Cooking has always worked for me as a survival tool. I learned at a young age that I could please people by delighting their palates and satisfying their stomachs. It always worked for me. There are many other media that you can employ to help you survive by your wits. You just might need help in identifying what those talents are. What tools have helped you survive? What skills did you rely on to help drive you to pursue your goals? How did you combat your early fears? Do you remember stories of any inappropriate actions that you might have taken, or desperate attempts to win your way? Have these experiences built bridges and developed communities for you to continue your pursuit, with crowds cheering you on, even through the roughest storms?

I know I have come a long way, winning many battles with many different alligators. Still, I particularly treasure my stories of the early alligator wrestling that evolved from my life as an artist and as a creative cook. These stories reflect the preposterous behavior of my young adulthood, and I have put them in the front of the book so that you may get to know me a little better. I hope that once you have read this chapter you will then be able to read the rest of my stories with my unique experiences and perspectives in mind. You, too, have your own stories of youthful outrageousness, though you may not have used a live model to serve food, given yourself a wedding, or appeared as a giant peacock in Central Park. Remember that the roles we play at any given stage of our lives are shaped by the social climate of the times. All those acts of extravagance practiced in our young adult years made us into the people we are today. After all, people mature, settle down, and raise children. Perspectives and behaviors change with age.

We all possess an extraordinary gusto in youth. Remembering our early pranks, lofty ideas, and creative resourcefulness not only entertains our children and friends, it also reminds us to be more accepting as we view the dramatic displays of today's generation. Tattoos, purple hair, and pierced navels are merely costumes for the expressive artists of today.

Dinner Questions

❏ How did you handle obstacles in your life differently than in your youth?

❏ What abilities have surfaced as you have determined your path in life?

Breakfast in Bed

*I have not ceased being fearful, but I have
ceased to let fear control me. I have accepted fear
as a part of life, specifically the fear of change, the
fear of the unknown, and I have gone ahead despite
the pounding in the heart that says: turn back, turn
back, you'll die if you venture too far.*

— ERICA JONG, IN JANET STERNBURG.ED.,
THE WRITER ON HER WORK

My first attempt at business came at the age of twelve, a business based solely on scaring children. I frightened them with tremendous delight and incredible financial success. That year, my mother and I had designed a haunted house as a fundraiser for my music teacher's "club" to foster music appreciation. The location was perfect—a dark, log cabin, perched on the edge of a city drainage ditch. We filled the cabin with stuffed dummies posing in different horrifying scenarios, apparently overtaken by fuzzy tarantulas, rubber rats, and man-made cobwebs. A touchy-feely maze of cardboard tunnels required visitors to crawl over various foam rubber sponges in the dark while nylon stockings scented with perfume, ammonia, and turpentine taunted the nostrils and tickled necks and faces. A mad teenage scientist, a wildly beautiful fortuneteller who resembled my music teacher, and a decaying body in a real coffin offered dramatic confrontation amidst our various bloodcurdling offerings. Real rats inhabited the old cabin, along with live spiders, crawling roaches, and a bat or two, further enhancing the effectiveness of our shadowy venue. The drainage ditch nearby, famous for snakes and other creepy crawly things, contributed excellently to the overall ambiance.

Advertising consisted of strategically posing a stuffed dummy, complete with a wicked face, straggly hair, and outstretched arms extended in a menacing threat, in front of the log cabin. Lit with a ghoulish green spotlight, the dummy drew the attention of the entire neighborhood. We sold over a hundred tickets. Many kids paid several times for the privilege of having themselves scared silly. That haunted house was such an overnight success that we continued to reproduce it for several years afterwards, to growing crowds and leaping profits.

From that experience, I deduced that the market for novelty and surprise offered me a niche. I tested my theory in college when challenged to earn money for the band's trip to Washington, DC. The band director divided us into small teams and motivated us with friendly competition. My team served breakfast in bed in the women's dorms. Our pancakes, bacon, and coffee, brought to the bedside of our client-coeds, made so much money that our team won the contest before most of the teams ever got their ideas off the ground.

At the age of thirty, I decided to apply the concept of novelty and surprise to a real business. I combined my love for drama with my ability to cook. Customers could order a French dinner party (which I served while only speaking French), large, edible sculptures, and the college favorite, Breakfast in Bed. The latter, I reasoned, would be perfect for couples on their wedding anniversary. The only glitch in my master plan consisted of my trepidation about working with customers who I did not know. Cooking for girlfriends in a dorm was comfortable compared to cooking for total strangers and serving them in their bedroom. I knew I could adroitly handle the food preparation and the service, but I was not nearly as confident about my ability to handle the customers. I worried that they might not like me, that I might mess up, or that some unsavory person, wanting more from me than the food I was offering, might hire me.

The latter was a big concern since I was, after all, basing my business in their bedroom. A simple written policy handled that: "Nothing gets into bed except the breakfast."

I had great fun coming up with my menu choices, which included Eggs Benedict and Bananas Foster. I had never eaten Eggs Benedict *or* Bananas Foster but they sounded exotic and elegant. Why not experiment? If I served champagne, I figured that no one would notice mistakes. I printed a brochure announcing this unique experience, distributed the brochures to several locations, and waited for the phone to ring. An older friend, Peggy, volunteered to be my first customer. We arranged the time and agreed on a menu of Cheese Omelets and Cherries Flambé.

As the event approached, my anxiety mounted. The very thought of cooking for Peggy's husband, a man I had never met, petrified me. I pulled up to their house in the early morning darkness, stealthily unloading my supplies. Peggy wanted the breakfast to be a complete surprise for her husband, but I didn't want it to be *too* much of a surprise. What if the surprise triggered a heart attack? What if he kept a gun under his pillow? I looked at my long, white gauzy dress. In the dark, he could easily mistake me for a ghost.

After fumbling nervously with the house key, I let myself in the backdoor and into the kitchen, taking my shoes off like a guilty teenager returning too late. I silently unloaded my supplies and surveyed my resources, which included one of the first microwave ovens made. Though I had heard of microwaves before, I had no idea how to work it. I fidgeted with the knobs, put in my crescent rolls, and closed the door. To my horror, that state-of-the-art technology turned the crescent rolls into hard stones. "These are not edible!" I gasped. "I've made weapons!"

Spying a loaf of bread on the counter, I reluctantly toasted two pieces in the regular oven on broil. Cheese omelets I managed with ease, much to my relief. Arranging my tray artistically, I slipped into the hall and approached the bedroom, holding my breath. My heart was beating so loudly in my chest that I was sure it would give me away.

Tap, tap, tap. Knocking timidly, I opened the bedroom door. Without looking at Peggy or her husband, I hurriedly entered the room.

"Here's your breakfast," I stammered.

Setting the steaming plates on TV trays, I poured juice in fancy glasses with a shaky hand.

"Here's a little bell to ring when you're finished," I continued in a whisper.

My demeanor communicated as much embarrassment as if I had asked them to use a bedpan.

Bolting from the bedroom like a scared rabbit, I actually heard myself panting with fear in the kitchen, my heart throbbing high in my chest. I listened timorously for the inevitable "ding" of the bell. My hands continued to quiver as I lit the Cherries Flambé, and once again served and ran.

A week later, I received the verdict from Peggy over a cup of coffee. "We enjoyed the food," she proclaimed kindly, "but we really wanted an experience of YOU. You were practically invisible! We never saw you!"

Her words stuck in my head. Me! They wanted an experience of me! I thought they wanted romance, to enjoy breakfast in bed together as a couple! Okay, I told myself, if my customers wanted me, they'd get me. I went to work, adjusting my entire approach to my Breakfast in Bed scheme. I replaced the white dress with a red one, adding a fluffy feather boa and a blonde wig. A trumpet fanfare on a kazoo would announce my entrance and give the drowsy couple warning, in case they needed to cover up.

"We'll start with champagne," I announced. No one missed the orange juice.

I brainstormed additional ways to make each breakfast different, adding little touches based on the interview with my customer. Serving the second Breakfast in Bed seemed much easier. No microwave oven this time. To my amazement, my heart didn't beat as loudly as the first time. The success stirred more business. My phone rang with calls from women who wanted to surprise their husbands. They loved to be included in the planning.

"Can my children come?" one lady asked.

"Let's get them in the act!" I replied.

Armed with more kazoos, the kids paraded in behind me, and then scampered onto the bed for the delectable feast, enthralled with the idea of a family party occurring in the most unlikely room in the house.

The novelty of serving Breakfast in Bed attracted a young journalist who wrote a story about me and sent it to the Los Angeles Times. Again my phone rang, only this time a television producer was on the other end.

"You serve Breakfast in Bed?" she inquired.

Within a month, a national television crew taped my gourmet service. By now, I had no inhibition. Waltzing into the bedroom of my customers, I twirled a feather boa and played my kazoo, mugging for the cameras while plopping cherries into the champagne.

Ultimately, no one cared what I served. Their delight depended on how I served it. I hired another caterer to cook. Like the haunted house, people bought the surprise and novelty of my presentation. The funnier the presentation, the more popular the breakfast. I drove to another city to serve the family of a corporate executive. This time, I changed costumes for each course. The family followed my lead! In between courses, we all changed our clothes in a mad scramble.

Serving Breakfast in Bed taught me several valuable lessons about life. When afraid, push through your fear, over and over, until you find you no longer feel apprehensive. Add little touches to anything you undertake, and try new approaches to old situations. A comfort level comes with practice, bringing with it freedom for creativity. I remember these lessons as I forge ahead in my new career as a professional speaker. At times my old shyness still surfaces around new people. Whenever I join a new organization, it takes time for me to feel comfortable. New jobs, new clients, new challenges all require practice and repetition before self–confidence replaces fear. The Breakfast in Bed experience even helps me as I coach my children in their school presentations, assuring them that speaking in public loses the grip of fear the more they do it.

Another valuable lesson from my Breakfast in Bed days continues to make an impact as well.

"We want an experience of YOU," my friend had proclaimed.

Personalization, warmth, and spontaneity bring magic to any service you render, whether you serve fast food to customers, lead a Girl Scout troop, or sell cars. Sometimes my determination to perform a task perfectly actually gets in the way. I discovered that everyone has more fun when I relax and give more of my personality in the process.

New entrepreneurs continue to claim the market with unusual services and theatrical pizzazz. Women continue to cook up ideas to sell from their kitchens, combining traditional abilities with business innovation. I applaud their creativity and guts, admiring their spunk and wishing them the best. Meanwhile, my children relish spook houses during Halloween in other locations or while visiting the fair.

"You would have loved my spook house...," I tell my children. Where it all started.

Dinner Questions

❑ What childhood adventures have led you to magical experiences as an adult?

❑ How have fearful situations brought you valuable lessons about life?

The Human Buffet

I think most artists create out of despair...
— LOUISE NEVELSON, *DAWNS + DUSKS*

I had no idea how to select a graduate school. After high school, I had attended Maryville College, a family tradition on my mother's side. I graduated without a career in mind, so I figured, for lack of better ideas, graduate school came next. Since I wanted to live in Florida, I thumbed through a catalogue from the state school and was satisfied with a picture of a campus decorated with swaying palm trees. I applied to Florida State University, without really considering whether or not the school offered what I needed.

Now I had to determine what I should study, since there are no liberal arts degrees given out on the graduate level. I assessed what I liked to do and what I was good at, and concluded that art seemed to be my best bet. Florida State, like most art graduate programs, required me to send slides of my art with my application. After a few weeks, the slides returned with a letter that said something to this effect:

"Dear Ms. Tampanna, We are not the school for you."

It should have been a red flag, warning me of troubles ahead, but I chose to ignore it. I went off to FSU anyway.

Moving to Tallahassee, I secured a secretarial job at the First Presbyterian Church and enrolled in a painting class at FSU as a special student. I guess God felt sympathy for me because my passion for color, and my liberal use of it, caught the eye of the British artist-in-residence. Trevor

Bell arranged for me to be admitted into the graduate program, after which he promptly returned to England, leaving me to deal with the FSU art faculty on my own.

In the early seventies, the art faculty of FSU was made up of hippie cowboys. They wore boots, big belt buckles, pigtails or longish hair, and walked around campus with a macho swagger. A token woman managed to survive in that faculty, and she smoked a cigar. This all should have been another red flag, but still I plowed on, intent on completing my masters in art. Rumor had it that, unless you drank beer at the pub and worked in the foundry, you would not receive attention as a serious student. I shared a little house on campus with four other women, where we painted and created and plotted for our degrees. It didn't take us long to learn, however, that this plot would be foiled every time we tried to present our work to the faculty. The cowboys, apparently, didn't keep appointments with female students.

The professors there shared a perspective of art totally foreign to me. They talked of complex installations, and larger-than-life reality that spared no detail. Shock value seemed to be important, too, usually sexual in nature. I persisted in painting traditional portraits and openly loved the Impressionists. I did not fit in this department.

The women painters who shared my studio also shared my frustration. For days we would toil on our paintings, eagerly awaiting feedback from a professor who rarely bothered to show up to view the results of our efforts. His brief, erratic visits inevitably brought messages of doom for us. He spoke in cryptic sentences, leaving us stumped and confused about what to do next. Our work never received approval, especially mine. He obviously felt disdain for my portraits, which were, in his opinion, boring and lackluster.

"Look at painting as an adventure," the artist cowboy said one day. "Take a risk, go where no one has gone before."

"But how?" I stammered. Too late, he had left.

How dare he offer nothing but rejection? We plugged away, floundering without instruction. Since he missed more appointments than he kept, we felt belittled, bewildered, and powerless to improve. Finally, I had enough. This situation required drastic action—Aikido. In the martial art of Aikido, one is taught to move the same direction as the attacker, and then take him in another direction. It seemed to be a perfect strategy to reach my recalcitrant art professor. I would have to make it appear as if I was finally doing what he asked by looking at painting as an adventure. But then, I would take it in a direction that even he never dreamed of going with art. He clearly didn't like my portraits or my painting skills, so I would have to use something else to hook him in. My mother used to tell me that the way to a man's heart is through his stomach. Maybe I couldn't paint, but I could certainly cook. I would use food as my art, adding a touch of shock value, decidedly sexual in nature. I felt like the Pied Piper, preparing to play for the rats.

First, I baited the hook. I sent invitations with dinner mints, requesting the presence of the art faculty to attend "The Human Buffet." Whet their appetite! The location for my event concerned me. If I carefully cleaned up afterward and refrained from outside promotion, I found out that I could prepare my art in the church parlor. Somehow a church room setting did not seem to be congruent with the male professors from my art department. I couldn't imagine any of these men in a church. They dressed in grungy clothes, used vocabularies that could melt crayons, and had a particular fondness for alcohol. My location, however, had a nearby kitchen and a gracious atmosphere that would lend itself well to what I had in mind, so I scheduled my event for the church.

Next, I needed an assistant and a model. Without hesitation, two women from my studio enthusiastically volunteered. Nancy, a quiet young woman, surprised me when she agreed to be my model.

On the day of the event, Nancy showed up ready to change into her bikini. Surrounded with bags of cut-up vegetables, plastic grapes, sundae toppings, cocktail breads, and other crudités, I went to work on creating my masterpiece. I covered the table with a paper tablecloth and the model's torso with plastic wrap, then tackled my first challenge: how to make Nancy's feet appetizing. Feet required a major transformation.

I mixed my acrylic paint in soft celery green and began painting Nancy's legs, feet and toes as she giggled. Gingerly, she climbed on the table and lay on her side. My assistant, Josie, and I packed handfuls of a sticky granola mixture all around the base of her for support. Next we lined little hors d'oeurvres up her legs. We worked fast, since the table did not offer a comfortable resting place for Nancy. While I layered roast beef, cheese, and turkey around the torso, my assistant used big curvy lettuce leaves to cover her behind. We decorated the granola base with rings of onions, green peppers and cherry tomatoes. I crowned Nancy's head with the plastic grapes sewn to a swim cap. Only Nancy's bust remained undecorated.

At this point Nancy quivered in her awkward position. I began to worry about my model, the base for my entire artistic creation, and her precarious position on the table. What if Nancy develops muscle spasms and shakes the food off? We gingerly massaged her, hiding little wedges of foam rubber in strategic places between her hipbone and the table, and rushed to add our final touches.

With a spatula and a jar of marshmallow cream, I successfully slathered the sweet, white goo all over the plastic wrap protecting the upper body curves of Nancy's petite figure. The maraschino cherries, nuts, and chocolate chips stuck beautifully to the marshmallow cream. Josie covered the remaining table space with cocktail breads and little bowls of mayonnaise and mustard. Graham cracker squares were placed near Nancy's dessert-laden bust. I topped this section with whipped cream. Voila! We were ready for guests. But, would there be any? Would the professors even consider attending a dinner served in a church parlor?

I quickly changed into a long peach-colored dress and a big garden hat, for a Southern Belle hostess appearance. Slowly opening the door to the entrance hall, I froze in astonishment. A long line of professors filled the narrow hallway. I didn't even know them all. "Gentlemen," I announced, "dinner is served."

The professors entered the parlor slowly. Their eyes popped open as they circled the table like vultures. One snapped photographs from every angle with his camera. No one spoke. I tingled with delight. I had succeeded in creating a visual adventure using a woman's medium.

One by one, the men began to assemble sandwiches from Nancy's décor. I feared that soon she would begin quivering again. In my mind's eye, I could visualize all that food falling off as Nancy's legs trembled uncontrollably. What if she collapsed onto her front? What a mess that would be! Meanwhile the professor, who had so cavalierly neglected our studio appointments, had firmly planted himself in front of Nancy's chest. Carefully scraping off the gooey dessert with pieces of graham crackers, he devoured them by the mouthful. As if in some sugar-induced trance, he ate cracker after cracker, each laden with the sticky sweet conglomeration. Finally, he realized that he had consumed every last dessert scraper. "I don't even like graham crackers," he proclaimed with disbelief.

The Human Buffet created a stir four more times in four different cities. Each time the reputation grew and the excitement intensified. I varied the production, adding men's heads on vegetable platters, requesting that guests be formally dressed, scripting quips for the models, and donning an opulent costume myself. National television featured the Human Buffet, viewed in foreign countries hosting American armed forces. To my surprise, a producer of prime time television in Japan requested another installation. I wonder if the negligent art professor ever received such international attention for his art? I suppose, in a way, I am grateful to him. If I hadn't felt driven to meet his challenge, even in revenge, I would not have stepped out of my comfort zone and experimented with something so bizarre. I had what I needed all along; I just had to take a risk. The Human Buffet led to a business called Edible Adventures, to my debut swinging from a crane, to meeting my husband while I was dressed like a salad, to having a daughter who wears ten-foot bat wings. Life would never be the same after I served up my very first Human Buffet.

Dinner Questions

❑ What adventures did you orchestrate in your youth?
❑ When have you retaliated in defiance?

The Wedding

*A wedding isn't for the bride and groom, it's for
the family and friends. The B. and G. are just props,
silly stick figures with no more significance
than the pink and white candy figures
on the top of the cake.*

— SUSAN CHEEVER, *LOOKING FOR WORK*

I have been a bride in four weddings; four incredible weddings that were each happy celebrations with friends and relatives, weddings planned with meticulous detail and filled with surprise for the guests, weddings that promised a lifetime of happiness. The most opulent wedding, however, had no groom. Now, don't get me wrong, I loved all my grooms, at least when I married them, but the wedding without the groom had a distinct calmness to it. I felt in complete control, most of the time.

As a graduate art student during the feminist seventies in a school of strong male leadership, it seemed only natural to question this event of events in a woman's life.

Freshly divorced, I contemplated that pinnacle of maidenhood that promised "living happily ever after." The groomless wedding would honor traditional wedding rituals while at the same time guarantee that there would be no unmet expectations. There would be no vows to make, no dreams to risk breaking, no divorce threatening in the end. I threw myself into the creation of the greatest groomless wedding ever known to humankind, designating it as my finest work of art.

Women have been programmed since preschoolers to dream about our weddings. We acted out weddings with our dolls, giving each a part to play in a usually traditional ceremony. Most of my dolls had a bride dress, even my baby doll. Mother gave me my first costume, her own wedding veil, consisting of miles of tulle cascading from a beaded head-piece. Surely she felt a pang of sorrow when I took her scissors and cut off the trailing veil in order to make an accessory just my size. I paraded around the living room for hours, imagining a never-ending aisle that didn't necessarily lead to a groom.

As a three-year-old flower girl in my aunt's wedding, I discovered my love for an audience. I wore lavender organza with pearls that matched my mother's and carried a giant yellow chrysanthemum. Painfully shy, I tucked my head into my shoulder and followed my mother down the aisle. I remember standing there in the front, awestruck and timid, as people winked and smiled at me. Then my aunt emerged, looking like a fairy queen who stepped from the pages of a storybook. She was glorious in her long white gown and magnificent veil. Immediately after the ceremony, I suggested, "Let's do it again!" My relatives laughed but I was serious; I had experienced the excitement of being in the limelight and I wanted more. The sweet taste of stardom had cast its spell.

The "wedding without the groom" fulfilled my little girl fantasy to play wedding with all the rituals, props, and clothes that I could ever dream about.

The first announcement was my photograph in the newspaper, the one where the bride conspicuously displays her hand next to her face so that the world might notice her diamond ring. To emphasize my forthcoming prosperity, I flashed five rings. Since many people don't read the paper, or might have missed that section, I utilized a billboard in a high traffic area, featuring my enlarged picture surrounded by lights, to announce my upcoming nuptials to a far larger audience. No one ever asked whom I was marrying; no one seemed to notice the absence of a groom.

To finance this wedding myself, I sold beautifully engraved invitations, which covered the entire cost of the event. I immediately commenced working on the wedding, which seemed to consist mainly of making tiers. I sewed tiers of ruffles into frothy pink dresses, built tiered tables, and fabricated gigantic round bases out of fiberglass to simulate layers of wedding cake. One included three tiers, the base for the real wedding cake. The other would be the bride's platform. Each base was adorned with swirls of faux icing. Using a bathtub-caulking gun, I draped white garlands around the sides, and held each strand in place with white roses. I purchased four sizes of cake pans for the actual wedding cake, the bottom layer being so large I would have to borrow the use of a professional oven. I hoarded miniature swans from party goods stores and purchased packages of tiny doves and edible white glitter. I rented candelabras, procured white runners for the blue carpet, and looped miles of ribbon into bows for oversized corsages. Martha Stewart, the queen of such elaborate decorating schemes, had yet to make her national debut. I did this whole thing without her help!

I searched for the cast that would play the parts of my ideal wedding party. A delightful couple from my church filled the role as my perfect parents. Petite, outgoing and plump, Kay blessed people with her warm smile, and her husband, a retired professor, offered wisdom and wit. A nurturing couple fond of young people, the Campbells often invited young friends for meals in their home. I had worked part-time for the professor and since his wife had arranged for my scholarship, these parents supported me emotionally and financially, just like real parents do.

Next, two lovely grandmothers, their soft faces wrinkled with age and kindness, completed the family picture. I easily recruited the bridesmaids and a flower girl. The four brunette bridesmaids beamed with engaging smiles, boasting a total of twenty weddings experienced amongst them. The young flower girl, a winsome blonde of six, projected a sweet well-mannered demeanor that I knew I could trust in any public situation not to upstage me, the bride. I auditioned groomsmen who could master the art of gracious small talk while escorting guests into the wedding hall. My cast for my production completed, I was ready to tackle the costumes and props.

A consignment store offered a profusion of heavenly bridal attire, overlaid with lace and encrusted with beads. I selected a divine white satin dress and studied my choice of veils. Such decision-making demanded meticulous consideration. I mulled over floral arrangements, wedding programs, and music selections. I bought molds for mints shaped like tiny bells and doves. The anticipation for the big event mounted as I checked off each detail. My biggest challenge loomed ahead: my first attempt at a wedding cake.

The entire confection, including the base, would tower over six feet tall. The top three tiers, comprised of Italian cream cake, required a full day to bake. The fourth layer and middle layer, in the specially ordered cake pan, caused a calamity that nearly ruined the wedding.

Since the pan didn't fit my oven, I located an institutional kitchen available to me on a Friday night in the university student center kitchen. The six-foot oven rotated shelves like a Ferris wheel. It had the capacity of baking twenty oversized cake pans. Closed on Friday nights, the kitchen became my laboratory for the evening. I mixed my expensive ingredients, multiplying the recipe by three to fill this enormous pan. When I opened the oven door, I had just enough time to slip the pan onto the shelf before it disappeared from view, another shelf coming down from above. I began cleaning up, waiting for my incredible concoction to transform from a runny batter to a delicate golden confection fit for the gods.

All bakers test a cake to see if it is done in the middle. With potholders in hand, I opened the oven door and carefully pulled my cake halfway out. Unlike amateur bakers, however, professional bakers know how to stop a rotating oven. I no sooner pulled that cake halfway out from the oven shelf when CRASH! the next shelf demolished the fourth layer of my deluxe Italian cream cake, neatly slicing pan and all. In a panic, I pushed a red button near the oven door, but it was too late. As the oven grinded to a halt, I retrieved the crumbled mess and crushed metal: an Italian cream cake catastrophe. At eight o'clock the evening before the wedding, I drove home frantically, my disaster in a cardboard box. Mentally, I reviewed my Rolodex, eliminating all the friends who could not solder cake pans.

An hour of frenetic phone calls availed nothing. I quickly moved to Plan C, which required me to find a local bakery downtown. Surely, the baker would have a cake pan the size I needed, and of course he would be baking all night, I rationalized. With my heart pounding in my throat, I dashed to the grocery store for more flour, eggs, and pecans and, for the fifth time that day, whipped up another batch of Italian cream wedding cake batter, again tripling the recipe. At one in the morning, I banged on the door of the bakery, hoping to be heard over the radio music from inside. A middle-aged man with a mustache and an apron covered with flour abruptly opened the door. He stared at me incredulously, a wild, red-eyed woman with messy hair and clothes covered with cake batter, hands clasped for mercy—an unlikely desperate beggar appearing at his doorstep.

"I need help!" I pleaded in a pitiful voice.

I guess the world saves a soft spot for women with wedding dilemmas. Accepting my bowl of batter, the baker instructed me to return in five hours.

The fourth tier, along with its six companions, emanated perfection as I rapidly glued them together with cream cheese frosting. I had, by the grace of God and a sympathetic baker, produced a six-foot-six-inch tower of heavenly white wedding cake bedecked with swans, doves, and garlands. I generously sprinkled the bottle of edible glitter, fairy dust for connoisseurs, over the entire pièce de résistance before hurrying to the dressing room to slip into my fairytale gown and to douse myself with fragrant perfume. I was ready.

The wedding rituals commenced. Ushers in their smart tuxedoes oozed professional charm to guests and delivered them to the reception line. The beautiful bridesmaids blushed and giggled, the parents proudly beamed as they shook hands and thanked guests for coming. The grandmothers hugged everyone, their generous corsages carefully pinned to their shoulders. Hungry guests gobbled sandwiches from the white-tiered tables and sipped champagne from the fountain. Hostesses sliced wedding cake and presided over the guest book, offering an ostrich-plumed pen for signatures. The organist played love songs sweeter than the candy mints. At the end of the room, guests gazed upon the bride. Dramatically bathed in light, I stood on my pedestal, a round tier that matched the cake, festooned with garlands and swans. I beamed radiantly, looking down on the room full of guests, my white dress and bouquet a bridal dream come true. Women gathered around me, sighing in unison. One lady reached up as if to touch, then pulled her hand back. No one missed the groom. My wedding experience had filled my sweetest dreams, without the added nightmare of another husband.

All girls should have a wedding. It is the culmination of social programming throughout one's childhood and adolescence. A rite of passage to adulthood, it satisfies parents' expectations, entertains friends, and provides the bride with a sense of achievement. People come to pay tribute to her beauty, her style, and her ability to pull off such an incredible celebration. It's not all that difficult because the social rituals we go through are almost second nature and we all know our parts. The event we have rehearsed with our dolls can finally take place. We are given permission to purchase a myriad of magazines, to try on dresses of extravagant expense, and to plan a party just for us. Every bride becomes royalty for that one event, the storybook princess who lives, hopefully, happily ever after.

Most girls plan for this moment all their lives. We are better prepared to pull off weddings than we prepare ourselves to pull off our marriages. This should come as no surprise, for what little girl even considers the groom beyond his role in the ceremony of her dreams. The wedding is just a performance; a marriage is a life, requiring clear values and commitment. As for me, I didn't get clear about my values until I was in my forties. I didn't understand the ground rules for a relationship with another person any more than I understood how to use a professional, rotating oven. Like my precious cake, my marriages were smashed beyond repair.

What no one ever told me as a child was that in order to be successful in relationships with others one must first be successful in understanding oneself. There were so many areas I needed to work on to become a better person, able to give of myself to another. I discovered as a young adult that I lacked numerous skills that were crucial to a satisfying marriage. I had never practiced standing up for myself. I didn't know how to be independent, how to manage the details of life, or how to find security. I couldn't say "no" without feeling guilty. I didn't know how to argue or how to fight fairly. I couldn't be true to myself, much less to another person.

I had everyone's support to create a wedding. I had access to consultants, volumes of etiquette books, an empathetic baker, and generous friends who all contributed to my successful celebration. But a marriage took resources I didn't have. I'm still learning about give and take, commitment and values, love and forgiveness. One person can effectively design an incredible wedding. A marriage requires two.

Dinner Questions

- ❑ What are your stories of wedding disasters?
- ❑ How have you handled the pressure to get married?

Salad Lady

Let's dare to be ourselves, for we do that
better than anyone else can.

— SHIRLEY BRIGGS, IN SUE PATTON THOELE,
THE COURAGE TO BE YOURSELF

Some find life a succulent banquet. For me, life tosses a salad. I eat salad, paint salad, wear salad. You could say that salad made me famous. But I never dreamed that salad would bring me love.

Florida sizzles with fantasy. The long Southern peninsula delighted my soul with its exotic colors. The splendor of the opulent Don Cesar Hotel, a confection of pink icing, thrilled me with its hundreds of steps delivering guests to an endless strip of sand known as St. Petersburg Beach. My heart seemed to beat faster in Tampa's Ybor city amidst the neon lights and the red ruffles of Flamenco dancers. There the heavy, sweet scent of Cuban cigars perfumed the night. Across the state in Miami, swaying palm trees enhanced the pastel corals and soft greens of the beach hotels near by. Neighborhood yards guarded by plastic pink flamingos were not to be outdone by the wild parakeets that perched on overhead wires. I loved it all.

Here was a place where I could truly express my performance art. Butterflies, with their brilliant colors of fluttering silks adorned by patches of cobalt blue inspired my first metamorphosis. With the passion of a madwoman, I bent wire into giant wings, cut neon-orange silk, and glued on fuchsia sequin trim. Once finished, my wings sparkled and

26

fluttered with the resplendence of a real butterfly. Oscillating down any street, I drew a crowd. Children waited breathlessly for me to take flight. Such exhilaration! I wanted more.

My next colorful creation was a peacock. My addiction for sensationalism motivated me to build a magnificent creature with the tail span of ten feet. Sewing a turquoise mesh screen together and inserting aluminum slats, I bolted the giant tail to a copper cake plate mounted to the end of a frame that I strapped on my back. I carefully covered the cake plate with turquoise lame to match the bodysuit I would wear beneath my faux feathers. Dazzling eyes of gold and purple lamé sparkled with dark blue sequin centers. Like a real peacock searches for a peahen to display his glorious feathers to, I searched for parades to strut in.

As a Peacock, I flew to The Big Apple. I carried with me a long, sitar-like case with extended zippers, and checked it onto a plane for New York. The fragile headdress, with its glittering feathers, sat in my lap. Everyone back home had agreed that Central Park would be the best strutting ground.

I found a quiet shaded area to assemble my tail, then removed my raincoat and strapped on my magnificent plumage. Slowly I extended my arms, cocked my head, and took a deliberate step out onto the path in silver high-heeled sandals, pointing my feet like a dancer. Within seconds a crowd of onlookers surrounded me. Thirty, then seventy, then hundreds of people pointed, smiled, and stared. It was such a supremely sweet moment. People scrambled up trees to get a better look. Intent on my performance, I strutted down the park path, just wide enough to accommodate my tail.

Suddenly, someone screamed, "Look out! Here they come!"

With terror I realized that I was blocking the path of an oncoming bicycle race. A mass of cyclists in helmets bore down on me with alarming speed, allowing no time for me, encumbered in such a massive costume, to clear the road. In a frantic moment, I turned sideways and held my breath. I no longer presented a roadblock to the racing bikers, just a bizarre obstacle in the middle of the road. The cyclists parted down the middle, whirring past me for what seemed eternity. When the last of the wheeled cyclone disappeared, the crowd cheered and clapped. Not exactly the performance I had planned, but crowd-pleasing just the same. I strutted off the path, not willing to wait for the slower stragglers in the race.

I didn't stop with creatures with wings as my only costume creations. At the circus, spectators sought my autograph, my silver-and-white feathers cascading from my bejeweled headpiece.

"My elephant is sick. I'm just watching today," I explained to my curious fans.

For more sophisticated events, I would appear in a black wool Geoffrey Beane dress edged in striped frou-frou feathers. I completed the ensemble with a black lampshade hat and matching black gloves. The outfit came alive, however, when I glued Velcro to the feet of a stuffed cardinal and perched him on my shoulder.

My hats made a commotion everywhere I went. During a routine check-up at my gynecologist, the nurse led me to an examining room and ordered me to "Take off everything, except the hat."

The doctor, a mild-mannered Jewish man, breezed into the room and froze in his shoes. Wrapped in a sheet, I sat under my straw hat blooming with flaming red hibiscus and tropical birds-of-paradise. The good doctor recovered his composure, then burst out laughing as his nurses ran in from the hall to get a peep. He completed my exam with me still wearing the hat.

The collection grew as I added feather boas, tiaras, wigs, and a gay queen's gown from Mardi Gras. I was best known for my headdresses. Borrowing ideas from my book of Carmen Miranda paper dolls, I built citrus headdresses, studded with little mirrors that glittered in the sun. There is an art to making ornate headdresses light. I can empathize with Queen Elizabeth who must get headaches from wearing her heavy crown. But headdresses give a woman added height so that she becomes bigger than life. Almost untouchable. I liked that. I actually felt safer. Men don't know how to handle a woman in a headdress! Bananas cascaded from one, lemons and oranges from another, and silver grapes from a third amidst festoons of turquoise marabou feathers. People referred to me as "The Fruit Salad Lady."

This reputation caught the attention of the bank president in Belle Glade, Florida. As president of the local Chamber of Commerce, Rupert Mock was determined to bring national attention to the tiny farm community just north of Fort Lauderdale. Celebrating the winter produce

harvested from the area's "black gold" dirt, the festival supplied the setting for a *Guinness Book of World Records* accomplishment: creating the
World's Largest Salad. Local promoters succeeded in securing sponsor-
ship of Kraft Foods and Disney Cable. Motivated to build this media
event into one of historic proportions, Rupert searched for affordable
celebrities.

For the parade, he secured Miss Florida to ride in a convertible
flanked by two high school bands, three floats, and decorated farm equipment. Not enough. Rupert foraged for something outlandish to draw
attention to his small town. He called me.

"Miss Tampanna," he began, "My name is Rupert Mock but folks
around here just call me Bubba. Are you the lady who dresses like a fruit
salad?"

The negotiating began. I assured Bubba that I could dress like a
vegetable salad as well as a fruit salad, but for a large and crowded festival, I would require an appropriate vehicle to display me and a bodyguard
to protect me.

"No problem," Rupert, a.k.a. Bubba, assured me.

I briefly met with the bodyguard before the festival. A local Army
recruiter, he suggested that he wear his official dress blues for the parade. Sgt. Robert Reister took his job seriously, showing up for my early
morning run while entertaining me with stories about his efforts to
motivate other soldiers.

Belle Glade obliged my request for an appropriate vehicle. I inspected my "float," the biggest, most awesome piece of farm equipment
in South Florida. Usually covered with mud, the sugarcane combine is
as monstrous as an army tank. A John Deere tractor towed the combine
designated as my float, cleaned up nicely and polished to perfection. It
was, indeed, an impressive throne for the salad queen.

Wearing a lavishly sequined headdress of tomato wedges, carrots,
and an onion ring, I felt exceptionally glamorous in my costume. Sparkling lettuce-green organza cascaded from one shoulder while a green
satin train trimmed in ruffles was fastened to my hip. I perched twenty-
seven feet in the air atop the gigantic combine while Sgt. Reister,
breathtakingly handsome in his dress blues, anchored himself below
me. He understood his job well: to protect, defend, and promote.

"Miss Tampanna," he would announce, "there are cameras coming up on the right."

I whipped around to my right and waved my queenly parade wave. Sgt. Reister learned his job quickly.

No First Lady or European queen has ever received such rapt attention as I did from my military bodyguard at The Belle Glade Salad Festival. Sgt. Reister kept the crowd at bay as I posed for photographs. As I held local babies and greeted eager families, he guarded the train of my dress from muddy feet. He scheduled breaks for me in an air-conditioned trailer and brought me drinks and lunch. Finally, over dinner, my head weary from long hours under my headdress of stuffed vegetables, he entertained me with stories. We ended our long day together with a goodbye hug. No kiss. Just a hug.

Two weeks after the salad festival, Sgt. Reister showed up at my apartment with two bushels of fresh corn, his running shoes, and more stories. A detail man, Sgt. Reister lacked formal education beyond high school. But he embodied the Army motto, "Be all that you can be," with impeccable manners and a desire to please—a diamond in the rough. One thing for sure, anyone smitten with a lady dressed as a salad had to possess a sense of humor.

Sometimes we need to look beyond labels, appearances, and trappings of success. We need to look into a person's heart. Beyond the uniform, I recognized a man with dreams, sensitivity, and a strong work ethic. Sgt. Reister didn't see a crazy woman under that headdress of salad. Fortunately for me, he recognized a creative spirit with ambition for goal setting and a love for life.

As our friendship grew, so did our respect for each other's spirituality. Robert and I became students together, attending church, classes, retreats, and lectures. We shared music that spoke to our souls, and made friends with other seekers on the path. Eventually we participated in a Marriage Encounter Weekend where we broke through more barriers for deeper intimacy. Our marriage continues to grow in depth and commitment as we approach another anniversary and fantasize about our lives in retirement.

Though I am no longer concocting wild costumes, my creativity expresses itself through motherhood, speaking engagements, and volunteer work. Robert has traded in his uniform for casual clothes, a soccer coach whistle, and a clipboard. Instead of supporting me from a parade vehicle, he supports my lifework with encouragement and his involvement as a parent. He cheers me on as I reach out to other women, he participates with me in multi-cultural activities, and he fixes grilled cheese sandwiches for hungry children.

Our past mistakes in marriages have taught us to value the richness of what we share together. We've stuck by each other through some pretty tough times and never take the glue that keeps us together for granted. We know that our marriage continues to require work, romantic dates, and play. We display our photograph of the Salad Queen and her Army Escort in our living room as a reminder of the uniqueness of our marriage. For us, the banquet of life is spiced with dreams, our sense of humor, and yes, a salad tossed with creativity.

Dinner Questions

- ❏ What qualities endear you to the special people in your life?
- ❏ How do you support each other with your unique gifts?

The Sugar Plum Fairy

I suppose you can't have everything,
though my instinctive response to this
sentiment is always, "Why not?"

— MARGARET HALSEY, *SOME OF MY BEST*
FRIENDS ARE SOLDIERS

"What do you want to do when you grow up?"

While little boys dreamed of constructing bridges, conducting trains, and fighting wars, little girls in my time dreamed of modeling designer dresses, slinking in sequins on a movie set, or pirouetting in tutus on Swan Lake.

Not me.

I preferred to be a superhero. A creature of magical capabilities. Someone whom everyone adored. Yes, I desperately wanted to be The Sugar Plum Fairy.

"But the Sugar Plum Fairy is a ballerina!" my mother had exclaimed. "Do you want to be a ballerina when you grow up?"

"No, Mama," I corrected her. "The Sugar Plum Fairy is an angel."

My obsession with angels began at the age of three. Since my mother had disappointed me with the arrival of a baby brother instead of the baby sister I had secretly hoped for, I created my own playmate, invisible to anyone except me. Baby Angel, as I called her, had wings and whispered the loveliest secrets into my ear. When she grew up, she would become the Sugar Plum Fairy. I longed to be just like her.

The world needs a superhero like the Sugar Plum Fairy. She is an ethereal creature who sprinkles magic over hopeful children and whispers sweet thoughts into troubled minds. Her presence instantly makes you feel good, knowing that she would always protect you and surround you with goodness and light. These are happy vibes for any age. The Sugar Plum Fairy was exactly as you perceived her to be, tiptoeing around in her wings and halo. There were no deceptions, discrepancies, or false promises like with Santa Claus. There were no teeth stealing, with an unfairly random distribution of coins, as with the Tooth Fairy. The Sugar Plum Fairy, promising sugary utopia for all who believed in her, embodied the very essence of benevolence and love, and promised the realization of lofty dreams for everyone, especially young girls like me.

I don't know how long it took Clark Kent to figure out that when he pulled open his shirt and exposed his blue leotards, people treated him differently. But at twenty-five, I realized that the clothes, particularly extravagant ones, made the person wearing them. I found that I could get on with my gallant mission of the day after a morning at my sewing machine. A quick purple tutu and wings stapled together from scraps of gold satin did quite nicely. A wad of tinsel glued to a stick and voila!

The children at The First Presbyterian Preschool in Tallahassee received my first visit as the Sugar Plum Fairy. I breezed in on tippy toes while the room shushed in awe of my new persona. No one moved. The wide-eyed children sat motionless, their mouths open in wonder. I sprinkled magic on their little heads and slipped a chocolate kiss in each chubby hand. Their euphoric looks reflected pure rapture. My heart melted. This was my first love affair with an audience. I knew, fluttering before the adoring faces, it would not be my last. As a child I had always hoped that the Sugar Plum Fairy would transport me to the world of my dreams; now I realized that she had!

During my early thirties, the Fairy matured into a more sensuous creature, befitting my stage in life. A strapless, jeweled bodice topped a diaphanous lavender organza skirt, figuring that one should play up one's best feature, which for me was my voluptuous bust. A purple, ruffled petticoat from a square-dancing supply store added a backbeat swish to my walk. Tiny sparkling birds flew around the crown of lavender crystals and beaded sequins that perched on my long ash blond curls. I had outgrown the wings at this point, since there was no longer anything on my shoulders to attach them to.

The act of making wishes speaks to the child in all of us, whether we are two or one hundred and two, for we all secretly hope that wishes can and do come true. When circulating a party as the Sugar Plum Fairy, sans my wings, I was aware that every guest watched me, eagerly anticipating their turn to be granted a wish. No one would be overlooked as I carefully made my rounds. Old ladies, businessmen, mothers, and even teenagers closed their eyes and wished their hearts' desires while I dusted their heads with a precious sprinkle of magic dust. It is a delicate transaction, this wish granting procedure, and I took my role in it quite seriously.

I began moonlighting as a fairy for many events, distributing wishes and perpetuating dreams. But even the Sugar Plum Fairy herself doesn't get all her wishes granted. After demonstrating my popularity at a certain ritzy establishment, I negotiated with the manager of an exclusive gourmet French restaurant to let me entertain diners on Christmas Day in return for a deluxe dinner for my boyfriend and me. He agreed. After five hours of individual wish granting, and smiling my most charming fairy smile, I changed into my fine dining clothes and waited for my date to join me for the promised dinner of a lifetime: succulent Chateaubriand for two elegantly served with all the scrumptious accompaniments. But alas, my wish was not to be granted, and my boyfriend stood me up. The fairy ate her Christmas dinner alone.

In my forties, the costume evolved into a white satin version of Glenda the Good Witch from *The Wizard of Oz*. The dress hangs in my closet today. On occasion I wear this garb of magic that allows me to grant wishes to dreamers and believers. The skirt has panniers with bouffant clouds of white tulle. Gold poufs drape like delicate curtains over the skirt studded with lots of tiny bows and festooned with golden stars. I glued giant rhinestones on my gold shoes and wore long golden lamé gloves. The debut of this new image included a feather headdress that lit up for the New Year. Since I had to wear a belt full of batteries around my waist, adding to my girth, I must have looked more like The Gilded Cream Puff. Now the headdress has been replaced with a saucy little gold-and-white marabou hat poised over a wig of platinum curls. It is ravishing in spite of the fact that much of the costume is hot-glued together and anchored with safety pins. I never fail to enjoy a chorus of "ahhhhhhh's" when I glide into a room.

My performance as The Sugar Plum Fairy has evolved as well. Instead of just granting wishes, I whisper affirmations into children's ears. Sometimes I suggest that they are mother's best assistant or that they will grow up to help thousands of people. Children seem to know when they have heard divine words of wisdom and often take my proclamation straight to their hearts. Many keep their affirmations a sacred secret, but I have been told they believe in them always.

I'm fifty now. Will the Sugar Plum Fairy appear again? I don't know. But I have a three-year-old grandson with a big wish in his heart. His mother is leaving for active duty in Saudi Arabia soon and he will definitely need some extra wish-granting to get through. We all need a Sugar Plum Fairy from time to time, someone who affirms our dreams for kinder days, our wishes for a better tomorrow, and our aspirations for a magnificent future.

Dinner Questions

☐ What future did you dream of as a girl?
☐ What future do you dream of now?

Family Alligators:
Once Upon a Culture

We had codes in our house.

— LOUISE GLÜCK, *SCRAPS*

A young man I know has been disowned by his mother. An eleven-year-old friend of my daughter's waits for sporadic visits from her father, knowing full well that his promises have little credibility. In a nearby area, a fourteen-year-old girl was arrested for drugging her grandmother because she had grown tired of the old woman calling her fat and good-for-nothing.

Families hurt each other, often.

A new daughter-in-law hesitates to bring her daughter to visit Grandma in North Carolina. As a white German married to a black American, she feels harsh prejudice when visiting the United States, preferring the more open acceptance of her friends in Germany. Families and their prejudices foster the alligators of rejection that can easily maim, and kill, anyone in their path, even small children. Such prejudices are carried on from generation to generation, silently infecting the offspring, creating even more rejection and exclusion. A family's proclivity for perpetuating certain beliefs is what creates the family culture—a unique blending of perceived values, genetic make-up, national heritage, and personal histories. Each family's culture is slightly different than that of their parents and their community.

Whenever Robert and I visit the home of one of our siblings, we experience a kind of culture shock as a result of these incongruous family cultures. Even though we love our relatives, we feel uncomfortable in many ways because of their vast differences in lifestyles. This is true for most extended families. Some families run around in the nude at home while others embarrass easily in front of a nursing mother. One family might maintain piles of packrat stuff, casually stepping over their collections and blithely ignoring the clutter; another throws away the same stuff as junk with great discipline, incapable of existing in a home without order. Some families formally dine together; others seem to thrive on the run, with fast food containers littering the floor of the car.

Every household acquires its own culture based on certain standards and the mutual decisions of the people who inhabit the home. As we grow up together, we fine-tune this culture until it becomes distinctively ours. When our offspring leaves home and marries, a new culture must be cultivated, blending the two lives together. Problems arise when there are conflicts over this new-formed alliance, particularly from the parents. Often a spouse is accused by his or her in-laws of influencing the son or daughter to live differently. This seems to invalidate the original family culture. Some parents even ostracize the spouse as an outsider, refusing to let them share in their culture by shutting them out.

I have personally seen and heard horror stories of such family abuses based on conflicting cultures. My friend Jana had in-laws who chose to speak French in her company, even though they spoke fluent English. Another friend visited in-laws at Christmas and discovered that she had been left out of gift giving. Siblings easily find family support when criticizing an in-law among them, and some families even encourage it. I have witnessed family situations where the favorite leisure activity consisted of gossip regarding the daughter-in-law.

When you think about it, there are so many factors that contribute to the culture within the home, including the values the family holds dear. There are numerous elements that influence how a family chooses their values beyond those that they brought into the marriage. Who makes the decisions? How and where does the family worship, if at all? What prejudices are taught? What are the attitudes towards sex? The answers to these questions, and many more, largely determine your family's culture.

In the beginning of a marriage, however, it is often difficult to establish a family culture if the spouse's values are dramatically different from your own. During my first short marriage, I witnessed a shocking behavior practiced by my husband's family. The mother enjoyed watching afternoon TV. One day, one of her children walked in front of her and switched the channel to another program. No one bothered to ask the mother if she minded. The entire family accepted this practice of insensitivity towards the mother's feelings! How could I expect a husband to respect me if he and his family treated his mother as a non-entity?

Even if you successfully blend your two cultures together, forming your own set of values and standards, there are times when it is difficult to maintain these practices, especially in the home of an in-law. Sometimes this can cause tremendous stress, particularly if the other family exhibits values you find abhorrent. For example, it disturbs me to be around people who make racist remarks, even when I was young. I remember visiting my grandparents as a child. My grandfather would make terrible racist generalizations that embarrassed my mother. Mother would take us children aside and explain to us that Granddaddy didn't know better and that we should never repeat what we heard him say. It took a lot of parenting to "undo" the damage caused by my grandparents' contradictory culture.

Cultural differences within families are a major concern, as proven by the thousands of letters Ann Landers answers each year on the topic. One of my teachers pointed out that most conflicts in relationships, even in the workplace, boil down to sibling rivalry (jealousy or competition) or rebellion toward authority or parent figures. These conflicts are centuries old, represented in the Old Testament of the Bible, and a never-ending source of hurt on every level. If we could just learn to heal within our families we could go a long way in healing our society.

It is difficult enough to accept cultures within families here in America, but consider the complications that women from other countries face when they try to adapt to American lifestyles. Smeeta, an outspoken woman from India, has a doctorate in psychology. She knew that she could not accept the low position of a wife in India so she emigrated to the United States.

"In India, a woman doesn't marry a man, she marries a family," says Smeeta.

Women in India are expected to live with the husband's family and to serve under the management of his mother. Some women come with dowries of money, televisions, and VCRs. A woman is the sole property of the husband and his family. Many families used to believe that if he should die, then, by rights, so should she. Traditionally, the wife would throw herself upon the funeral pyre of her husband, so that she may join him in death. This is illegal now and only practiced in rural areas. As property, men are free to treat their wives however they like, which sometimes includes getting rid of them altogether. Since divorce is disgraceful, another method was sought. Although illegal, bride burnings still occur when a wife's sari "accidentally" catches fire. The husband and his mother are hence free to choose another wife servant, complete with another dowry. Even though Smeeta has married a progressive, Westernized Indian man, she still struggles with the traditions and duties imposed by both families upon the young couple because of their culture.

Neang came to America from Cambodia. As she grew up, her mother took her to market, training her to never look at men or boys. By the age of nine, Neang became an object of close observation by parents of sons. At the age of thirteen, her parents arranged for her marriage. Neang came to her two-day marriage ceremony without having met her sixteen-year-old husband. Neang and her husband have lived together as a team for nineteen years. American couples cannot understand the terms of arranged marriages, and certainly can't comprehend that an arranged marriage could work. But Neang and her husband share the same family culture, and found happiness together.

Sometimes in-laws click. How wonderful when a man or woman is accepted as a true daughter or son by parents-in-law. My parents love my husband this way, even though they already have three sons. He honors that relationship in return by being a good son, finding things to fix for my mom and providing devoted assistance to my feeble father.

My friend Martha firmly tells each of her sons, "If you divorce your wife, you had better make friends with her, because she will be my daughter from now on."

Sure enough, Martha brings younger women to committee meetings and introduces them as her daughters, even though they are no longer married. She remains involved with her grandchildren and refuses to join in any couple squabbles.

Sara remained close to her in-laws in spite of her divorce. When her father-in-law died, Sara spent many days with her mother-in-law as she grieved.

"She needed to talk about him with somebody," said Sara. "You can't live with someone for fifty years and never talk about him again when he dies. I wanted to give her that opportunity to talk as much as she needed."

Our lives grow richer when we practice respect and acceptance for each other's culture. This does not mean that one has to give up personal beliefs in order to embrace another set of values, in fact, it is very important to remain grounded in the culture that your parents imbedded in you. It is vital to remain connected to our roots and our ancestors. My friend, RaVonda, continues a strong relationship with her ancestors even though they are no longer living. Sometimes she loans one to me.

"RaVonda, I am feeling anxious about my long drive to Atlanta," I say in a quick e-mail.

"Take my aunt with you," replies RaVonda. "She will sit on your shoulder like a little bird and bring you peace."

RaVonda's aunt, a calm spirit, did accompany me on my trip, bringing me a decided sense of peace!

This chapter demonstrates ways that we attempt to incorporate a respect for diversity in our family. We still feel challenged by family criticism, but we need to feel confident that our choices are right for us, and for our own nuclear family.

Dinner Questions

- ❑ How do you live differently from your parents and siblings?
- ❑ When have you been deeply impacted by a culture other than your own?

The Body Lesson

I was climbing up a mountain-path
With many things to do,
Important business of my own,
And other people's too,
Then I ran against a Prejudice
That quite cut off the view.

— CHARLOTTE PERKINS GILMAN, "AN OBSTACLE"
IN THIS OUR WORLD

Slim and pretty, Corine had a bubbly, friendly personality, cat-eye shaped glasses, and an inquisitive nature. She also had black skin. It took a lot of guts to be one of the first five African American students to attend my all white high school. I liked Corine. She flattered me with an invitation to visit her home—a girlfriend visit. The invitation resulted in a serious, parental discussion about the safety of going to the "colored" side of town.

In the fifties, white West Memphis, Arkansas, pretty much ignored the "colored side of town." Small wooden houses were crowded together along unpaved streets, the dirt yards filled with barefooted children. White people considered the black community dangerous, especially at night. Even the white police force didn't willingly venture into it. The community was left to handle its own disputes in whatever way they could. We rarely, if ever, drove through the area, and when we did, my curiosity and empathy left me in a state of conflict.

My parents, progressive for their community and the times, finally gave me permission to go for an hour. I could visit Corine for only one hour, but that hour made a lasting impression as I discovered more about myself than I did about Corine. I discovered the resistance that people experience in changing their beliefs about other people based on outward appearances, such as skin color. Little did I know that this same prejudice also applied to the way I felt about my own physical appearance. You see, though my skin was not black, I could not accept my own body image. I cursed myself as fat and ugly based on society's standard of thin beauty.

Corine lived in a small, neat house. Nothing about Corine, her home, or her family substantiated the stereotypes of blacks that permeated the attitudes of my white peers or the media in the 50s. After meeting the entire family, I followed Corine to her bedroom. In those days, the favorite activity with girlfriends consisted of dancing to a beloved record collection. Corine turned on her record player, and began to boogie as the strains of Motown filled the room. Gyrating her hips and clapping her hands, she shuffled to the fast beat with obvious enjoyment. Meanwhile, I sat like a wide-eyed statue on her bed, dreading the forthcoming moment of confrontation.

"Dance!" insisted Corine. "Come on!" She offered me her hand.

I panicked. Engulfed with embarrassment, I clung to the bedpost, steadfastly refusing to participate.

Corine persisted. "Do you want a different record? The Supremes? The Beatles?"

"It's not that," I stammered. "I like all of it. I just don't dance."

"I'll teach you!" Corine said resolutely.

I shook my head. This would be a long afternoon.

I couldn't tell Corine about the insecurity I felt regarding my body. Plump girls shouldn't dance. I chanted this familiar mantra in my head to remind myself again. The white world, as I knew it then, was stilted enough in the way it allowed its children and free spirits to dance, and this unspoken constraint for plump girls was always poignantly clear to me. I accepted this as a personal restriction without question and would adhere to it for fifteen years until I became thirty. My entire young adulthood would be plagued with a self-imposed, socially supported prejudice against my body, forcing me to the sidelines—never dancing.

After high school, Corine and I left for our respective colleges. My parents had selected for me an all-white campus with social clubs that organized dances. At first, I dressed up and went alone to the music-filled gym, standing on the sidelines in the dim light, desperately wanting a social life but praying that no one would ask me to dance. Finally, I found refuge in the safety of the girls' dorm, distracting myself with creative pranks. I dropped water balloons on love-struck couples returning from dates, wrote love notes to shy boys from the head cheerleader, and anonymously invited football players to attend Vietnam protest rallies.

The following year, I became a campus organizer, dreaming up special events and recruiting volunteers to contribute talents and manpower. Since I had organized the event, I never sat home waiting for a date. Of course, at my special events, no one danced.

Years passed. The country integrated publicly but not socially. Diversity became a popular goal of most nonprofit organizations and a buzzword in corporate cultures. I worked in a racially diverse office and committed myself to pluralism, although I could count my black friends on two hands. I had been in only three African American homes, including Corine's, over a span of twenty years, which were three more than most of my white friends. I entertained few African Americans in my own home.

My body image had not changed much either. Diets, pregnancy, exercise, support groups—nothing could erase the embarrassment I felt about my body. If anything, my list of rules for plump girls had increased. I acquired rules about dressing to camouflage a stomach, choosing dark hose to slenderize legs, and constricting myself with despicable undergarments. I hated my softness and added swimming to my forbidden activity list. I stoically believed this to be my life sentence, accepting life without physical fun as a prison I deserved.

The wake up call came when I met the Nigerian Queens. Invited as special guests to a Girl Scout leaders' banquet with a theme of diversity, the three Nigerian women, wives of university students, obliged us by wearing their native dress. Although not really queens, they carried themselves in the most regal manner I had ever seen. Each woman exuded serene beauty in her colorful head wrap and dress of native fabric. I studied them intently, noting with special interest their immense body sizes and how they wore their clothes. None of them dressed to minimize their size. In fact they emphasized round bellies and ample, rotund hips by tying wide sashes around their hips and stomachs. Assembling our group into a giant circle, they taught us to dance, Nigerian-style.

The image of those beautiful, robust women took root in my mind. An African American trainer in New York, hearing my story, gently reminded me that Africa is a continent of drought. Extra body fat is a sign of personal prosperity and desirability, a concept completely foreign to most white women. I continued to work out, skip desserts, and avoided wearing sleeveless blouses, but secretly I envied those beautiful Nigerian women who obviously felt good about their size.

Years passed again. At fifty, I am enjoying a new journey with two commitments to tackle the issues that I encountered so many years ago sitting in that bedroom watching my friend Corine dance. One is to heal racial relations in my community. The other commitment is to be fit but also to learn to accept my body for what it is and how it looks.

As I experience menopause and the aches and pains that come with aging, I spend increasing time walking, working out at the gym, and taking the magic supplements that promise longevity.

The fact does not escape my attention that there are fewer black women who go to the gym than white women, indicating to me again the difference between us in how we view our bodies. I asked my friend Cynthia why more African American women aren't attracted to the gym. After a long pause, she responded.

"In our culture, feeding people demonstrates your love for them. We feast at funerals, church functions, and social gatherings. Sunday dinner is sacred. And," she continued, "large women are considered sexy. One of the most popular songs is about the 'girl with the big thighs.' Men enjoy a woman with hips and thighs. We have fun dressing up regardless of our size." Then she added, "Besides, who wants to drive to the other side of town everyday to work out with white women who don't speak to you?"

There it was in a single statement—the two old prejudices together again. One Cynthia was free of (body prejudice) and one she was not (racial prejudice.)

I often think back over all the dances and swim parties I had missed growing up. I suffered so much at the time because I felt I was too plump, deserving the socially-acceptable prejudice against people like me. Looking back at old photographs of myself, I discover an attractive woman, not the grossly fat body I remember.

I am not alone, of course. I recall the thin, white beauty queen who told pageant judges that she fantasized about eating as much as she wanted. Her predecessor had caused great controversy by gaining weight normal for healthy women of her height. The contest sponsors wanted to bar her appearance unless she starved herself on a crash diet. I think about the unhappiness of Princess Di, her eating disorder pitied by millions. I contemplate Oprah, who can't eat a meal or gain a pound without being in the headlines of a supermarket tabloid; such is our obsession with weight.

When I look at my friend Cynthia, I envy her for not experiencing the body shame that is an integral part of my white culture. We both have a lot to learn from each other. Discrimination still exists and there is still healing to do for me personally as well as for the nation. That healing can start with dancing to a little Motown music.

Dinner Questions

☐ Have you ever felt discrimination?
☐ How do you personally feel about your weight?

Searching for Beauty

Beauty is not caused.

— EMILY DICKINSON

The President's Wives, my first set of paper dolls, left me disappointed. Looking for a glamorous role model, I discarded Mamie Eisenhower in her frumpy dress, and scoffed with disgust at Eleanor Roosevelt, an ugly old hag! What girl could be inspired by such a homely, unattractive woman, even though famous? A few years later, the political scene presented us with a chance to choose between Pat Nixon and Jacqueline Kennedy. We all chose the beautiful Jackie.

Meanwhile, my parents ingrained in me those indisputable attributes that determined the worth of women and girls. Clearly, the ideal woman should be subservient, attractive, and slim. She should cook and serve wonderful food, but refrain from eating it herself.

"Be quiet!" roared my father from behind his newspaper.

"Never talk back to your husband or your father." Mother modeled the unspoken message. Daddy reinforced it.

Daddy complimented attractive women. Flirting with waitresses, he always received bigger servings in restaurants, sending us children the clear message that being attractive equaled getting more attention from men.

Mother measured everyone's success in life according to body weight. She judged first impressions of new acquaintances based on the amount of poundage they needed to lose and what they ate at church functions.

"She could be so pretty," Mother would lament. "It's no wonder she's like that. She took the biggest dessert."

Food endeared my father to his own mother. Grandmother clearly knew that her role in life consisted of cooking what people loved. Visits to the family home in Sweetwater, Tennessee, promised the smell of chicken frying for dinner and plates of fudge cooling on the porch. No longer considered an object of attraction, Grandmother's weight didn't seem to matter, although she needed to lose about one hundred pounds.

My own mother worked hard to have dinner on the table at six. She diligently attempted to imitate Grandmother's sage dressing patties, which my dad loved so much. Daddy's tastes pretty much determined all family menus and set the atmosphere for the meal. We children ate family dinners in silence while mother recapped the day's accomplishments for Daddy's approval.

Helping me achieve the perceived standard of attractiveness was not always easy for my mother. She did her best to coif and dress me on a stringent budget. Stinky home permanents and tight sponge rollers on Saturday nights guaranteed what I called " the weenie roll look" I detested. I also hated my clothes. The sewing machine buzzed its familiar sound as mother sewed night and day to provide necessary pants with knee patches for the three boys and a homegrown wardrobe for me. My choices of styles were limited to what mother felt suited "plump girls." No stick-out petticoats, skirts with ruffles or gathers, and nothing in gray, the color unflattering to plump girls. The dreaded ordeal of trying on an unfinished outfit, filled with pins for hemming, included mother's ritual of mashing down my stomach so the hem would lie straight. I detested this ritual, a recurring reminder that I had an unacceptable tummy.

Mother's body type and mine came from entirely different genes. Slim and small-waisted, Mother told stories of a skinny childhood. She had no need of "self discipline" because of her high metabolism, yet deemed people without such self-discipline as flawed in character. My curvier "vintage" figure obviously hailed from my father's side of the family, but that knowledge never made me feel better about my curves.

Female baby boomers never lacked for ladylike role models among television peers. Beautiful Annette Funnicello smiled shyly to reward the cutest boy, Sandra Dee maintained girlhood innocence as she developed into womanhood, and Haley Mills sang about being "demure, sweet and pure, hide the real you." Television programs featured saintly mothers in aprons and blondes with special powers. These women, including a witch and a genie, loved to hang around the house while they relied on mischievous means to manipulate their men. Mother and I eagerly watched the annual "Miss America Pageant," predicting the most perfect smile, the flattest stomach, and most selfless answers as the winner. Talent had the least amount of pull, but it had to be there. Piano players never won. I played the piano, lacked both a perfect smile and a flat stomach. I could not think on my feet to answer anyone's questions, much less a man's. The Miss America Pageant, and all the success and acceptance that the title implied, was out of reach for me.

Junior high school introduced the coming of age for girls. Kotex, "ponytail pink" lipstick, and high-heeled shoes led us into adulthood. As women, we had more secrets to learn as we dressed for show. My "beginner" girdle, a light turquoise band of spandex sported garters that ripped off the first time I wore them during my parents' Christmas party. Running to the bathroom when I felt the "pop" give way to a droop, I pulled rubber bands up my legs and succumbed to the pain. Shaving with razors resulted in numerous self-inflicted injuries. I stuck pieces of toilet paper to the multiple nicks on my legs. I gritted my teeth as I tweezed eyebrows, horrified at the masculine look of hair growing across the top of my nose. In spite of my efforts to "obey the rules," I knew in my heart that I was homely and not thin enough, destined to be unloved forever. It was an unhappy lot for most girls at that time, for almost all of us had one perceived flaw or another that caused us to deviate from the perfect, albeit unreal, image found in magazines, on TV, and in the movies.

For me, Barbra Streisand changed everything. A close up of Barbra Streisand on television stunned me as I realized that homely could still be glamorous. With her crossed eyes, long bumpy nose, and large lips, Barbra would have never qualified for Miss America. Her magic emanated from her phenomenal singing voice, her personality, lots of makeup, soft lighting, and ample breasts. I had hope. I couldn't sing like the great Barbra but I had personality and ample breasts. And I would buy the makeup. I studied my new and improved role model.

Barbra wore opulent costumes. I could do that, too. Barbra aggressively pursued the career she wanted, poked fun at her characters, and was actually considered adorable even in her most awkward moments. I could do all that, too! It was a new image for women that I could, in fact, have hopes of achieving.

Glamour became an illusion within my grasp. I perused the makeup counters. Pancake, liquid matte foundation, cover up, lip liners, and a rainbow of eye shadows weighted down my makeup case. Sponges, brushes, and eyelash curlers became my ready tools while lipsticks in many hues, lined up like little soldiers, filled countless receptacles in my bathroom. Longline bras became a necessity while girdles assured me that my tummy would be hidden from the public. I insisted that my lovers turn out the light before proceeding and I forbade them to touch my stomach, fearing their repulsion at my softness. I formulated my new motto, "If you can't lose it, decorate it."

In my forties, I lost myself further in the futile search for beauty with the discovery of yet more appearance enhancers. False eyelashes guaranteed a glamorous look without smudging the skin under my deep-set eyes, while shoulder pads provided the balance for my large bosom. I was obsessed. I even took my eyelash glue and hot foam rubber shoulder pads camping. Both of these indispensables caused alarm on important occasions.

False eyelashes come unglued, or stick to your eyelid, requiring immediate repair in the ladies' room. I found myself in this predicament before a presentation to a state committee. The large, immaculate stainless steel bathroom in the new state office building offered a haven with its wall-to-wall mirrors. After rummaging in my purse, I pulled out the small tube of glue that contained the answer to my problem. This particular glue, colored black, guaranteed me instant eyeliner. I squeezed as hard as I could, but the stuff refused to come out. Dried glue clogged the opening of the tube. Poised with my eyelash on a finger, I mashed the stubborn tube with all my might. Sploosh! A long string of black glue shot out a distance of five feet. Ribbons of black gunk spattered all over the stainless steel sink, the mirror, and the bathroom counter. Oozing and dripping on the mirrors, it looked like long spaghetti made of road tar. I panicked. What if someone walked in and caught me?

I scrubbed the mirrors and counters with wet paper towels, smearing the mess with frantic dismay as my watch ticked past my presentation time. The delinquent eyelash lay on the counter, looking like a dead insect. I rubbed it in a remaining puddle of glue and stuck it in place with my index finger and a sigh of relief. If my waiting committee only knew the nature of my tardiness, they would be surprised. The men, that is, because some of the women sitting there would have completely understood.

The shoulder pads caused another calamity. Made of foam rubber, they molded around my shoulders under my knit dress, offering me a body balanced with a silhouette of distinction, that is, when I could find them to wear them. As all busy working moms will attest, frantic schedules result in frantic searches for misplaced essentials.

On the day set aside for our family photograph, my shoulders of distinction were missing. After dressing two very resistant children in clothes they would never wear again, I grabbed a different pair of shoulder pads, unaware of the difference in shape and fabric and rushed with my husband to the photographer's studio.

This particular photo session required months of careful banking. It dictated great determination on my part to coax my family to agree to the session. The episode escalated once we entered the studio. My squirmy two-year-old son and active seven-year-old daughter severely challenged the talented photographer, in spite of her years of experience working with children.

"Why don't the two of you sit together on the floor," she suggested to my husband and me.

We obediently obliged.

"OK, kids, how about sitting still with your Mommy and Daddy ?"

Our children did not comprehend the meaning of "sit." Even more foreign was the phrase "sit still."

We insisted, cajoled, threatened, pleaded, and bribed. The photographer waved various stuffed animals to no avail. Simone wiggled and danced. John climbed me, with my head as his highest destination. He scrambled up my back, tumbled over my shoulders, and grabbed my neck with delight. As patience grew thin, John's clambering progressed. In a moment of sheer luck, John sat down for an instant. The photographer snapped the camera. An hour's work for one shot. Immediately, the family fell apart. John's mischievous attitude digressed to a fussy tantrum that also infected Simone. Our sitting had ended. My sigh mixed relief with resignation. As I looked down, my mouth dropped in horror. I discovered the shoulder pads. The left shoulder remained intact, but the other had nestled right between my breasts. I had the unfortunate distinction of being a three lumper, frozen forever in time by the single shot achieved by the photographer that day, a shot sabotaged by one of my most beloved tools of deception.

Following the painful years of childhood and young adulthood were many years of beauty success. Thanks to many tricks of the trade and judicious use of a plethora of beauty products, I grew accustomed to thinking of myself as beautiful, of turning heads as I walked into a room. Then I turned forty. Hurrying through a busy airport one day, I realized that I had become invisible. No one noticed me. No heads turned. Not one. I remember that moment clearly, the feeling of loss, the "what do I do now?" question. The years of "being looked at" were over. Forty years of preening, dieting, primping, plucking, sucking in, tucking under, and exercising, and for what? To be invisible for the next forty?

Barbra, who lived in seclusion in a world of plastic surgery and beautiful clothes, offered no help to me now. The lower rim of my right eye had developed a wart-like growth that grew back faster when removed by the ophthalmologist. My contacts gave way to bifocals and glasses provided better vision than the lenses. My weight slowly increased despite exercise classes. My hair changed in color and texture. My upper lip began to disappear. I ripped out an unwanted mustache with wax. With sadness, I watched my chin sag in crepe wrinkles. My parents didn't prepare me for this part of my life.

Yet, in my forties a deeper satisfaction took root. Though my surface beauty was clearly deteriorating, I discovered that I also possessed a certain inner beauty that started to radiate from within, a beauty that didn't need false eyelashes nor shoulder pads. Opportunities to develop a vision, teach skills, and learn about other cultures opened my eyes to new possibilities. Words like mission, vision, and corporate values guided my work. My employer invested in me with training, then complimented my achievements. My husband expressed pride in my work. I met mothers determined to raise daughters who could get dirty, enjoy sports, and set their sights on exciting careers. I began to search deep into myself for the lessons and values of my life's previous journey, planting the seed for a new career dream.

Now, I've reached my fifties. Women my age are scarce on prime time television, except as mothers, neighbors, and comic relief. Movies depict very few women my age in leading roles, compared to the large number of sixty-plus male actors who still play romantic leads, usually opposite twenty-something actresses. Women's magazines, published specifically for us common people, feature an occasional tall, skinny model with pre-mature, silver hair. I have become adept at recognizing facelifts, wigs, and dentures of aging stars. These women are afraid to show signs of their true age because their appearance is, quite literally, their life.

But my life, as well as most of the women I know, is based on so much more than my face and my figure. Unencumbered by adherence to or need to be considered attractive in order to feel successful in a typical, male-catching way, women are free at last to pursue interests of the heart and mind, rather than the body. What an exciting time for women with a sense of purpose! Women burn with their passion for social change, their motivation to succeed and their determination to make life better. I envy the young women who approach adulthood with a career path clearly marked, and I am inspired by women in their sixties and seventies who continue to contribute their professional experience and personal wisdom to society.

Finally, I have rediscovered Eleanor Roosevelt, an incredible woman who fought for human dignity of all people long before the Civil Rights movement deemed it a popular thing to do. Eleanor stood up for human rights and women's rights. When appointed to the United Nations, she persisted until the Human Bill of Rights was officially adopted, becoming the basis of the constitutions for over sixty countries. Eleanor didn't dwell on her appearance. She personified ageless beauty in the human spirit, which requires no makeup or shoulder pads. She was a heroine I wish I had recognized a long time ago when I first opened that set of paper dolls.

Dinner
Questions

❑ What silly routines do you follow to achieve beauty?
❑ Who do you think reflects the spirit of true inner beauty?

Cradle Trauma and Marriage Madness

*The tie is stronger than that between father
and son and father and daughter.... The bond
is also more complex than the one between mother
and daughter. For a woman, a son offers the best
chance to know the mysterious male existence.*

— CAROLE KLEIN, IN *TIME*

Deciding what to name baby launched one of the longest running arguments of our marriage. My husband, a mathematics lover, had named each of his three sons from a previous marriage three names that began with the letter R. Each name had five R's and nineteen letters. For example, Royal Rainerd Reister. Now, imagine three boys with such similar names. No one ever called the right boy the right name. This practice had been a family tradition, since Robert and his two brothers maintained the identical math in their names.

"If we have a son, we will pick another name with five R's and nineteen letters," Robert informed me.

Over my dead body.

"Michelangelo. We'll call him Michelangelo," I hissed in defiance.

Robert refused to budge. A spiritual teacher of mine once said that arguments must be resolved with an inspired solution. I prayed fervently for a brilliant answer to my dilemma. The enlightenment came.

I introduced my concept excitedly to my husband. "Robert, you presently have three sons. Their initials form three R's cubed."

$$R\,R\,R$$
$$R\,R\,R$$
$$R\,R\,R$$

I drew the picture for him.

"If you named our son with R's it would disturb the mathematical perfection. Your first three sons need to keep this special."

It worked. I had appealed to Robert's mathematical mind.

The next hurdle: the baby's gender. I badly wanted a girl. After growing up with three younger brothers, I found their endless arguments, rowdy wrestling, and loud burps abhorrent. I successfully ignored them and their activities with the exception of attending an occasional Cub Scout Pack meeting to win points for my competitive mom. Thinking back to my impressions of her role as a mother of sons, all I remember are noisy little boys hammering footstools, Mother pitching a softball for hours on end as my brother swung the bat, fishing with Daddy who insisted on long hours of silence in the boat, and dirty Boy Scouts who wore the same clothes and ate hot dogs every day on a four-day campout. No way could I enjoy any of that.

Fortunately, my first baby *was* a girl. Friends gave me frilly pink dresses, lacey hair bows, and tights with ruffles on the bottom. But when this daughter turned three, she absolutely refused to wear dresses ever again except after a knockdown drag-out fight in the photographer's studio. At four, she stomped around in monster feet, at seven she gave herself a pirate party, and at eight she dressed in full Darth Vader regalia. Dolls never received her affection, she hates the color pink, and she wouldn't be caught dead in a hair bow.

When pregnant with the second baby, I lay on the sonogram table looking at the monitor image as the nurse pointed out appendages with her pen.

"Nope, that's not a leg. You have a boy!"

"Oh no," I sighed. "The inevitable has happened. What will I do?"

"Boys are so sweet," the nurse reassured me.

Watching a mother rush out to the street to stop her son from throwing rocks at his friend, I felt dubious. "Sweet" did not describe any little boys that I knew.

Looking back, I realize that I had focused on the wrong issue. Having a boy would not be my problem. Like other mothers of boys, I, too, soon became smitten with his affectionate personality, his caring ways, and his insatiable curiosity. Having a boy at the age of forty-two, however, would have repercussions. No one warned me about going through menopause when my son turned seven. No one suggested that at the age of fifty, I might be required to play offense on the Mothers' soccer team, a ball smashing me in the stomach. I failed to visualize newts and salamanders escaping from their jar of creek water into my son's bed sheets. And no one painted a picture of a birthday sleepover with four young boys bored by James Bond.

Actually, it has turned out all right. God has a way of making all babies adorable no matter what the gender. The truth is, my son really does have the best hugs and sweetest kisses. I don't mind newts and salamanders, and encourage him to explore the treasures of the creek. I even embraced Cub Scouts, now that my own son is one. Their camping experience is still not my style. I prefer latrines to squatting in the weeds, and I will never develop a love for eggs scrambled in black bacon grease. But I can definitely contribute a little drama to their ceremonies. My costume collection easily accommodates adult Boy Scout Indians. As a consultant of ceremonies, I insist on flaming torches and real drums filling the night skies with the echoes of past powwows.

Although I failed miserably at entertaining the boys at their sleepover, they left me with my favorite compliment. The three seven-year-old guests, having decided that I am extremely old, huddled to discuss my age at length. (Okay, I am something of an anomaly, since no other second grader at our school claims a fifty-year-old mother.) Reaching a conclusion, they confronted my son, John.

"John, we figured out just how old your mother is," announced the young spokesperson. "She must be thirty-six!"

My son, in his young wisdom, simply smiled and saved the secret for me. As for the Mother's Soccer Game, I played at 110 percent, screwing up my face to intimidate the seven-year-old defender, actually kicking the ball, and whooping as if I enjoyed it. We lost, of course. (What mothers' team would not lose to their sons?) But I made myself a medal for my valiant efforts on the playing field.

Dinner Questions

❑ What kinds of expectations or attachments did you have for your children regarding names, gender, and behaviors?

❑ How did these family preferences impact your life as a child?

The Quest for Respect and Bula-Bula Berries

*Fantasies are more than substitutes for
unpleasant reality; they are also dress rehearsals,
plans. All acts performed in the world
begin in the imagination.*

— BARBARA GRIZUTI HARRISON,
"TALKING DIRTY," IN *MS*

Not everyone appreciates the privilege of living with a five-year-old. With unlimited imagination, they are enthralled with any adult willing to enter their magical world. I treasure the private events experienced with my five-year-old daughter, Simone. These events needed only a few basic elements: food, costumes, and specific character parts for us. Frequently, we became Native American. I braided Simone's blonde hair adding feathers or beads while she made her fringed dress out of a grocery bag. As soon as Simone donned her beaded buckskin, we assumed our Indian names as well.

"You look lovely, Little Sparrow," I said admiringly.

"Thank you, Woman Who Swims in Rivers," Simone responded.

We referred to Simone's infant brother, John, as Buffalo Boy. He lay on a lambskin to sleep or play with his toes while he watched us.

Our living room became the forest in which Simone learned how to walk toes first without making a sound. We practiced etiquette for wigwams, respectful salutations for elders, and caution for nature's dangers. We created ceremonies for receiving courage and wisdom and invented animal stories for campfire entertainment. Our living room teemed with wildlife, as furniture became trees, rocks, and riverbanks. I summoned Little Sparrow into my wigwam with my special birdcall meant just for her. I described the perilous journey she must take in order to find my medicinal herbs. Her Quest.

"Little Sparrow," I commenced, "you must run to where two rivers meet, then climb the boulders until you get to the purple berry bush. There the kind owl will show you a big cave. Across from the cave find a large log covered with mushrooms. Do not pick the mushrooms but look for the red leaves of the bula-bula plant nearby. Gather them up in your dress and hurry back. Be sure that no one sees you. Now go!" Simone bowed in respect, then said, "Yes, Woman Who Swims in Rivers."

Simone disappeared on her personal adventure that sometimes lasted twenty minutes. Meanwhile, I prepared our picnic of sunflower seeds, apples, raisins, and crackers to celebrate her successful return. Simone always found the bula-bula leaves but only after encountering a dangerous bear that left her out of breath with a big story to tell.

In the years that followed, Simone delighted her teachers by creating characters in costume to deliver book reports. She gained a reputation in her school as she transformed into Sakajawea, Nefertiti, Daniel Boone, or the Boy with Bat Wings. Even in middle school she mesmerized her Spanish class as a confident matador, resplendent in silver-fringed epaulets and a jeweled jacket, her red cape at her side and a rose in her teeth. She described the grandeur of the bullfights and the bulls she had killed. Her class responded with resounding applause.

Our Little Sparrow game not only fostered imagination, it fostered respect. Respect for a child's need to be a hero, for people who live differently, for a five-year-old's insatiable appetite to learn, explore, and be whomever she pleases. Little Sparrow and Woman Who Swims in Rivers lived in a world all their own, an intimate bond precious to us both. As a teenager, Simone continues to invite me to be a part of her world at an age when other kids don't want to be seen with their parents. She explores new activities, returning home out of breath with stories to tell. She enjoys babysitting because it gives her the opportunity to play imaginatively with her young charges, just as I played with her. I feel confident Simone will create an imaginative world for her own children when she becomes a mom. I am especially proud that she embraces wisdom and courage beyond her years, which I attribute, in part, to the brave Little Sparrow persona she envisioned when she was a small girl.

Dinner Questions

❑ How have you fostered important values in your children?
❑ How do childhood playtimes impact your children as teenagers?

John's Gift

Her child was like a load that held her down, and
yet a hand that pulled her to her feet.

— EDITH WHARTON

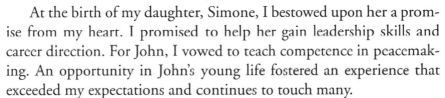

At the birth of my daughter, Simone, I bestowed upon her a promise from my heart. I promised to help her gain leadership skills and career direction. For John, I vowed to teach competence in peacemaking. An opportunity in John's young life fostered an experience that exceeded my expectations and continues to touch many.

Having just moved to Winston-Salem, we debated over our choices concerning John's preschool. As we looked for a summer preschool before kindergarten, another parent told us about the extraordinary impact her son experienced at a special school for handicapped children. The school addressed the needs of children with birth defects and severe physical disabilities. Devoted teachers, aided by assistants and volunteers, taught small classes in cheerful rooms loaded with highly stimulating toys. Special funding enabled students to enjoy swimming, bowling, and trips to the mall. The teachers discovered that normal children interspersed in the classes were beneficial to all. They developed a new program for promoting the involvement of "The Typical Child."

In order to fill one of the few "typical child" slots, the school tested prospective students. Sitting on the sidelines, I watched four-year-old John perform a variety of physical challenges such as jumping, throwing a ball, and turning a somersault. Then he completed simple tasks such as sorting and stacking for the patient teacher administering the test. As John's comfort level with the teacher increased, so did John's mischievousness. The teacher placed a small block on the table, then under the table, then next to the table. Each time John correctly described the position of the block until she placed it behind the table.

"Where is it now, John ?" she asked gently.

"In your underpants!" teased John.

My face turned many shades of red as my body heat rose. The calm teacher smiled at me.

"It's OK," she said assuredly, "that's an age-appropriate answer."

I comforted myself often with the phrase "age-appropriate " as a verbal tranquilizer. Fortunately, the school admitted John as a "typical child."

The first day of school, I took John in with some apprehension. Children in wheelchairs, walkers, and leg braces filled the halls. Some children wore helmets. John's class included a child with a faulty esophagus and a paraplegic boy, bound to his wheelchair.

"That's Tyler," the teacher informed me. "We strap a stick to his forehead and encourage him to point to the buttons."

She demonstrated his special keyboard of colorful buttons, which lit up, played music, or set things in motion. I looked over at John who was busying himself with the flashing lights of a small police car. I left him with the teachers, feeling a sense of awe while I considered the challenges that Tyler's parents must face.

John loved the school. Everyday he came home with stories of new adventures; violinists who played for the children, a trip to the museum, a big fish with scales to touch, computers with their interactive games. But, more important to me, he made friends, especially with Tyler.

About a week into the summer session I walked John down the hall towards his class. Seeing Tyler sitting motionless in his wheelchair, John broke loose from my grasp and ran to him excitedly.

"Tyler !" he greeted the child with gusto. Taking Tyler's face in his hands, John pulled Tyler's head closer. The two boys stared eyeball-to-eyeball, nose-to-nose.

"John !" I gasped in horror, worried my son might be injuring this fragile child.

But Tyler's face broke into a beaming smile, as he looked at his adoring buddy. The children communicated in their own age-appropriate way. John had taught me my first lesson about his gift of acceptance.

My "typical child" spent only a summer at the special school before receiving a letter of acceptance to the kindergarten of our choice, and another lesson lay ahead.

At the Downtown School, children remain with the same teacher for two years. John's four-year-old class had been together the previous year. John quickly fit in and enthusiastically came home with stories about his new best friend, LaKeisha. John played with her at recess and enjoyed having a little girl to entertain with his antics.

One day the phone rang, John's teacher requesting a conference.

Oh, no, I thought, what "age-appropriate " thing has he done this time? I recalled how, in an earlier playgroup, John had named the wrong boy "Doo-Doo Head." John wears a scar to remind him of that mistake.

Three teachers waited for me at the school. With my heart in my throat, I sat down and nervously clasped my hands, expecting the worst. The teachers wore serious expressions on their faces.

"We want you to know what John has done to our class..." the teacher began.
I held my breath.

"We have a child with Down's Syndrome," she said. "Last year this child was violent. She bit other children causing everyone to dislike her. When school began in September, the children remembered their fear from last year and avoided her. Since John came to us as a new student, he didn't know about her history. They became friends!"

LaKeisha ! I thought to myself. They are talking about LaKeisha!

The teacher confirmed my realization. "John chooses LaKeisha when it's buddy time. He asks her to be his partner when we play games, and he entertains her outside on the jungle gym."

One of the other teachers wiped away a tear.

"It's amazing! The other children have been influenced by John to accept LaKeisha as a friend. John turned the whole class around! This healing has touched the entire staff! We've never seen anything like it," she said, shaking her head.

I felt deep gratitude for the Children's Center for the Physically Disabled.

That night as I tucked John into bed, I asked about LaKeisha.

"I just like to make her laugh," he said matter-of-factly. "She's my friend."

LaKeisha and John enjoyed their friendship for a long time. Teachers arranged for her to be in his class the following two years. They attended each other's birthday parties, and enjoyed many games of chase. John even asked LaKeisha to marry him. But in her own age-appropriate way, LaKeisha shook her head with disgust.

"Yuck!" said LaKeisha, pretending to slit her throat with her finger. End of that.

Shortly afterwards, John taught me a third lesson about acceptance. My dad has a disease similar to Parkinson's disease. He lives near us with my mom, his caregiver. He also suffers from memory impairment with limited speech and a slow shuffling walk. Beginning at the age of six, John loved to be "Boppo's" special buddy. During family outings to restaurants, instead of running ahead as most small children would do, John patiently takes baby steps next to Boppo, his little hand in Boppo's large shaky one. It's John who climbs into Boppo's lap, instigating cuddle time on the sofa, which brings a look of tenderness to Boppo's normally vacant face. John insists that Boppo join in a family game, while he carefully shows him where to move the game pieces.

My son's special affinity for people of all ages who are different, and often less fortunate, than himself continues to astound me. John's best friend in the neighborhood has a speech impediment. John listens carefully and treasures their times together. He plans to celebrate his next birthday with his list of guests, mixing race, ability, and economic class. A newscast about the Ku Klux Klan staging a rally here reduced him to tears with fear for an African American friend.

We are proud of John's sensitivity to other people. He still has many lessons to learn, and so do I. Sibling rivalry challenges him, and peer pressure awaits him in middle school. But he has taught many of us about a child's unconditional love and ability to see past people's differences. They say children are teachers in small packages. I say they are also healers.

Dinner Questions

☐ How do you and your family break barriers and build bridges?
☐ When has your child taught you a lesson about life?

How A White Man Found His Passion in Kwanzaa Drums

It's not the men in my life that counts;
it's the life in my men!

— MAE WEST

Unfamiliar territory. I felt nervous.

"We might be the only whites there," I forewarned my family as my husband drove us to the other side of town.

"What's it going to be like?" asked John. My children like to know in advance if they will be bored or not.

"There will probably be some refreshments," I replied, knowing what really matters to them. "There will be a ceremony like the one you had at school."

In spite of the widespread promotion of Kwanzaa and the children's exposure in school and scouts to multi-cultural celebrations, my decision for the family to attend the African American festival of harvest required a bit of coaxing. The children did not look forward to being a minority.

"Imagine how *they* feel, being surrounded by whites all the time." My suggestion fell on deaf ears.

Fortunately, my husband responded willingly. He drove as I navigated my finger on the map lit by a flashlight. Passing the airport, we noticed that community neighborhoods took on a different personality. I couldn't put my finger on it at the time, but the frequent large,

66

modern grocery stores and bustling small businesses of local entrepreneurs on our side of town were missing. I recalled hearing black community leaders lamenting the lack of commitment to economic development on the east side of town.

We spotted our destination, an African American Presbyterian Church, and turned into the crowded parking lot. Dismayed by our tardiness, we rushed to the back church entrance, passing friendly teenagers and exuberant adults welcoming new guests. They received us warmly as we entered. The Fellowship Hall overflowed with animated African Americans dressed in flowing caftans of multi-colored prints, many heads wrapped in turbans or topped with small kufi caps. My family investigated the gifts thrust into their hands; a Kwanzaa lapel pin and a snack-size bag of Motherland Potato Chips, with its brightly-colored map of Africa on the front.

Colorful wares simulated the spirit of an African marketplace. A rack of multi-colored caftans, embellished with swirling stitches, enticed customers to try them on. African costume dolls, calendars, and Kwanzaa candles in traditional colors of black, green, and red attracted browsers. Ebony statues carved by African hands awaited new owners.

A panorama of T-shirts presented motifs validating the varied sizes, shapes, and colors of African American women. You would never see shirts like these for white women, I thought.

My daughter recognized the bronze-skinned lady sitting next to me as a school chum's mother.

"Hi, Mrs. Turner! I'm Simone. Markeitha is in my class."
Mrs. Turner responded with a smile. Since we comprised the white minority of the audience, it felt comforting to have a connection with someone next to me.

"Markeitha and the family are still in Washington, D.C.," she explained. "We celebrated the first night of Kwanzaa there, with ten thousand people!"

We felt duly impressed.

"They stayed for the rest of Kwanzaa while I came home to go back to work," she added.

I thought of my own resistance to attend functions alone.

"What are you doing on New Year's?" I asked with sincere curiosity.

"Going to church," she replied matter-of-factly.

My admiration deepened. Many of my African American friends had similar plans to spend the traditional party night in religious contemplation with fellow worshipers.

An earsplitting noise interrupted our conversation. Boom! Boom! Boom! Our attention was riveted to the back of the hall where African drummers pounded tight-skinned drums, eliciting deep, explosive sounds that resonated throughout the room. The crowd froze as the majestic drummers paraded up the center aisle, their powerful presence demanding reverent homage. Three women followed, African dancers in short dresses of flowered print, their dark hands shaking carved gourds, encased in nets of tiny shells, rattles of swishing rhythms. As the enticing dancers smiled and shook their simple instruments to the drums, the audience jumped to their feet and joined in, clapping and stomping in joyous celebration.

The fast-paced variety of the ethnic program held our rapt attention. Distinguished elders and youth took turns giving welcomes, pouring libations, and explaining Nia, or purpose, the theme of the evening. The audience applauded community leaders and children. I thought back to my own childhood church services, where children were ordered to be still and silent, invisible in a program geared to adults. Not here. Children sat in front row seats, while adults hoisted their precious toddlers on their shoulders for better viewing. Other youngsters performed in the program, presenting their talents confidently, refined from hours of careful practice.

After a piano solo and an impeccable recitation about pride for the black experience, three young ladies in purple sequined chiffon pirouetted with flawless timing. Finally, the drummers returned accompanied with the African dancers, their hips keeping the beat of the drums while their undulating arms and upturned hands pushed the air out to each side. Long braids of hair cavorted about their smiling faces as they pounded the floor with a frenzied stomp. A grandiose finale for a magnificent evening, the perfect completion to this cultural experience, I thought. Wrong! The biggest surprise for me was yet to come.

After demonstrating African dancing, the dancers went into the audience. My daughter, realizing that they were seeking volunteers, raised her hand and pointed to me. She knew I usually loved a stage.

Grabbing her hand, I yanked it down with maternal authority.

"No, Simone," I hissed, "that's not appropriate. This is not a white person's dance."

The dancers continued to pull people up. After a moment of confusion and shuffling, I realized that my husband no longer sat with us. Drafted by an insistent dancer, he followed her to the front of the room.

"Oh, no!" I gasped.

Too late. Robert stood expectantly with five other men at the front of the room, watching the head performer intently and listening for directions. A line of six women stood on the other side of the hall, a competition brewing, men versus the women. I stared at my husband, anticipating an anxious glance in my direction, his face red with embarrassment and panic. He always preferred to remain backstage, leaving the spotlight to me. But this time, Robert did not look to me for a rescue. Instead, he remained focused on the head dancer. My bespectacled husband is conservative, a reserved member of our white American culture, a fifty-two-year-old computer nerd. He made gallant attempts to swing dance with me years ago during our courtship, but never progressed beyond a good-natured shuffle. I prayed fervently for a secret trap door in the floor to open up and swallow him, an escape from his approaching humiliation.

Two by two, the dancers paired up and took the spotlight. The first couple danced with sexual energy, hips swaying toward each other in suggestive invitation. I held my breath.

"Please, Robert, look at me!" I whispered. "I'll give you a thumbs up for encouragement, sweetheart!" He must need it desperately, I thought. But Robert remained focused on the lead performer.

The next pair gleefully approached center stage, obviously experienced in this art of African dance. Competent, fully enjoying their energy, they danced with the ease of accomplished athletes. The third couple continued and so on. Finally, the dreaded moment arrived. The drums paused as Robert stepped forward, removing his jacket. The head performer took his hand and that of an older woman, pulling them to a squatting position and whispering a few words as we waited in pregnant expectation.

With a resounding staccato of tribal punctuation, the drums began their mesmerizing beat. In an explosion of energy, Robert bounded up, his head bouncing to the rhythm and his arms flailing while his feet kicked to the front, the side, and behind, like some sort of funk aerobics class at super speed. Robert danced furiously, a look of rapture on his face as if in a state of altered consciousness. The drums had kidnaped him! As I watched his delirious performance I realize the entire room was focused on this lone white man. My white man! The clapping rose to a tumultuous crescendo as my mouth dropped in astonishment. Robert had brought the house down.

My 12-year-old daughter grabbed me, her eyes wide with disbelief.

"Mama! That's Daddy ! Can you believe it? That's Daddy!" she repeated.

The drums picked up speed and strength, excited by Robert's exuberant energy. As his performance ended, he faced the audience, stunned by the applause, yet looking very pleased with himself. I continued to sit in speechless stupor. How would I ever describe this experience to his mother? What a moment!

Most African programs end with a feast, we learned, and this one was no exception. As the drummers made their exit, the emcee delivered the evening's instructions for orderly buffet service. Robert made his way back to us, accompanied by a crowd of admiring well-wishers.

"Good job!"

"Nice going."

"You can sure dance, man!"

Our family will never forget that evening. We watched Robert take a huge risk in front of a hundred-and-fifty people. We watched as his body became one with the beat of the drums, something none of us ever thought possible. Without any words being spoken about the subject, my children had learned that night a lesson of acceptance and friendship. Kwanzaa is a celebration of pride and respect, precisely my feelings for Robert.

Dinner Questions

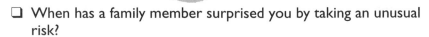

- ❑ When has a family member surprised you by taking an unusual risk?
- ❑ What multi-cultural experiences have enhanced your life?

Sudden Alligator Attacks:
Women Protect Their Young

A mother's love for her child is like nothing
else in the world. It knows no law, no pity, it dares
all things and crushes down remorselessly
all that stands in its path.

— AGATHA CHRISTIE, *"THE LAST SÉANCES"*
IN THE *HOUND OF DEATH*

Sometimes our most feared alligators are intruders, uninvited strangers who threaten to bring traumatic disaster. As we tend our offspring, our mothering instinct makes us protect our young, the weak, and the infirm amidst the unforeseen dangers that we know surround us. As a small child, I asked my mother if she could ever kill another person. I'll never forget her answer.

"Only if that person tries to hurt my child."

My mother knew the depths of her unbridled passion and her utter resolve to safeguard us against any attack. Her answer deeply reassured me of her love and protection. Fortunately, no one tested my mother's commitment, but I never once doubted that if an intruding alligator had even so much as bared his teeth at us, my mother would have without hesitation rapped him on the snout and sent him scurrying back to the swamp.

Thank God, so far no intruder has ever threatened my offspring, but I have the same commitment as my mother and know I would kill if that happened. But not all intrusive alligators are easy to recognize.

Sometimes they are disguised as something delightful and entertaining, and yet they can do as much damage to our children as if they are being physically attacked. Deadly poisonous, they prey on us as children and infants. These alligators might be painted in pastel colors and sold in fancy department stores and elite boutiques, deceptively promoted by the media as a necessity for every girl's success. Clothes and makeup, promising instant sex appeal for little girls, and dolls with enormous breasts, setting the standards for our young children, are such innocent props for these deceptive alligators. Verified by magazines, television, and movies, our children eagerly embrace the images of females as well-endowed, nicely-dressed victims waiting for rescue.

In the African savannahs, mother hippopotami teach their vulnerable babies to avoid the alligator's jaws by covering themselves with mud. Maybe we should learn a lesson from them about survival in a proactive way, rather than waiting helplessly in the bushes while our children's self-concept is devoured. Maybe it would be better if we humans could devise a way to mask our young girls protectively, keeping them safe from the predators lurking in the department store or on the pages of their fashion magazines.

Still other alligators disguise themselves as accidents waiting to happen: mistakes, misjudgments, and impulsive actions that threaten our children's safety. If only our limited experience had the vision to warn us. Haplessly we plunge ahead, while disasters, crises, and tragedies relentlessly attack us, leaving us to grapple for survival.

We are not totally helpless. Together, we can intimidate these alligators if we organize ourselves. We need to educate each other regarding the incognito predators, cunningly disguised as toys, femininity, or status quo. We need to give each other courage and support. Women who have successfully defeated these alligators develop into strong, capable leaders. Others, who are equally successful at fending off the hidden beasts, quietly influence and support thousands of other people in their communities: children, the sick, the elderly, and the disabled. These women have recognized the veiled alligators around us and have found ways to overcome their damaging influence.

Dinner Questions

❑ What alligators might prey on your children, disguised as toys or desirable image?

❑ What ground rules do you maintain to guide your children in spite of peer pressure to participate in activities you think are detrimental?

The Lioness Instinct

*Patience and endurance were not virtues
in a woman; they were necessities, forced on
her. Perhaps some day things would change and
women would renounce them. They would rise up
and say, "We are not patient. We will endure no
more." Then what would happen to the world?*

— MARY ROBERTS RINEHART, *THIS
STRANGE ADVENTURE*

In every mother there lives a lioness, a primal instinct to feed, protect, and defend her children at any cost. Not all animals make such devoted mothers. In the animal kingdom, every species has mothers who abandon their young, including ours. Even human mothers who don't abandon their children physically or emotionally find living in our culture makes doing their job more difficult. We want to protect our young, but what about the normally protective mothers who become blind to the predators? Our culture tricks our lioness instinct, forcing us to run with the others in order to fit in, sometimes in the wrong direction and, occasionally, into the river where the alligators wait hungrily.

My lioness instinct became apparent to me when I first nursed my children. Having attended La Leche League in Augusta, Georgia, before my daughter arrived, I committed myself to breast-feeding. Never have I experienced a stronger group of women than among the women I found in La Leche League. With their friendly meetings filled with education and tender kindness, they offered compassion, patience, and interest in the nesting mother. I soaked up their values for motherhood, enjoying the peaceful friendships of women who held their function as mothers with reverence. I learned to relax and to see the world from a child's perspective, a major shift for a working professional.

La Leche League offered a protective environment for a new mother. Social gatherings involved entire families. Mothers nursed openly in front of teenagers, husbands, and children. I quickly felt at home in such a setting where everyone considered nursing a baby a natural, acceptable behavior. While many of my friends chose not to nurse because of busy schedules or the perceived embarrassment, I treasured the close bonding with my child and even considered it a convenience. As a matter of fact, because of my wonderful La Leche introduction to breast-feeding, I felt no embarrassment at all.

Everything changed when I moved to Florida, leaving my cherished support group for the lifestyle of a professional career woman and a busy mom. The protective safety of the La Leche League community out of my reach, I continued to nurse my children in public and in locations deemed inappropriate by my peers. I offended, embarrassed and angered some people. Sometimes I juggled a hot blanket for modesty, but many times I did not. When my infant or even my toddler, felt hungry or distressed, my instinct as a lioness took over. I could not adhere to anyone's rules or protocol; I nursed that child. Nothing else mattered to me.

My father-in-law, his limited knowledge of babies a bit out of date, advised me to give the baby pabulum. Whenever the whir of the breast pump motor became audible behind my locked door, the office manager at work referred to me as "The Cow." Women who didn't nurse looked at me with disdain, and married women accused me of tempting their husbands. I ignored them all, and nursed my child with a strong and defiant lioness' instinct. I knew in my heart what was best for my child and, with all the strength of my convictions, I was determined to ignore social conventions to follow my beliefs.

This instinct takes other forms depending on need. My friend, Maxine, gave birth to a child with a defective heart. An optimistic, gracious woman, she fought for that child's life with every fiber of her being. She worked two and three jobs and juggled the activities of two other sons while scheduling endless medical appointments, which included flying to New York for his heart transplant.

Vickie, a former co-worker, sat through countless surgeries as doctors fused a rod to the spine of her retarded, paraplegic son. She created costumes for his wheelchair on Halloween, concocted teenage-inspired tastes in a blender, and installed a hydraulic lift over his bed as he grew too heavy for her to lift him. Like Maxine, her love for her son has no limits. Another friend, Gail, firmly held her severely autistic toddler, clad in his protective helmet, tears running down her face, as she defended him from himself. She visited him regularly at his group home, threw birthday parties for him as a child with family and friends, although mentally he could never appreciate the effort. She lovingly tended to his medical needs, which included scheduling dental appointments when he knocked out his tooth as a teenager. With pride she treasures his handsome features while at the same time grieving the fact he will never know adulthood. These mothers, all challenged by the physical impediments of their offspring, live with their lioness instinct running on high all the time.

The lioness instinct also thrives in mothers who fight to protect their offspring from invisible predators. No amount of light can illuminate these stealthy monsters, cunningly disguised as they move subtly around their vulnerable prey. The monsters come in the form of attitudes and prejudices that rob the young of their strength and courage. These invisible enemies can't be touched but are felt in the most painful way.

Sandra, the mother of a Down's syndrome infant, her arms displaying her child in all of his newborn splendor, ignored the negative doctor who openly disdained her child when taking his first breaths of life. Savannah fought a teacher's prejudice toward her daughter's weight, rejecting the woman's premise that talent, feelings, and achievement were somehow less important than physical appearance. Tawanna battled for her son's right to be tested for academic advancement, refusing to let his mental ability be dismissed because of his skin color. Delores, her lioness instinct supplemented by years of education, experience, and organizational skill, has stared the predator of racial harmony in the eye, contesting the enemy of generations. As president of the local Urban League, she initiates programs to instill pride, motivation, and knowledge to a community struggling to succeed economically. She understands that racism enslaves and tortures its victims with cruelty, denying them a life of privilege, dignity, or justice.

Simply recognizing the obscure alligators that prey on our children is not always enough. Many frustrated lionesses pace back and forth in lonely despair, disappointed in the lack of interest or support demonstrated by their community and peers. I contemplate in solitude the predators of my own children at all stages of their lives, particularly as they age. My daughter loves to read teen magazines where anorexic models dress in glamorous clothes, air-brushed to perfection, promising early sexuality when wearing a specific brand of makeup. Others guarantee popularity when sporting expensive, designer-label jeans, composed of worn-out, shredded fabric.

My son faces a different pressure as his playmates tempt him with their material abundance: items for trading, toys that encourage violence, and technological entertainment that teach him to fight, zap, and decimate the "enemy" with raw abandon and glee. I watch as video games suck the imagination from my child's mind and gobble up his time. Movies depict male heroes who chain-smoke cigarettes, drink alcohol, use drugs, embrace violence, and engage in unprotected sex. It is hard for my son to resist the allure of such cool role models, no matter what I teach him.

Financially successful role models unfortunately often breed contempt for professions dedicated to teaching children. Flashy super stars, paid millions of dollars by the sports or entertainment industries, knock their women around, speak casually of rape, and hire high-priced, high-profile lawyers to guarantee their freedom. Meanwhile, burned-out social workers, getting by on minimum incomes, struggle to protect the young from the very things these famous people flaunt.

Yet it is these super stars that our teenagers long to be like, imitating the skimpily dressed pop-singers they see on MTV, and the tough talk of the gangsters they admire in the movies. Their heads are so filled with these desirable images that few teens seriously consider the aspirations of Madeleine Albright or Janet Reno as a more appropriate role model for them. Who can blame them? We fill the sports stadiums, race car tracks, concert halls, and movie theaters in adoration of these questionable symbols of success. We give large allowances to our children to buy an endless stream of CD's with negative messages of violence and despair. We placate them with video games and video movies as babysitters. It is amazingly easy for me to give in to these temptations as well, and I know in my heart that the predator is winning, even in my own home.

We lionesses grieve for our children and all the horror that happens to them. Victims of guns, unprotected and unwarned, fall dead. As a parent, it is hard to determine who or what the predator might be. Who will introduce our children to such dangers? The video games? The movies? The media? The public who supports them? The working parent who is trying to make ends meet? The community that doesn't want to get involved in social action?

The change must start in our hearts, in our homes, and in our pocketbooks. We have to learn to put the parental foot down hard, in order to protect our children from all the alligators who thrive in our society by preying on the young and the innocent.

The mother of the son who shot and killed several innocent victims also grieves. Her pain and loneliness have no end as she tries to make sense of this devastating act by her own flesh and blood. She, too, is a friend, a woman I worked with closely. I keep her agony in my heart, knowing that her own life changed forever by this violence, her family destroyed, her reputation ruined, and her dreams of grandchildren shattered. I quietly cry with compassion for her while she weeps an ocean of tormented tears.

This war to save our children is too widespread and too big for any one individual to tackle. We must connect as women and support our children together. As we feel the pain together, we will find the strength to draw the boundaries and find solutions to our problems. We must refuse to buy any toys that are a detrimental influence to our children. We need to find time to evaluate what our children are watching, both on television and in the movies. We should be each other's eyes and ears when our children are concerned, being on the look-out for dangers for not only our own children but for each other's as well. Most importantly, we need to organize ourselves to make a difference into associations such as Mothers against Drunk Drivers, the Million Moms' March, or

Sisters for Racial Healing. We must tap into that lioness instinct that lies, sometimes dormant, sometimes unaware, in all women.

Unite Lionesses of the World! Never give up. Sing to your Sisters that they might awaken and recognize your song as their own instinct, deep inside. Find your inspiration from your ancestral mothers who tucked herbs from their homeland in the cornrows of their hair; the mothers who planted the fields and fed their children while the men fought for freedom; the wives who won prohibition to reform drunken abusers; and the sisters who joined arms in abolishing slavery. All these things were done in the name of the children. All the battles fought by these women were fought to win a better life for their offspring. We need to continue the battle; the war is not over.

Dinner Questions

❑ When have you felt your lioness instinct?
❑ How do you participate with organizations of women or parents to protect children?

Slippery Sledding

This downhill path is easy, but there's no turning back.

— CHRISTINA ROSETTI, "ARMOR MUNCI" IN
*THE POETICAL WORKS OF CHRISTINA
GEORGINA ROSETTI*

Accidents can supply us with our greatest lessons in life, if we are able to recognize the positive side of negative occurrences. Though I have gained wisdom from the careless mishaps of my life, I have always paid a big price. It doubly hurts whenever my children must also pay a price for my mistakes. Then there are the blunders they will inevitably make themselves, causing accidents that may not have the positive, albeit high-priced, outcomes my mistakes have had thus far. I fear these mistakes the most of all, recognizing that the potential for making these errors in the first place is steadily increasing for my children, each generation's mistakes bearing much bigger price tags. If only the lessons from my mistakes could be transferred to them automatically, without the pain that accompanies the knowledge! Fortunately, accidents, with their lessons learned, also contribute to parenting skills. One of the most dramatic ones came with our first North Carolina ice storm.

Cra-a-a-ck, Crash! Cra-a-a-ck, Crash! Cra-a-a-ck, Crash! Tall trees, heavy from ice, fell around our house throughout the night keeping us awake with excitement tinged with anxiety. The ice storm left us without electricity for five days, a new experience for my technologically-dependent family. We warmed ourselves around the gas logs in our basement fireplace and snuggled together under piles of blankets on our air mattresses at night. We quickly learned to use our sleeping bags for insulation underneath us, or freeze our backsides.

The extreme winter weather entertained us somewhat since our children only knew the balmy winters of Florida. Challenged by the severe and unfamiliar weather, I felt proud of my resourcefulness. I made foil dinner packets of meat, carrots, and potatoes, and heated them on the gas logs. We ate s'mores until we consumed all of the chocolate then resorted to toasting the remaining marshmallows. We told stories in the dark, and listened to "The Prairie Home Companion" until the radio batteries ran out. Finally, we found the fourth day of cold a miserable bore. My husband cautiously drove us to my brother's house in a neighborhood rumored to have electricity.

A dramatic change of pace welcomed us! The hot showers, steamy bowls of homemade soup, and red-cheeked laughing children raised our spirits immediately. I settled into a captivating book as my family donned their hats and coats to join in the neighborhood merriment outside.

"Mom, come quick! You should see what they're doing!" The interruption came from eight-year-old Simone, excited and insistent. " Mom, you've gotta come, NOW. Daddy and John are going to sled down this really long hill. Come on! NOW!"

Strong-willed, Simone usually persists until she gets her way.

Grabbing my coat and hat, I followed Simone to the street corner commotion. The neighborhood streets intersected at a four-way stop. Beyond the stop sign, the street took a nosedive down a steep hill in a straight line. Athletic youngsters had deemed this icy runway as a perfect sledding hill. A sixteen-year-old boy lay stomach down on his sled, then pushed off mightily with his hands, and rocketed straight down the street. The crowd cheered with delight.

"We're next, Mommy!" My three-year-old son John, his eyes wide with pure exhilaration, jumped up and down next to my husband.

Robert grinned like a kid himself, eager to show off for me. The two of them took their places on the sled, John sitting in between his Daddy's legs. One big push and whoosh—down the hill they went with amazing speed, traveling down the street until we could barely see them.

"Let's you and me go, Mom! Please?" Simone flattered me by selecting me as her buddy for adventure.

I have to give myself credit here. As an indoor child, I did not even learn to ride a bicycle until the fourth grade. I preferred paper dolls to roller skates. But as a mother of an athletic, high-energy daughter, I attempted sports with as much gusto as I could muster. I went horseback riding, skating, and even climbed a tower at the water theme park. There I said a prayer before shooting down the water slide, a human log with arms crossed, screaming "Aeeeiiiiiiii" before the torrential splash at the bottom. I could not let my daughter down this time.

"OK. I'll do it."

Simone squirmed with impatience. Robert and John trudged up the hill toward us dragging the sled behind them, their faces flushed with excitement and pride.

"We're next," I announced.

Simone took her place in front of me, with the sled posed at the very pinnacle, the steep incline before us, promising an immediate rush of adrenaline. I had never sat on a sled before. This wooden one looked like an antique as I placed my feet on the front bar. My husband handed me a piece of rope.

"This is what you steer with," he said.

I tugged on the rope and noticed the front runners moving to one side. When I tugged with the other hand, the runners shifted in the opposite direction. Unnecessary information, I thought, since we only needed to go straight down the hill and would never need to actually steer.

"OK, give us a push." I felt as ready as I ever would.

Robert shoved with all his might, propelling us down the icy road. Unfortunately, we were not headed for the bottom of the hill. We found ourselves careening toward a giant tree on the left-hand side of the street. I jerked the rope with my right hand. Like a scene from a fast-paced Indiana Jones movie, our sled cut sharply to the right, narrowly missing the tree, twisting around to instantly face more danger. Our sled veered abruptly across to the opposite side of the street at an impossibly high speed. We watched helplessly as our sled zoomed toward a parked jeep, my frantic hand on the rope pulling too late. With absolute horror, I tensed myself for the oncoming crash, the menacing steel fender looming large in front of my daughter's face. The final split second occurred in slow motion. I reached out with my hand. WHAM!

Silence. The world seemed to stop when we did. Pain rushed in bringing with it Simone's hair-raising scream. I reached down, preparing myself to see her lovely face in pieces, with crushed bones and blood spurting in every direction. I couldn't move my fingers, but felt a rush of relief as I studied her face, still with its lovely shape even though momentarily contorted in painful sobs. Blood gushed from her lip, but that was all.

My husband dashed quickly towards us, immediately asking one of those irritating questions that husbands tend to ask at inappropriate times. "Why didn't you steer the sled away from the car?"

Picking up Simone in his arms, he carried her to the house as I followed, my hand throbbing, a pain I almost welcomed, feeling racked with guilt and knowing at the moment that I deserved this small, painful punishment. We felt fortunate. Simone's worst wound consisted of a chipped tooth and bloody lip. I had a jammed finger, while we both sported tender lumps and bruises. Robert and I carefully observed our daughter until we were convinced there were no signs of a concussion.

That night, Simone and I both dealt with the emotional bruises of our accident. Lying in my arms on our padded air mattress, she clung to me, reliving the trauma of the crash.

"I'm so very sorry, so sorry, honey," I repeated over and over, rocking her gently and stroking her hair.

Guilt ate at me like a hungry rat, permitting neither sleep nor peace of mind. How stupid of me! Why didn't I ask somebody to show me how to steer? Why didn't I practice first? Why didn't I roll us off? The questions ate at my mind like a relentless animal throughout the night. I found it practically impossible to forgive myself for injuring a child. I struggled with an avalanche of morbid possibilities, worst scenarios of what could have happened because of my lack of judgment. I felt fortunate to have my precious child alive, in my arms, her lovely face intact.

Five years have passed since that icy winter. Life healed our accident with time. To avoid any future sledding mishaps, I compiled a mental list of the lessons that I might learn from our catastrophe. Ask questions. Practice. Think about possible dangers. Master the skill alone without endangering the life of my child. Let go and move on.

Simone is thirteen now, and faces risks of a different nature. She sleds down a slippery road where I can't accompany her—the road of relationships with the opposite sex. Seventh graders discuss these relationships, particularly sex, in vivid detail. They test each other's knowledge of sexual intercourse, reviewing slang terms for oral sex, masturbation, and genitalia. Couples "go with each other" in the school halls, passing notes of passion and possession. At thirteen, Simone has experienced the euphoria of "belonging" to someone and the empty hurt of rejection. I listen helplessly, feeling like a spectator at the sledding hill, having no clue how to teach her to steer before it is too late.

How can I prepare my daughter to avoid the mistakes of my own relationships? I reluctantly answer her questions about my past, afraid of her judgment and more afraid of offering undesirable examples of behavior by her role model mother. I provide her with sexual education, and encourage mentoring and career exploration that I hope will take some of the pressure off of her as she develops her own sense of self. I work with our church to bring in a religious sex educator. I listen with restraint as she recounts her conversations and flirtations, and I comfort her when she grieves at the loss of a boyfriend. My heart aches as I hear her cry herself to sleep. I know too well the pressure of peers, not to mention the promises and threats of ardent suitors. But for some reason being armed with this knowledge cannot help me prevent my daughter from slipping out of control and crashing into a jeep/boy parked by the side of the road.

Thinking about my own lack of preparation for dealing with sex, rape, STD's, divorce, and all the emotional baggage attached to relationships with the opposite sex, I wonder about my effectiveness as a parent to prepare my daughter. The gap between what we had to deal with when we were young and the new dangers that young women face today, such as cyber-sex, date rape cocktails, and AIDS, make me shudder in despair. Will Simone make it to the end of the road, or will she veer into early marriage and quick divorce or crash into unwed teenaged pregnancy? Will she be able to figure out the way things work with little or no experience, learning to steer straight and stay on the path leading to happiness and success? Or will she hit a bad patch in her life or ride down the hill with a bad peer who will encourage her to leave the straight path and start using alcohol, drugs, and sex? How can I help her if I am not on the sled with her?

The lessons of the sledding accident have become my parent guide. What appropriate role models could help her steer? How can she practice decision-making in relationships first before heading down that slippery slope? How can I help her to explore options for getting to her destination? What other questions need to be asked to make her a stronger, more effective sledder? How do relationships provide lessons for life for her, and will she learn from them or be defeated by them? Just as I let go of my guilt for causing our accident, I am trying to release my fear for future ones, mine *and* Simone's. Life will always offer more sleds and more hills to conquer, and we have to expect a certain amount of crashes. Accidents and mistakes are a positive part of growing up and learning, so long as the crashes are never permanently damaging, or, God forbid, deadly. I pray for the ability to accept both my mistakes and Simone's, and for the willingness to enjoy the ride.

Dinner Questions

❑ What mistakes do you need to let go of?
❑ What life dangers threaten your child while you helplessly watch on the sidelines?

The Nest falls Apart

A woman is like a teabag—only in hot water
do you realize how strong she is.

— NANCY REAGAN

Sometimes, just when you think you've got it all together—your health, your career, your marriage, your life—a big old alligator comes snapping at your heels. And then, just as you turn to face that menace head-on, you spy another lurking in the shadows, waiting to strike when your back is turned. Yet another awaits your first wrong move behind the bushes. It seems as if all of a sudden your perfect life is rife with alligators in every direction, waiting to drag you down, roll you around, drown you, and eat you.

Our biggest alligator attacked Robert just as he was anticipating with great excitement his college graduation. At forty-three, my husband had tackled the immense challenge of returning to school for a college education. He had completed the first phase, the two-year community college, and we were celebrating his accomplishment by attending his graduation. The attack came unexpected by either of us.

"I've got cancer!" Robert gripped the steering wheel, his eyes refusing to look at me as he drove. Tears streamed down his face as the reality of his disease hit home in full tragic force. Now, just before attending Florida State University for his chosen field of study, he had received the devastating diagnosis of testicular cancer.

My heart hurt for him while my mind spun out of control with visions of a bleak prognosis and an uncertain future. For now, I harnessed those nightmarish thoughts and managed to say, "Let's stay focused on the information, not the 'what ifs.' We'll take it one step at a time."

"You're right," Robert agreed, regaining his composure. We had a graduation to celebrate.

At the graduation ceremony, we received another shocking bit of news. While not exactly an attack, it did threaten to complicate our fragile lives even more.

"Hi, I'm Rhonda Smith," an exuberant stranger introduced herself to us. "Our daughter is marrying your son, Russell, in two weeks. He's adopting her son. We're so excited."

What ensued could only be described as unbridled craziness. Alligators in every direction. We tackled a wedding, maintained our heavy work schedules, while Robert crammed for his university exams and prepared for surgery.

"Cancer." The doctor, in his green scrubs, confirmed his fears with me in a private hospital room after Robert's surgery.

"The good news is," he continued, "this is the most treatable kind. I tried to remove it all, and for extra precaution we will start radiation. Are you through having children?"

"We wanted one more," I stammered. An older mother, I felt a little embarrassed to admit my desire to have a second baby.

"When treatment starts," the doctor said gently, "your chances of ever getting pregnant are over."

Robert recovered quickly from the surgery, although his ego seemed somewhat altered.

"Can you still find me attractive?" Robert asked down fallen.
The question surprised me. It seemed amusing to discover that a man would think a woman judged him by his testicles. I assured him that a missing testicle would not effect our relationship in the least. He didn't seem convinced.

"Could you love me if I had only one breast?" I asked. Robert held me close. Cancer forces a couple to engage in serious discussions of real significance.

The first radiation appointment loomed ominously on the calendar. Getting pregnant had to happen now or never. My Catholic girlfriend explained the basics of natural family planning, and how to identify my most fertile day. I hurriedly plotted my husband's seduction. In spite of the years it took us to get pregnant with our first child, we succeeded in one try before Robert's treatments began. A miracle baby!

Radiation left Robert feeling tired and nauseated, his skin itching from the harsh rays. He continued to work nights although he missed a semester of classes. After the final radiation treatment, we celebrated at our favorite restaurant. We could put cancer behind us and move forward. My mother made professional maternity clothes for me to wear to the office and Robert attended the university's orientation. The anticipation of the new baby grew with my size. I sedated all other stresses, including conflicts with Robert's insolent teenaged son, with my pregnancy. I planned my natural childbirth experience like a director making arrangements for opening night performance.

"We'll have no cold delivery room and harsh lights, only candlelight with soft music," I explained to my two girlfriends at a luncheon prior to the event. "After the baby is born, we'll eat frozen yogurt pie and open presents. A birthday party."

My endless details provided an escape from the unpleasant dealings with the teenager.

Sometimes our efforts to control life are like an attempt to grab running water. The little surprises and unplanned events that change our destiny are almost ironic in nature, forcing us to discard unrealistic expectations for the perfect outcome. As my due date approached, so did the incredulous challenges. I kept a journal throughout, and later compiled a list of events that occurred the week of my son's birth. It went like this:

Came home with the new baby
Robert's stepfather died of a sudden heart attack
I have Bell's palsy, leaving my face half paralyzed
Robert's son ran away, taking the yard equipment with him
The grass surrounds my knees
The IRS audited us and wants $900

Simone has bronchial pneumonia

Robert's cancer has returned

Everything could be handled but the last item. The day I brought the new baby home from the hospital, Robert complained about a lump in his neck the size of a pea.

"It's just a swollen lymph node," I assured him, "nothing to worry about."

The next day, it had grown to the size of a marble and the following day it swelled to the size of an egg. Robert called our family doctor.

"Come in RIGHT NOW!" the doctor commanded.

By suppertime, an oncologist had examined Robert and scheduled emergency surgery with chemotherapy to begin the next day. My milk had just come in. The newborn and I struggled with nursing. How would I find time to care for a sick husband, a five-year-old daughter, and a hungry infant? I held my sleeping baby and went into a deep meditation, praying to God for guidance. I recited Psalms 23 to myself for personal comfort, but I needed to be more proactive if I was going to help Robert. The answer came in a flash of insight. I opened my eyes with excitement for my new plan. I decided to use humor to build his endorphins, keep his attitude positive, and to raise our morale. We were a team and we were going to fight this together!

Robert's friends agreed to participate in my humor project. We collected comic videotapes, cartoons, and an audiotape that promised nothing short of sidesplitting laughter. I prepared a care package to accompany Robert to the hospital for his daily intravenous treatments: pictures of our new baby and our daughter, jokes, and short spiritual messages—soul food.

Robert's gratitude for my teamwork, however, was not overwhelming. In fact, he refused to participate.

"Sweetheart," he said weakly as he crawled into bed, "Don't make me laugh. I get hiccups that hurt. They last for hours. Please just let me rest. I need to be alone. These chemicals make me smell bad."

Robert retreated under the covers. Darkened by the closed blinds, the bedroom turned into a lonely cave for a sick animal.

My master plan rejected, I felt powerless again, frustrated by the isolation of Robert's disease. I listened to him thrashing around. Bad dreams and delusions plagued him, chemicals playing havoc with his mind. I brought him soft relaxing music and peppermints to overcome the metallic taste in his mouth. Helpless to do anything further for him, I retreated to nurse the baby.

We knew Robert's hair would come out. The first big clump washed down his face in the shower. "I'm going to the barber," Robert announced, "to have my head shaved."

Sobering feelings of the cruel reality of cancer overcame me as Robert left for the barbershop. I needed to be with somebody immediately. I mentally searched my neighborhood, desperate for a sympathetic friend amongst the working professionals who lived around us. Gathering the baby in my arms, I knocked on the door of a woman I barely knew.

"Hi, I'm Ana from down the street. Would this be a convenient time to visit for a minute?" I asked.

The lady opened her door without hesitation.

"My name is Nancy," she said, "How about a cup of tea?"

The companionship of a compassionate woman during such a vincible time helped me gather the courage I needed to greet Robert when he returned. He entered the house, his white head looking vulnerable. Locking my eyes with his, I silently embraced him.

Evenings began to torture me. My worry about Robert corroded my ability to deal with the demands of the other members of my life. By sunset, I was exhausted physically and emotionally. After a particularly stressful day, I simply could not cope with the demands of my children. My ravenous five-year-old whined for dinner and the baby cried without ceasing. He seemed to become more upset by the minute. No amount of nursing or rocking could stop the baby from screaming at the top of his lungs. Frazzled to the end of my rope, my head throbbed relentlessly. I could not stand another minute of the deafening noise or tolerate my daughter's incessant tugs on my skirt. I began to understand the insanity that overcomes mothers who do horrible things to their children just to achieve some peace and quiet. Again, I sought support in our neighborhood. I grabbed the children, fled to our next-door neighbor's house, and rang their doorbell.

"Help me, please!" I pleaded in panic. The baby screamed even louder.

My neighbors, Susan and Richard, seeing the open desperation clearly in my face and voice, reacted immediately. "Don't worry about the children, Ana, go take a long bath and relax." Susan took the baby in her arms while Richard steered Simone to their family dinner table.

Never have I appreciated our dear friends as much as I did that moment. Relaxing seemed impossible, but just having a moment of quiet to myself provided heavenly relief. As the warm, comforting bath water lapped around me, I took slow deep breaths, listening to my quiet inner voice instructing me to find my peaceful center and to nurture myself. I knew right then that my own survival and the care of the children that depended solely on me had to be my major focus. I thought of Robert lying in the dark bedroom, the look of pitiful anguish on his face. I imagined a white, healing light surrounding him, glowing from his skin. I knew at that moment that I had to trust God and Robert's medical team, and then let go of that persistent, all-encompassing worry that was dominating my life. I had to pull myself out of this quagmire of despair and stand on firm, sane ground for my children, and for myself.

That evening, after kissing my daughter good night, I pushed a videotape into the VCR and settled into a recliner. The Billy Crystal movie I selected belonged to the abandoned pile of materials in my cardboard box marked "humor project." This movie, borrowed to hasten Robert's recovery, provided me with the first laugh I had enjoyed for months. What a release I felt, just laughing! I refused thoughts of guilt for laughing so raucously. Though this might not be an appropriate time to laugh, it was a necessary time! From that moment on, I have turned to humor as a coping tool in times of undue stress and trauma. If humor could provide such a healing release for me then, it could for any crisis.

Another tool that brought comfort and peace came from a past health crisis of my own. Remembering the power of the spiritual journey I experienced earlier in life, I chose to take that journey again throughout Robert's illness. Every morning, after dropping my daughter off at preschool, I settled in for meditation and reading, nursing the baby at the same time. I read Alan Cohen's *The Dragon Doesn't Live Here Anymore*, and *You Can't Afford the Luxury of a Negative Thought* by

John-Roger and Peter McWilliams. I enjoyed Unity's Daily Word with its uplifting thought and scripture for each day, as well as *The Course in Miracles*. During that time, I gave up all professional goals and personal plans, focusing on each present moment as if it were all that existed.

Friends came to visit, offering homemade treats for Robert, which we ate since he couldn't. Katie brought pictures of her women's trip up the Amazon River. She transported me to the jungles of Brazil as she described the excursion led by natives, with ceremonies, snakes, and swimming in cold springs—an awesome experience for the group of women who became best friends as they adventured together. What a pleasant distraction for me! Garnet, our future babysitter, bathed the baby, giggling with him as he splashed the water. My boss, Pat, cooked dinner and brought her family to enjoy it with us.

Robert attended church in the dashing Humphrey Bogart hat I purchased for him. The ladies complimented him in spite of the dark circles under his eyes, his missing eyebrows, and tired demeanor.

We tend to focus so much on the needs of the cancer patient and our needs as the caregivers that we often forget cancer's youngest victims—the children. Children have the hardest time understanding the complications of living with cancer. Simone found her dad's disease disconcerting. Not only had she lost her place of honor to a new baby brother, she lost all attention from her daddy. No longer did he swing her in the air or cuddle her in his lap. Her tickle sessions disappeared along with Robert's bright smile and wide-eyed expression of delight he always wore for her.

"Why doesn't Daddy play with me anymore?" Simone pouted. "I don't even get to see him!"

"Daddy is sick, honey." I explained gently. "He needs to sleep a lot so he can get well. He'll be able to play with you in a few weeks."

"But I want Daddy now!" Her eyes filled with big watermelon tears. So did mine.

We counted the days until the treatments ended. After each chemotherapy session, Robert reported the progress of fellow cancer patients. Some tolerated the discomfort while others couldn't bear the treatments and quit coming. He also resisted the treatments, forgetting his route to the hospital.

"Why don't you let me drive you, sweetheart?" I asked.

"No, I can get there," Robert replied. "The chemicals disorient me, but I'll manage. You stay home with the kids. "

That night, Robert drove around the neighborhood, completely lost. The type of person who refuses help, he didn't tell me until several weeks later.

We began to notice that Robert's reaction to the chemotherapy occurred in cycles. A week of intravenous treatments upset Robert mentally with hallucinations and forgetfulness. Next came the expulsion of chemicals through his sweat glands, urine, and saliva. Robert smelled and tasted chemicals all the time. Robbed of these important senses, food lost its appeal.

"Please don't get close to me," Robert pleaded. "I know I smell bad. I don't want to offend you."

I never smelled the metallic odor that seemed to plague his senses.

Robert needed to talk about his treatments. It must have been difficult for our Marriage Encounter friends who patiently listened to his descriptions of physical torment. One couple, Jay and Wonja, succeeded in eliciting chuckles from Robert with small medicine bottles labeled "Hair Growing Tonic" and "Stress Removing Pills."

At work, Robert's co-workers formed a sick-leave bank. By donating their sick leave time for the use of anyone with a life-threatening illness, the workers supported each other. It comforted us to know that back up time waited for our use. Robert continued to work whenever he could, his dependability never wavering despite the physical anguish he endured.

Robert was too sick to celebrate the completion of his treatments.

"Your chances of having cancer again weigh far less than for an average person with no history of cancer," the doctor assured Robert. "Still, the five-year checkup makes a landmark you can really celebrate."

After being on hold for three months, we picked up where we left off. Robert called Florida State University and scheduled classes for the next quarter. Three years later, Robert walked down the aisle of the Leon County Civic Center in a cap and gown to receive his diploma as the first college graduate in his family. Never in my life have I been so proud of him, and us. Tears flowed freely down my cheeks as I thought of Robert's determination and persistence, working nights, cramming for exams during the days, meeting with fellow classmates to finish projects, and attending classes with his little tape-recorder. Our friend, Shary, custom-ordered a bronze medal and hung it around Robert's neck at a party for his friends and family. That medal hangs in a place of honor today.

I, too, received a life-altering education. I learned that together, with God's help, Robert and I can pull through anything. God gave me a place of peace and calm amidst the storm. I needed only to go there. I learned to use humor as a crisis tool, resulting in sanity and release from unbearable stress. Surrounded with opportunities to make friends, we learned to reach out to others that we might be nurtured in the process.

Finally, I made a special medal for myself.

Dinner Questions

❑ When have you felt helpless around a loved one's crisis?
❑ What have you learned from the times you lost control?

Breaking Bread Together
(Dinner Alliances)

*We are eating as a medium for social
relationships: satisfaction of the most individual of
needs become a means of creating community.*

— MARGARET VISSER,
THE RITUALS OF DINNER

The proposal couldn't have come at a worse time, and it took me
completely by surprise. We were being invited to attend a dinner party
every six weeks. Preposterous! Host this group in our home? Unthinkable! We didn't even have a dining room table. Juggling work schedules
while raising a toddler and a first grader left us overwhelmed at best.
Our house served merely as a habitat for our family, not a public entertainment center. Yet, we let this woman from our church talk us into
being a member of a "dinner group." It was a simple concept, she patiently explained to us. Four couples, including Shary and her husband
Ken, would fix dinner together every six weeks, rotating homes as the
"host." Shary had selected couples within the same age bracket that all
had young children and attended our church.

The "dinner party" included specific ground rules. The host would
supply an appetizer, the main dish, and beverages. One couple would
bring salad and bread, another two vegetables, and another the dessert.
This should be manageable for working professionals such as ourselves.
My assignment consisted of bringing the salad and bread for the first

dinner. I purchased a wonderful bread we could just heat up and enjoy fresh from the oven.

Although we eagerly anticipated the first dinner date, we discovered that the plan was anything but simple. The process of locating a babysitter for five hours on a Saturday night presented a new, expensive challenge. Childless couples can't imagine the routines required of parents as they prepare babysitters. How the oven works, where to find the phone number for poison control, what to do with dirty diapers, which stuffed animal is required for sleeping necessitates an entire orientation session! All three guest couples had infants or toddlers requiring frantic preparations, and we all arrived at Shary and Ken's breathless from the struggle. We settled into a plush sofa and chairs while Ken poured glasses of wine and Shary offered a stuffed mushroom appetizer.

Shary led us on a tour of the house, while their family story unfolded. We walked down the hall lined with pictures of the children and a framed proclamation celebrating their adoption. Childless up until the adoptions, the demands on their household tripled when they brought home three special-needs siblings.

"I like to acquire things in sets," smiled Shary.

Showing us "before and after" pictures of the modest four-bedroom house, we marveled at the transformation they had achieved. Shary and Ken nurtured the restoration of their house just like they nurtured the newly created family, with total love, devotion, and enthusiasm. There was so much evidence in the house that Shary had embraced her penchant for both entertaining and motherhood. She had conjured up visions of family pool events, adult dinner parties, and children's birthday parties. Her talents included finding a way to pay for these visions as well. She sniffed out amazing bargains, scouring yard sales and retail closeouts with calculated mastery. While Ken oversaw the building of a spacious deck around the pool and totally gutted the darkly paneled kitchen, Shary designed luxurious cabinets, masterminded storage in the pantry and the garage. She filled plastic bins labeled with children's clothes for a variety of ages, themed decorations, and accessories for every activity imaginable.

Shary couldn't wait to exhibit her dream kitchen. Light and modern, it demonstrated Shary's organizational skill everywhere. Her pantry shelves edged in white eyelet trim had stacking units to maximize the small space. A family communication center, job chart, children's snacks jar, and pretty glass containers filled with gourmet utensils impressed us all. The kitchen counter sported bar stools on one side where children could perch to talk to Shary while she cooked. On one end the counter displayed an elaborate beach party with Barbie and Ken dolls. Fifty pounds of rice became sand surrounding the dolls posed in miniature lounge chairs, and while a nearby sailboat suggested the ocean. A tiny radio sat on Barbie's beach towel.

"We change the scene constantly," Shary explained matter-of-factly.

My mouth fell open at this imaginative shared family activity. I did well just to change bed sheets every other week. Brightly-colored napkins and centerpieces with floating candles created magical drama for Shary's dining room table. She themed this room every month with different mobiles, colored lights, and displays. This month, stuffed animals dressed in the summer-related theme posed on a shelf, while whimsical figurines reigned among food dishes on the buffet.

Although Shary and Ken made entertaining look effortless, the rest of us panicked at first. Each couple confessed to being faced with meticulously cleaning off little fingerprints, painting over crayon marks, and gathering up small toys strewn throughout the house to stuff in some hidden closet. We all purchased table clothes, and ordered replacements for our dishes. Soon, though, we stopped focusing on our material possessions and relaxed into the growing friendships, feeling accepted regardless of our simple furnishings and cluttered environments. The initial curiosity of home decor shifted quickly to discovering individual personalities and learning about family cultures.

Each home offered different stories of family challenges that were often inspiring and sometimes even amazing. We discovered ideas for organizing children and their busy lives. We shared discipline techniques and empathy for problems with in-laws, teachers, and babysitters. Together, we celebrated individual accomplishments and mourned a family's loss. We admired family pictures, reminisced our first dates, and explained family rituals.

Within a few months, the dinner party became intertwined into our lives. Each set of hosts began to impact our day-to-day lives with their own unique gifts. Shary taught me the art of bargaining at yard sales, one of the men in the group updated our wills, and another woman in the group contributed her talents to the Girl Scout council where I worked. All of us began volunteering together at church.

Suddenly, our bustling lifestyles came to a halt with a development that touched us all deeply.

"We have a crisis," Shary's voice on the phone sounded strained. "We need to postpone our December dinner party."

Problems with their oldest adopted daughter had escalated. Intense counseling for the family and the child could not curb her violent behavior. Shary and Ken were running out of options and coping techniques. Their amazing patience seemed to find its limit with this young child.

"There's a bonding problem," Shary explained to me. "This child came from an abusive home. When a baby does not have her needs met, she doesn't learn about trust. This child can't trust and, therefore, can't be trusted."

The girl roamed the house at night, stealing from Shary's purse. Discipline problems intensified at school, forcing the parents to leave work to rescue a desperate teacher. While the two younger children bloomed under Shary and Ken's care, this oldest, profoundly disturbed sister manipulated and bullied her way with her family as well as other people, constantly discovering new ways to challenge her adoptive parents. My husband and I could relate all too well with the anxiety and frustration caused by a troubled young person who lies, steals, and resists any act of loving support.

The situation deteriorated. One day, I stared incredulously at the black-and-yellow bruise encompassing Shary's entire upper arm.

"She bit me again," Shary sighed. "And that happened after I found her initials carved in my new dining room furniture."

Taking a chunk from their family savings, Shary and Ken borrowed boots and winter clothes, and packed the family suitcases for a winter trip to Colorado.

"We are attending a clinic for children with rage." Shary announced. "This is our last hope."

Shary and Ken left with their children, leaving their home and the Christmas season they loved to celebrate.

The commitment, persistence, and selfless love of Shary and Ken had touched our little dinner group. We began strategizing support for the Colorado trip and our dinner group sprang into action.

First, we collected compact Christmas decorations to fit into Shary and Ken's suitcases. The children would surely need a little spirit for their hotel room. As soon as the family left for the airport, our church generously joined in to help us send long distance support. Purchasing an Italian crèche, we express-mailed a different nativity figure each day, accompanied by notes and cards of encouragement. Prayer groups met daily to pray for Shary and Ken.

After their strenuous week at the clinic, Ken and Shary prepared to return to Florida with their children on Christmas Eve. Coordinating our many church volunteers, we filled their home with poinsettias, Christmas breakfast, and Christmas dinner to welcome the family's return on Christmas Eve. We couldn't relieve their problem, but we could certainly communicate our love.

Shary and Ken struggled for a long time before admitting the need to find another home for their oldest daughter. Today, they are a happy, vibrant family of four, providing as much opportunity as possible for the two children who have flourished under their care.

When I think back to that crisis, I remember the special feeling of community we all experienced throughout Ken and Shary's ordeal. The feeling doesn't always have to follow a crisis. We can also discover the warmth of community in small acts of togetherness. It reminds me of Greek folk dancing. While holding each other's hands the dancers expressed communal feelings experienced by the entire village. Shary and Ken gave us the opportunity to hold hands and express our concern for their struggle.

Somewhere in all of us lives a frightened child, a desperate parent, and an individual wanting family. We came together and bonded as friends, providing comfort for the child in us, respite for the parent in us, and family for those of us longing for this connection. We felt the deeper meaning of Christmas love in a world filled with fear, desperation, and loneliness.

Our dinner group lasted another year until Robert and I relocated to North Carolina. We cherished our dinners together, expanding our views of the world and deepening our own personal family values. Shary taught us a lesson about connecting—about risking the vulnerability of sharing our imperfect personal space with other people and discovering our commonality while breaking bread together. Although she originally wanted to increase the meaningful friendships for herself and her husband, she created a deeper support system for us all. We all became richer for it. In our busy world of tight schedules and growing demands on our time, it is important to break bread together on a regular basis, especially with people who seem different from us. What better way to build bridges across racial, cultural, and economic chasms than with mashed potatoes and gravy!

Dinner Questions

- ❑ When did you rally around another family in distress?
- ❑ What did they teach you?

Lurking Alligators Await their Victims:
Women's Wit and Wisdom Save the Day!

*I always knew I would turn a
corner and run into this day, but
I ain't prepared for it nohow.*

— LOUISE MERIWETHER, *DADDY WAS
A NUMBER RUNNER*

Alligators hide in the swamps, very still, waiting to catch their prey off-guard. Blending in with water vegetation or appearing to be a floating log, they fool the vulnerable animals that come to drink or play in the refreshing water.

My alligators catch me by surprise almost every time. Since I am always on task, determined to accomplish a goal, I fail to consider possible dangers that might be lurking in my own territory. Alligators, hidden in my own bedroom, easily catch me off guard, with my soft underbelly exposed.

Two of these stories deal with the element of surprise. The third represents the danger that we overlook in our own nest. A woman's strength, her ability to fend off these alligators, and to survive alligator-infested territories, lies in her inner character. It is in her attitude of determination, her use of wit and humor, and her willingness to discover her capabilities that enable her to fight these hidden threats.

Dinner Questions

❑ How much of your fear is related to the fact that you are a woman?

❑ What do you do about it?

Babes in the Woods

*You don't realize what fine fighting material
there is in age… You show me any one who's lived
to over seventy and you show me a fighter—
someone who's got the will to live.*

— AGATHA CHRISTIE, *DUMB WITNESS*

Six Girl Scout leaders in the outlying areas of north Florida requested training in camping skills. As the training director for a Girl Scout Council that encompassed six counties, I instructed volunteer trainers. They, in turn, provided Girl Scout leaders with the knowledge and skills to work with the girls, learn about the organization, understand safety standards, and perform first aid, if necessary. This includes program training, such as how to teach arts and crafts, and of course, camping. My hardy outdoor trainers relished the experience of pitching tents and identifying animal tracks while baking a cake in an outdoor oven made from a cardboard box. Real outdoor women, they felt at home in the woods amongst the ticks and poison ivy. They often traveled throughout our Council to spread their infectious love for this aspect of Girl Scouting.

This particular weekend, I learned that all of my camping experts had caught the flu, left town, or had family emergencies except for one. Since Outdoor Skills training required a team of two trainers, I would have to go myself. The six leaders in the outlying area of Florida deserved to be trained and I would not let them down. As a mother of two small children, however, the logistics of a two-night expedition out-of-town required some juggling since their father worked nights.

A sweet, grandmotherly woman named Garnet cared for my infant son and five-year-old Simone. Committed to nursing my baby while I worked, I managed to pump milk, or come home at lunchtime for his feeding. Clearly, my son needed me close by throughout the night.

Garnet, herself, enjoyed Girl Scouting. For the latter half of her seventy-six years, Garnet camped and played as a leader with hundreds of little Girl Scouts, keeping her own spirit of adventure intact. It seemed like a wild idea, but Garnet suggested we all go camping together. She and the children would share my tent, entertaining themselves while I worked with the adults.

I called the one available outdoor trainer. "Katie, we need to train some leaders out of town. Can you come?"

"You know me, Ana. I'm always ready to camp!" Katie never turned me down. "All I ask is that you drive."

Katie could not drive at night. The oldest of my trainers at seventy-eight, Katie's positive attitude and knowledge of the out-of-doors contributed a terrific asset to my training team. She took pleasure in teaching Girl Scout leaders how to identify animals in the dark by the shapes of their eyes. Katie feared neither insects, bears, nor snakes.

Although I hadn't camped for several years, I figured that collectively Garnet, Katie and I could pull off a relatively decent experience. I crammed my head with policies and procedures while packing tents, sleeping bags, and diapers.

Our drive through the Florida countryside carried some anxiety. Garnet possessed a rare talent for remembering conversations in their entirety, as much as sixty years ago. Everything we said, looked at, or thought of reminded her of a long story filled with substantial conversations. She even quoted herself. Katie, sitting up front, strained to hear with her slightly deaf ear. Simone interrupted frequently with "When are we going to get there?" and Baby John did not enjoy his car seat. I contemplated my bizarre cargo, not the typical camping crew, as we pulled over for our third bathroom break on a two-hour trip.

We arrived as the dark of night settled over the state park. The ranger assigned us our campsite where we found a young African American

Girl Scout leader waiting for us. A quiet woman in her twenties, Claudia had never been camping and was obviously out of her comfort zone. We greeted her enthusiastically and hurriedly pitched two tents.

Simone and John simultaneously announced their hunger, creating a noisy disturbance. My role as a Girl Scout training leader gave way to my role as a mother. Maintaining my professional countenance in front of our young trainee, I disappeared with them into my tent so no one would see me fall apart. I lack the ability to stay calm when two fussy children compete for instant gratification. Simone's indignation flared up with the defiance of an only child uprooted by a baby brother. Clinging to me desperately, she whined even louder for her dinner. I frantically opened sandwich wrappers while unfastening my bra to nurse at the same time. I was multi-tasking better than most executives ever manage. John latched on with the gusto of a starving child. I could hear Katie and Claudia making small talk and envied them for being able to eat their own sandwiches in peace.

"I wonder where the other leaders are," mused Katie. "They are bringing our groceries for tomorrow."

"Maybe the news scared them off," ventured Claudia.

"What news?" Katie became suspicious.

"Rain," responded Claudia. "Lots of rain. Maybe a flash flood. If it starts raining, I'll be leaving."

Flash floods! I had forgotten! We had entered the part of the state where flash floods were notorious for washing out roads, bridges, and entire communities. I had no personal experience with such phenomenon.

We had planned to set up camp, eat our sack suppers, and invent campfire skits. But we needed participants. Was it true they were absent because of the news of an impending storm? Or had they gotten lost searching for our campsite? I decided to go alone to the park entrance and watch for the late arrivals. Leaving Katie in charge, I drove my car to the gate.

The park entrance consisted of an empty guard booth and a single streetlight. Leaning against my car, I watched for motorists. As an approaching car motor grew louder, I recognized trouble. A large van entered the gate, filled with Boy Scouts.

Boy Scouts and Girl Scouts are two totally different organizations. While Girl Scouts have strict safety rules and requirements that are followed to the letter, Boy Scouts operate by a much looser standard. With our new program of sports and rugged outdoor ventures, Girl Scouts take pride in being every bit as competent as Boy Scouts, including our leaders and trainers. The competitive spirit between the genders has not lost any of its vigor. So, when the Boy Scout van stopped at the entrance to inquire if I wanted a ride, I stood erect and politely refused.

"I'm on the look out for late arrivals," I responded matter-of-factly. "I can drive myself to my campsite."

"I hope they get here soon," replied the pipe-smoking scoutmaster. "It's going to rain."

He sped off as I felt the first sprinkle. Looking at my watch, I realized that if we didn't have participants by now, two hours late, they would never show up. What on earth happened to everyone? How could they stay home after I practically brought a nursery out here to teach them camping? I hurried to my car and thrust the key into the ignition.

Dead. No coughing, no chugging, nothing. I sat at the steering wheel, dazed with disbelief as the rain splattered down on my windshield, the drops gaining momentum and circumference. Headlights blinking in my direction interrupted my trance. Leaders! I jumped out and ran to the approaching car. My feeling of relief disappeared quickly when I saw that it was the Boy Scouts again.

"Looks like you need some help," they offered. "Hop in and we'll take you to your campsite."

Reluctantly, I submitted to their chivalry, my tail tucked firmly between my legs. The sky no longer sprinkled, it now showered us with endless curtains of rain.

"I hate to say this, but it looks like your tent is pitched in a gully," informed the scoutmaster as we approached our site.

"We arrived after dark," I mumbled defensively, silently cursing those know-it-all Boy Scouts.

The Boy Scouts peeled off as I ran to my tent. Inside, Simone and John wore their pajamas while Garnet adjusted her flannel nightgown. Sleeping bags covered the tent floor with pillows in place. I could barely hear Katie and Claudia in the next tent as the rain continued to pour down harder. Suddenly, loud thunder shook the earth.

What a dilemma! Here I sat, miles from civilization, with two women over seventy-five, a six-month-old infant, a five-year-old, and a brand new Girl Scout leader. I must be out of my mind. This downpour could never be mistaken as a harmless summer shower. Bolts of lightening and crashing thunder continued as I lay down to gather strength and plan an escape.

"Mommy," Simone whimpered. "My bed is wet."

Grabbing my flashlight, I surveyed the tent floor. Puddles joined together to form a moat around our sleeping bags. I adjusted the bedding, squeezing out sweatshirts, and stuffing our duffel bags. Garnet snored soundly.

"Garnet!" I shouted. "We have a crisis!"

"Huh? What's that?" Garnet raised her arm up to her forehead and groggily turned toward me.

"We have a crisis!" I repeated. "Water! In the tent!"

"Where's John?" Garnet asked. She never forgot her responsibility.

"He's here. Better get dressed, we're going to have to evacuate."

"Mommy!" said Simone grabbing my arm, "Someone is calling you!"

Everyone hushed, scarcely breathing. A man's faint voice could be faintly detected in the storm.

"Anybody here named Ana Tampanna?"

"Yes!" I yelled with all my might through the storm.

Unzipping the tent door and sticking my head out into the heavy downpour, I gasped at what I saw. Torrents of water surged by just inches from our tent. It reminded me of the animated movie, *Alice in Wonderland*, in which furniture and people rushed by, tossing in the waves of the Ocean of Tears.

The ranger lifted his lantern and hollered, "Your husband is coming to get you."

His words went straight to my heart. Thank you, God, for Robert.

Never in my life had I seen rain beat down as hard as it did on our tent. Our bedding had absorbed buckets of water seeping in from the ground. John's baby blanket sat in a puddle, sopping wet while his rattle floated nearby.

"Katie," I screamed to our neighboring campers, "We need to abandon our tent!"

"We do, too," hollered Katie. "We'll meet you in the bathroom."

How should we evacuate? Garnet and I both put on our hooded ponchos. Bundling John in his bedding, Garnet cuddled him inside her poncho and strapped the diaper bag around her shoulder.

"I'll follow you," she assured me.

Simone, larger and heavier, became my responsibility. Snapping up her raingear, I hoisted her on my back, my hands holding her legs securely.

"Simone," I instructed, "You'll have to hold the flashlight so I can see where we are going."

She relished such an important job and grabbed the flashlight out of Garnet's hands.

"Here we go!" Stumbling into the drenching darkness, I plunged into a small river.

"Simone," I yelled, "I can't see where I'm going. Shine the light on the ground, for Pete's Sake!"

The flashlight darted from tree to tree, never once lighting my path. I cautiously waded through knee-deep water, negotiating a ditch while tightly clasping my daughter, who grew heavier by the minute. Our dangerous trek uphill allowed no opportunity to search for the others. I had no idea if Katie, Claudia, or Garnet followed me or drifted further into the woods. The light from the wooden building fifty feet ahead grew brighter—a promise of shelter, running water, and toilets.

Fortunately, we all arrived at the same time, totally drenched. I counted heads, relieved that no one had drowned or gone looking for the Boy Scouts. At two in the morning, we had a long wait before Robert would arrive. Simone, wide-eyed with excitement, relished the adventure, anticipating the additional entertainment the deluge had provided. John even worked up an appetite and wanted to nurse. I settled in on the concrete floor, and took the baby in my arms. Sucking contentedly, he aroused our envy at his privilege to find such perfect comfort under such stormy conditions.

"Oh look," announced Garnet with sincere interest as she pointed to a corner, "here's a little spider."

As if on cue, veteran moms that we all are, we sang "The Itsy Bitsy Spider." Like most gatherings of Girl Scouts, one song led to another, then another. Garnet remembered a rain story from her childhood and began another personal saga. Katie produced two chocolate bars intended for our campfire and divided them into smaller pieces. Soon, Claudia's brother arrived to rescue her, and whisked her off to her family.

"Do you suppose Claudia will ever go camping again?" I asked my companions.

"She seemed like a really nice girl," said Katie, "but a flash flood is a bit much for a first time."

For two hours we amused ourselves, telling stories, singing songs, and playing games with Simone in the small camp bathroom while the storm raged around us. Finally the door burst open, and there stood Robert.

"Anybody seen some wet Girl Scouts?" he grinned.

Loading us in his station wagon, Robert drove his soggy cargo home. While the others dozed, I reflected on our adventure. Throughout our ordeal, not one person complained. No one got angry, or upset. No one blamed anyone else, or spoke unkindly to another. Everyone felt consideration for the group, looked on the bright side, and solved problems as they arose.

The flash floods of Florida's panhandle taught me a lesson about checking for storm watches before camping. But I also learned about the incredible pioneering spirit that enables women to endure crises and to nurture their families. Garnet and Katie, both skilled and experienced, possessed buoyant resourcefulness and unsinkable determination. These women had withstood war, the depression, and personal hardship during their earlier lives. Their tough fiber provided resilience for any situation they encountered. With such women as my companions, I knew I could weather any crisis.

Dinner Questions

❏ When have you weathered a disaster?

❏ What did you learn about yourself and others?

The Monster in the Bathroom

*By the time we are women, fear is
as familiar to us as air.*

—ANDREA DWORKIN, *THE SEXUAL POLITICS
OF FEAR AND COURAGE*

Trauma can paralyze, causing the victim to freeze long enough to be injured or killed. I used to wonder if I would be paralyzed, unable to scream for help in an emergency situation, such as an attack on the street. Now I know. I have stared into the eyes of a masked intruder as he hid behind my bathroom shower curtain. Instantaneously a scream tore out of my throat, a bloodcurdling siren alert, leaving me hoarse for over a week. This uninvited visitor proved to me that I would not panic in the face of danger, but it also changed my life forever.

Arriving home at 9:30, I remember admiring the coral and white azaleas filling the front garden, welcoming me back from my early morning appointment. I parked in our circular drive close to the front door to make a mad dash through the house since I had consumed too much coffee that morning. Once inside the bathroom, I froze. Behind my multi-colored shower curtain hid a grungy man, his head covered with a navy blue windbreaker. Through the sliver of a crack in the windbreaker, I identified white skin and greasy brown hair in loose curls. Grimy jeans covered the tops of dirty work boots. For a moment, I couldn't move. One thought permeated the shock—This person IS NOT SUPPOSED TO BE HERE.

Panic froze me only a microsecond before I fled, screaming and running, harboring no hope that the neighbors could hear me. I could feel the intruder gaining speed behind me. As I reached the front door, I fumbled frantically with the double locks, fully anticipating the impact of some metallic weapon in my back. Then I heard a voice in my head. Instinct? God? My inner voice?

"Pull open the front door and slip behind it," the voice inside me said.

Cornered between the door and the vestibule wall, I held my breath. The assailant, faced with an immediate exit, bolted out the door and took off. As he raced down the street, I shot to the phone. My fingers shook so hard, it took three tries to punch 911 correctly.

Police apprehended the intruder after he had violated four more houses in our neighborhood, his pockets filled with stolen jewelry. Rummaging through his victims' closets, he put on additional slacks, providing more pockets to fill. He even upgraded his shoes! This was not the first time for him. His cocaine-driven lifestyle included routine breaking and entering, getting caught, brief imprisonment, then back on the streets for another cycle. Although the police retrieved my belongings, the burglar left me with a broken basement window and the trauma and fear that tormented my thoughts for years after the incident.

It seemed impossible to lie close enough to my husband that night. I clung to him, still shaking with terror from my encounter. My mind pulled up mental files of other violent acts close to home. I remembered my girlfriend in Florida, returning home and startling a burglar. He beat her with a baseball bat, splattering her blood over the wall. She suffers with headaches time cannot heal. I thought of the mother of my husband's co-worker, killed by the burglar she surprised. I had been lucky this time; hopefully this would be my only encounter with violence. I ached for mothers in poorer neighborhoods familiar to the pops of stray bullets, breaking windows and piercing walls with holes. Violence and fear shatter the peace of everyday life, yet this has become accepted as the American way.

Coming home became a dreaded event. Each time I entered my front door, my heart raced. My hands shook as I dashed for the phone, calling women friends who could reassure me as I searched my house. I looked in closets, under beds, and in the downstairs guest room. I ordered the family to open shower curtains after every shower. I requested extra police protection for our quiet, shady street. I jumped at the slightest noise behind me. Anyone's shadow startled me. I knew I could not live like this; I had to do something to relinquish this fear.

Thinking back to past challenges in my life, I focused on my faithful coping tool. Humor has never let me down yet. Maybe humor could facilitate the healing that I needed this time. I prayed ardently, asking God to help me see the humor in this appalling event. I wrote my prayers in my journal, letters to God.

A burglary? Funny? Impossible. The act in and of itself could never be found amusing to me. However, it occurred to me that I had developed new, potentially amusing behaviors since the intrusion. Every morning I took great pains to make our bed, put away any underwear strewn on the floor, and straighten up my dresser, as if expecting another burglar, one who would appreciate my good housekeeping no less! Another new behavior took place whenever I visited a friend's home. I excused myself, went to their bathroom, and checked behind the shower curtain! I had to laugh at myself. These trauma-induced behaviors were pretty silly. This caused a tremendous release of stress. Life felt better after that.

Finding myself amusing was not going to be enough to put me at ease in my recently violated home. Many people keep weapons in their homes such as guns and pepper spray. I knew those would not be options for me. We adamantly refuse to use guns. I would have had no time to grab pepper spray. I settled on dogs as our new defense system. Our two new sweet and docile family pets resolved my fears. One has a loud bark and the other intimidates by size alone. Though I knew that pets should never be considered an ultimate line of defense against burglars unless they are trained guard dogs, I also believed that my furry friends would at least sound the alarm and potentially discourage another attempt because it would be too much trouble to even try with two dogs in the house. That, finally, made me feel safer.

We also developed closer relationships with our neighbors. Hosting two block parties each year has become a semi-annual fellowship time with lovely people who now look out for each other.

There remained one more hurdle to overcome. The burglar had robbed me of what used to be my personal retreat. My bathroom could no longer provide the private space for my own rejuvenation and enjoyment. A sickening negative energy lingered, especially in the bathtub. A short time later, the toilet leaked, the tub crack worsened, and my bathroom became an empty space, used only for arranging my hair. This continued for three years.

Some bathrooms are strictly functional—do the business and get out. But a bathroom can offer a sanctuary for many personal activities. Besides bathing, one can play, have sex, de-stress, read, look younger, relax, defoliate, shave, be sick, or feel rich. Bathrooms have their own personal meaning. I know a workaholic who sits on a clear, acrylic toilet seat filled with silver dollars. My friend Grace tested fifteen bathtubs before she found the one that felt right for her luxury baths. I once saw a picture of the Lone Ranger in his pink bathroom, shag carpeting everywhere and a matching pink phone. Bathrooms are a haven for a great many people. The burglar had robbed my bathroom of its unique definition for me. I wanted it back.

My husband recognized how important this little space was to me. He suggested a bathroom makeover—a major splurge. Choosing fiery reds, royal purples, and golden accessories, I designed my ideal refuge. New vanity, new tub, new everything. We contracted a team of skilled professionals for both bathrooms and trained the family to stumble downstairs to the basement for nighttime necessities and showers.

After three months of inconvenience, we began the process of painting, papering, and accessorizing. Finally, my brilliant bathroom ready for use, Simone and I conducted a healing ceremony. I gave Simone the turkey feather while I held the abalone seashell containing green sage. We lit the herb, inhaling its musky fragrance, and gently swept the scent with the feather into my precious space. A blessing for a room dedicated to personal balance, health needs, and transformation! I inflated my bath pillow, arranged my basket of aromatherapy, bubble bath, and water softeners, then raised a glass of wine to this environment of pleasure.

Only a memory now, the burglary sleeps in my subconscious without bothering me anymore. I relish my new bathroom, a warmer friendship with my neighbors, and my wonderful, loving dogs. I have experienced a deeper compassion for victims of violence, and sincere appreciation for the compassionate service of our community police force. How ironic that in a bizarre way, the burglar left me richer than before.

Dinner Questions

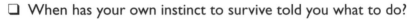

❑ When has your own instinct to survive told you what to do?

❑ How has a life trauma led you to a richer existence?

Heating Up the Marriage Bed

*The important thing in acting is to be able to
laugh and cry. If I have to cry, I think of my sex life.
If I have to laugh, I think of my sex life.*

— GLENDA JACKSON

*It was an old quandary for them. He needed sex
in order to feel connected to her, and she needed to
feel connected to him in order to enjoy sex.*

—LISA ALTHER, *BEDROCK*

"Fix me!" I begged. "What can I do to want sex again?"

Surely this therapist could help. I had desperately scheduled appointments with first one, then another therapist in a frantic attempt to discover the cure for my sexual malaise. Robert came with me to the second therapist, eager to help me find a magic cure that would provide him with an enthusiastic, willing partner.

I surmised that something must be wrong with one of us. At first, I blamed my husband. A computer technician, Robert specializes in logical thought processes, mathematical strategies, and problems with solutions. He works hard at troubleshooting computer programs with different formulas. Accurate in his work, he is a perfectionist. As a conscientious employee, he puts in overtime hours. He typically spends long hours alone working on his stamp collection or cleaning our kitchen to pass an imagined white glove inspection. Communication for Robert consists of reporting logistical information, such as what time the game starts and what the kids have eaten. Spending time together translates to him "let's clean the house together." He is satisfied with minimum discussion or mood-enhancing prior to sex.

I love to be seduced. Sensuous evenings, with candlelight, dinner, and background music stimulate me. I delight in intimate conversation, sharing innermost thoughts and feelings, but this is a foreign language to Robert. I love to sip a little wine and listen to jazz. Robert refrains from drinking anything other than Diet Coke and orange juice. Consequently, seduction never happened in our house. Robert expected a ready partner any time. Romance to me titillates all of my senses; to Robert it is simply a matter of waking up.

The first therapist looked at our busy schedules. "Schedule an afternoon date," he suggested to Robert. "Take her to a park where you can push her in a swing."

Robert dutifully did as he was told. Still no sex.

"Visit a romantic bed and breakfast," came the next advice. Robert, eager to please, found an old house furnished with antiques and booked a bedroom fit for royalty. A red velvet canopy came to a dramatic peak over the bed, topped with a gold crown for the best fairytale romance. He purchased my favorite champagne and chilled it in the refrigerator. Of course, that evening I menstruated, complete with racking stomach cramps. Robert became frustrated and I changed therapists.

The second therapist, a gentle, spiritual woman, urged me to be easier on myself. She also encouraged us to have fun, like camping, making sure to take a separate tent for the children.

"Unthinkable," I reacted, considering my daughter, barely six, and the one-year-old baby.

I also sought solutions from the multitude of books on sexual dysfunction. *How to Stay Married and Have Great Sex for the Rest of Your Life*, the title boasted. I looked at the exercises, and closed the book. I simply had no interest. In order to gain any benefits from these sexual sages, I had to be motivated to read them. What could I do to light the fire within me? Me, the lady with the wild costumes and abundant imagination, married to a devoted husband who would do absolutely anything to please me, and still I had no desire.

Somehow our marriage survived that bleak time six years ago. When I look back, I have to laugh at myself. I had failed to assess the big picture.

Following his recovery from a potentially life-threatening illness, Robert enrolled in his final year of school while continuing his night job. I worked as well, hiring babysitters for my odd hours. I also led a large Brownie troop for my daughter. Twenty-four little girls kept me busy planning camping trips, service projects, and cookie sales. Meanwhile, the energetic one-year-old needed his attention, too.

Exhaustion was both normal and expected. Robert survived on three hours of sleep each day. Many times I found him seated at the dining room table, dozing in front of his cereal bowl. Once he even fell asleep standing upright, the vacuum cleaner in his hands and running at a standstill.

To add to our impossibly hectic schedules, Robert's sixteen-year-old son was living with us, electrically charging our home life. Since this young man expressed his rebellion and confusion in violent ways, the police frequented our house. The violence continued to escalate, finally resulting in detention. We visited him in a juvenile facility out of town, adding yet another commitment of time and energy.

Our challenges continued as Robert's graduation approached. A car accident involving Robert and Simone sent me racing to the hospital to find my six-year-old unscratched while Robert lay in pain, a hairline fracture requiring bed rest throughout his Christmas vacation. We worked on résumés and long-distance job leads late into the night while hiring carpenters in the daytime to repair our house for the market. It was, by anyone's definition, a stressful year. And I wondered why I didn't feel sexy!

Robert continues to search for a quick formula for getting me in the mood, despite the interferences of our lives. It's not so easy for me.

"Seduce me!" I demand, envious of the romantic interludes enjoyed by childless friends.

"You keep changing the rules!" He complains. "I never get it right."

He's probably correct. Sometimes I need more relaxing time, sometimes more connecting time, and sometimes I don't know what I need.

After reading Anita Diamant's *The Red Tent*, I yearn for the close relationships of women in a tribe, women who share stories and advice for
the marriage bed. I am not the perfect lover, that's for sure, but with the
right support and encouragement I could learn to be better.

We looked for that quick fix, the sure formula, or magic therapist
that could provide us with a shortcut to achieving what we want. Our
quest for sustaining intimacy and excellent sex has forced us to investi-
gate a myriad of excuses: different communication styles, conflicting
attitudes about sex, old parenting messages, body issues, cultural differences in sexual banter, and various skeletons in our closets. We had to
peel away these layers to get to the core of our real selves, the spiritual
essence of who we are before we were able to achieve sexual alliance
with each other. We had lost touch with our own spirituality somewhere along the way, and, consequently, had become deficient in our
ability to enjoy each other sexually.

We weren't always so sexually deficit. A profound experience of intimacy early in our marriage came in the form of a lazy Sunday morning
in Augusta, Georgia. We skipped church and took beach towels and a
tape recorder to a park on a balmy day. Sprawling under a tall pine tree,
we listened to peaceful music and floated in our personal reveries of
nature. We experienced the wonder of the universe, the loving tenderness of God, and the miracle of our love. Maybe that was the magic
formula, the return to our spiritual centers, separately yet together. We
were searching for our spirituality and found that when we connected
on that wavelength, it could charge our sexuality.

Robert has read this essay up to now with considerable interest. At
last he put it down, clearly disappointed.

"Your title is a bit misleading," he said matter-of-factly. "You didn't
give a solution."

Masking my amusement at Robert's never-ending search for the
magic shortcut, I sensed my pragmatic husband may never understand.
My present therapist had challenged me to shift my thinking away from
the quick solution.

"What does *your* sexuality want, Ana?" She had asked.

I was stunned by her question. *My* sexuality? It had been a long
time since I considered my sexuality as being relevant to anything, much

less attached any significance to my desires. Previously I had only considered what I should be doing and how I should be feeling differently for Robert's sake.

"I guess I've lost touch with myself. I never think about *my* sexuality," I answered honestly.

"What would you enjoy?" she persisted. "What would you say yes to? If you could have Robert do anything you wanted, what would you ask him to do?"

She had turned the tables. I had new questions to think about.

The request elicited practically an instantaneous response from me. "No sex at midnight or at five in the morning."

"Most women raising children and building careers don't. So, pick a time, and plan for it. Tell Robert what you want him to do. I think he'll oblige." She made it sound so easy.

That left me to decide: just what would I like for Robert to do with me, to me or for me? My imagination took off. I fantasized about hot tubs and margaritas, of steamy jazz and cold strawberries dipped in chocolate.

My opportunity came three days later. Simone had been invited to spend the night with a friend. I informed John of his need for an early bedtime of eight-thirty.

"Robert, we are having time to ourselves tonight," I announced.

"But I need to get things done," Robert insisted. His inner taskmaster stays on overdrive twenty-four seven.

"They can wait. You go take a shower and shave, then meet me in the bedroom. And bring Simone's CD player."

Setting up candles, I started the water for a bubble bath. On the bed, I had laid out an outfit I had purchased for Robert to wear. Boxer shorts in a slinky, sensuous fabric were not the usual attire for a computer technician but for tonight he was going to be something different for me. I placed a bottle of massage oil in warm water next to the bed. I relaxed in my bath, reveling in its fragrant scent.

Robert knocked on the door, and came in, dressed in his usual pants and shirt. He smelled good. He practically radiated anticipation.

"Oh no, Robert. Your clothes are laid out on the bed. Now go put them on."

Robert dutifully retreated, and the fun began. I put on my outfit from Victoria's Secret that rarely left my lingerie drawer. I already tingled with long-forgotten excitement. My plan to rejuvenate my lapsing sexual appetite was working.

Simone's CD player emitted music accompanied by the sounds of a waterfall offering a comforting peaceful paradise in our bedroom. I lit the candles and handed Robert the warm oil. "Sweetheart, would you massage my feet?"

Nothing feels more seductive than a foot massage with warm oil. Completely relaxing the body, waves of sensuous pleasure tingled all the way to the scalp of my head. They say the foot and hand has pressure points leading directly to all parts of the body, and Robert was relaxing and stimulating all of them. I melted into a blissful euphoria, easy to arouse and ready for love. Our erotic evening lasted for hours. I learned that in asking for what I wanted, I discovered my passion and desire. That night I became an incredible lover.

Now that I had dissolved that barrier, I soon discovered a new hurdle in our intimacy—how to say "no" without feeling guilty. I'm still trying to conquer that one. I know to Robert it seems like I say "no" all the time. But each time I say "no," I think about what I would say "yes" to and make a counter proposal. I try to actively set up situations that I know I am more likely to be aroused by Robert's approaches. I allow for relaxing time together, I plan for my bath and Robert's shower, I ask for a massage. The result has been remarkable, helping us accomplish a new level of intimacy and pleasure that I look forward to after nineteen years of marriage!

The alligator here is not sex. The alligators of anxiety and frustration get in the way of communicating intimacy and love, important aspects of a healthy sex life. How strange that so often the male gender sees sex as an outlet for anxiety and frustration, but for women, or at least for me, stress drains my desire. Pressuring myself to perform out of a sense of duty destroyed my passion and excitement, and without it, I had no desire to ever make love.

Life has drastically changed for us. At times it seems idyllic in contrast to those earlier years in Florida. Robert works his ideal job. The teenage son fights his own battles as an adult. Our two children lead active lives in Scouts and sports, while I volunteer at their schools, taking my career at a slower pace. In our fifties, sex has offered some exquisite moments of ecstatic pleasure as well as heart-to-heart sharing. Still, like most people in our cohort, we struggle with the difficult task of life balance. Finding time to relax, talking together, and connecting in a playful way seems almost impossible at times. Our sex life continues to have dry spells but at least now we recognize the source and no longer blame each other.

The familiar alligators of frustration and anxiety visit us as if they were old relatives, ready to walk right in and kill our ability to relax and enjoy life to its fullest. Finances, career disappointments, aging health problems, and parental needs create a constant barrage of negative energy. We get so overwhelmed we forget to take time for our inner well-being.

Sometimes we need to be selfish in order to be better people, both in bed and out. Giving up the guilt and the sense of duty and obligation sex often implies, and considering our own desires encourages us to take charge of our sex life and change everything. A great way to wrestle a potential marriage-gobbling alligator!

Dinner Questions

- ❑ How does stress prevent you from enjoying life?
- ❑ How can you take charge, listen to your own sexuality, and become a better lover?

Alligator Wrestling with a Swamp Boat:
Taking the Right Equipment

*She had the loaded handbag of someone
who camps out and seldom goes home, or who
imagines life must be full of emergencies.*

— MAVIS GALLANT, *A FAIRLY GOOD TIME*

You would never venture into an alligator-invested swamp without the proper equipment to protect you in case you happened to encounter a less-than-friendly reptile. In the Florida Everglades, the mother of all alligator swamps, there are special airboats for navigating the shallow marshes and wetlands. These boats are designed for skimming over saw grass prairies and the mangrove wilderness where alligators congregate. They also provide a stable ride on a deep river. With a 350-horsepower engine, no propellers or wheels, the boats can speed through the Everglades without leaving residues in the water or scars on the landscape. They are even bulletproof!

One should no more attempt to venture unprotected into life than into an alligator swamp in Florida. How do you equip yourself to navigate through life amidst the alligators? Do you plan strategies for your journey, identifying times and places to stop and refuel? Do you have destinations in mind or do you cruise aimlessly around, going nowhere in particular? Have you thought about what supplies you might need?

All of us know people who wrestle with first one alligator, then another, then multiple alligators, getting nowhere, sinking fast. They

122

float in an unwieldy, unsuitable boat from one situation to another, without direction. Life swamps their boats and surrounds them with gators. Yet other people we know seem to embrace life as if it were some sort of sport—perhaps a race to be run or a game to be won. They are up for the experiences life offers them, relishing each new challenge, celebrating each triumph, and learning from each defeat. The key to enjoying the sport is to prepare. Determine your destination, then take time to acquire skills, tools, positive companions, and faith in a higher power. Prepare yourself mentally and physically for whatever obstacles life throws in your way. Your own boat will skim the surface at amazing speed.

The following stories represent a different category from my collection of wrestling tools: the ability to work with teams, the astounding results of goal setting and visualization, assemblage of a professional support team, and finally, the permission to fall apart once in a while.

Dinner Questions

❑ How do you prepare for the unknown?
❑ What kinds of life preservers do you have in place?

The Auction

After the earthquake and the fire
comes the still small voice.

— DOROTHY THOMPSON, *LET*
THE RECORD SPEAK

We always visualize our faith as being the stable, steadfast anchor in our life, something to retreat to in times of need. I think God provides an anchor for us, but I truly believe God demands action from us. I think He or She actually insists on it. When that quiet voice inside tells me to do something, I pay attention. This has not always been the case. In one instance, that little voice became a noisy, nagging nuisance before driving me to action. It taught me one of the most important lessons of my life.

I loved my little church in Tallahassee. With its eclectic mix of members and a dynamic speaker for a minister, I couldn't wait for Sunday. Robert and I enjoyed being with other couples our age that had young families as well as single adults and dear "community grandparents." Even more, we enjoyed being with people who shared like-minded spirituality. Worship brought joy, tears, awe, and mystery to us. It also brought a growing congregation and with that, growing pains.

We had no place to expand. The trailer utilized for an education building felt like a pair of pants too tight to zip. Children were packed into tiny classrooms with no room to turn around. Something had to be done. I watched with frustration as board members presented vari-

124

ous plans to buy a neighboring house, or to build an adjoining addition. Each time, the money failed to materialize. We lacked the older, established families that patronized other churches, and our young family budgets were already stretched to the limit. Our older population consisted mostly of widows who were just getting by. Every time a money-raising plan failed, a board member would fervently plead with the congregation to cough up the money, and I would sit quietly, wrestling with the voice inside me.

"*Volunteer to raise the money!*" the voice inside me urged.

"NO!" I insisted.

Time would pass, another attempt would fail, and the voice would speak again.

"*Volunteer!*"

"I can't," I would argue with myself. "I have a new baby and a full time job."

Again, another plan fell through, and another board member made a plea. We in our pews sat like bumps on a log.

"*VOLUNTEER TO RAISE THE MONEY,*" the voice shouted within.

I gave up, with the resignation one has just before jumping off a cliff. "Alright, I'll do it!"

Peace filled me immediately, an indication that I had made the right decision.

First, I had to come up with a great plan. *Make a commitment, the ideas will come*, the voice inside me whispered like something from the movie, *Field of Dreams*.

The Girl Scout Council where I worked planned to expand their capital campaign. After researching the successful auctions held by a Texas council, the creativity and fun involved grabbed my attention. I wrote down the names of active young couples in my church, hoping to assemble a team of dedicated workers for my project.

"We need money for this church. A major auction will do it. I want YOU on my team!" I recruited emphatically. Four couples agreed to join my campaign.

Next, I needed the church to get behind the project. The minister allotted time for me during Sunday morning announcements. Wearing a bright red suit with a yellow blouse, I sprang to the platform from my seat. Could I pull off a little revival to build the necessary support for my plan? My stomach turned somersaults as I made my way to the pulpit. One of my favorite ministers, an outrageous woman named Marge, called herself "God's Fool." I felt that way myself as I stood before the congregation.

"Ladies and Gentlemen, Brothers and Sisters, This is an exciting church. If you agree with me, say yes."

They all agreed, quietly mumbling, "Yes."

"And we want to see our church grow. If you agree with me, say yes."

They were catching on, their voices growing louder, "Yes."

"And our children want to learn…they deserve the best. If you agree with me, say yes!

The volume in their response mounted, "Yes!"

They were with me now one hundred percent. Whipping the air with my outstretched arms, I emphasized my words with reckless abandon, giving my all to my final declaration. "We need a building for these children! Say yes!"

The congregation yelled back unanimously, "YES!"

"Friends, we're going to have us an auction, and I need you to give what ever you can. We will raise $30,000 we need to build a new education building. Are you with me?"

"YES!" They shouted back, clapping as if they had all suddenly seen the light.

Glancing at my husband sitting in the third pew, my own enthusiasm wavered. Something was wrong. Robert sat perfectly still, his face glazed with shock. It dawned on me, standing there before God and congregation, that I had forgotten to discuss this with him. The amount we needed to raise just came out of my mouth, out of nowhere. I knew once the shock wore off that Robert would support my unexpectedly volunteering to lead the charge.

After church, excited people, impressed by my gutsy ambition, surrounded me. As a result, new people requested to join my team. These individuals would be lifesavers as our process developed. They would teach me another lesson: *Include people on your team who are different from yourself.*

"Come to my house tonight at seven o'clock sharp," I replied. "I'll supply babysitting."

Our first meeting involved visioning, something I knew how to do. I asked everyone to introduce him or herself by sharing what they felt were special qualities embodied by the church.

"I love it because it's family," said one.

"People love to sit in the silence and feel God working inside them," added another.

"This congregation agrees on the same principles, without judging others," another contributed. And so on. We had established our common foundation.

"Now, what do we want to see happen at this auction? Let's throw out lots of ideas."

I stood poised and ready at the flipchart.

"Outrageous items!"

"Our church musicians…playing jazz!"

"Katherine singing!"

"Outside guests finding out about us!"

"Wonderful food."

A group vision emerged. We brainstormed jobs and divided responsibilities according to talents and skills. We set up our meeting schedule, a time frame for achieving our goals, and set the date. Off and running, I thought. Wrong!

At first, activity flurried like a snowstorm. We generated forms for donated items, wrote letters to resorts, and made lists of prospective donors. By the third meeting, however, the energy of my team began waning. Fewer people showed up. One of our talented couples was struggling with marital problems. We could feel the intensity of their negative feelings as they glared across the table from each other. Other team members felt pressured for time commitments because of their jobs. Since Tallahassee is the capital, we had many state workers in our church and on my committee. State workers travel a lot. It is difficult to depend on them in committees since they don't always know when they will have to go out of town, and they frequently do. This phenomenon is a frustration known by anyone living in a capital city. Meanwhile, a pile of forms for small items waited for processing. I handle forms about as well as I juggle live fish.

Laboring for hours at night, I tried to shuffle paper, sinking deeper and deeper in despair. I was drowning in piles of donation forms requiring numbers and sorting. Items needed a value assigned to them. These small items—a free video rental, a haircut, and a massage—all needed other items to combine with them to form a package. Every package required a description. The donors were waiting for confirmation and thank-you letters. Night after night, I plodded through the pile with building distaste for my plan. I shared my frustration at the next meeting.

"I'll help you," volunteered a state worker. "I can assign value and descriptions if you don't mind taking down dictation."

Adapting to his style of working would be a breeze, I thought, compared to what I had been struggling with alone. Meanwhile, his wife, Vickie, lined up the logistics, taking advantage of her job at the civic center. Signing a contract with the expensive civic center terrified me, but I signed it in good faith, trusting in God and my team to pull this event off. Vickie shifted into high gear. She seemed to work best independently, and I gratefully let her take the reigns and run with it. Another lesson learned. *People have different strengths and work styles.*

Still, other volunteers had to be reckoned with. One woman blatantly refused to come to any meetings. Others came irregularly, or only wanted jobs at the event itself. Our marketing people seemed to be stuck and there wasn't any sign of progress being made by the rest of the team.

I can't count on anybody, I would grumble to myself. Nobody wants to do the dirty work. The voice inside of me spoke up again.

"Have faith. You can't always see what is happening. Stay positive and do your part. Focus on the vision."

As much as I wanted to complain or blame the team, I bit my tongue. When a team member called with an excuse for not completing his or her assigned task, or work required out of town travel, I simply passed the job to someone else. As I learned the strengths and personalities of the team, I began to delegate differently. I discovered that some people worked better in pairs, while others preferred working alone. Some initiated their own ideas while others wanted precise instructions to follow.

The next low point came when we analyzed our progress two months away from the auction date. Our stack of donations consisted of only small items such as haircuts, video movies, and furniture accessories.

We would never make our goal at this rate. We needed to get serious, to think bigger. In panic, I felt the need for drastic measures.

"Margarita will be joining us at church," I announced to my husband.

Robert smiled. He had enjoyed a few romps in the hay with "Margarita" himself. "Margarita" actually consisted of a gaudy costume and an outrageous wig of long brown hair. I had created this notoriously spunky gypsy character for parties years ago. She never failed to grab the attention of a crowd.

"Better warn the minister," Robert cautioned me.

Instead, I called another team member. "Paula, get balloons for Sunday's ticket booth after church. We need to put the air in this campaign or the auction won't happen!"

Margarita definitely caused a commotion Sunday.

"It eez time to buy zee tickets!" I unabashedly flirted and tossed about my affected accent from the center church aisle.

"You, wis zee legs," I pointed at a worshiper in Bermuda shorts. This church dressed in Florida casual. "You veel find a grrreat bargain at zee awk-zhun!"

Margarita had been my last trump card. We needed a miracle or we would have to throw in the towel. I prayed, God, if you want us to do this, then we need some help, soon.

The voice came again. *Oh, ye of little faith.*

Why do miracles always take us off guard, even when we have asked for one? The answer to my prayers came in the form of Joy, the team member who never attended our meetings. A mother of small children, Joy possessed imagination and guts. She dreamed up big prizes and pursued them relentlessly.

"Ana," Joy's excitement sparkled over the phone. "I secured two VIP tickets to the Jay Leno show, along with two airline tickets, and a weekend stay at the Hollywood Hilton."

My mouth dropped. This auction item would get the juices flowing.

"Wait until the team hears this!" I replied.

There is nothing like a success to light a fire under the team to get them moving again. The news was infectious. The entire team shifted gears and suddenly started getting results.

A staff assistant with the governor's office called. She, too, had been absent from meetings. "I'm back from a project that took me out of town." She explained. "Where do you need help?" A whiz at organizing, Colleen took the donation forms and efficiently worked her magic.

Vickie, a professional saleswoman by trade, reeled in more large value items, while church members donated a week's stay at a beach cottage, and a plane ride. One lady volunteered to bake chocolate chip cookies using Hillary Clinton's recipe, and another volunteered three formal floral arrangements.

Suddenly, dazzling donations poured in. We packaged small donated items and services together, then thought up catchy titles such as "Lovers Escape," "Dog Lover's Delight," "Pampered Car," and "Broadway New York Style." We saved bigger items for the live auction, including a full golf membership at the country club, an expensive painting, and frequent flyer tickets. We dreamed up patron donation levels in addition to our ticket sales, acknowledging the generous individuals inspired by our event. Our imaginations zoomed ahead as ideas and donations cascaded in. At full speed, we performed like a finely tuned race car.

Colleen and I worked at night in her office, pasting up programs and designing displays for the silent auction. Patty, a quiet individual who had volunteered to pick up items, refueled her truck over and over, driving incessantly to collect our booty. Larry, another team member, designed training for volunteers who would handle our payment process during the auction. Shary dreamed up an imaginative decorating theme while Vickie instructed the civic center staff to provide an impressive show of culinary treats. Church members with musical talent began rehearsing the entertainment. In spite of the long hours spent on the final preparations, the exhilaration of working on the event filled all of us with incredible energy. This flurry of activity and increased motivation actually carried over into my job, improving my productivity there immensely. To think that a lack of time had been my original excuse for not getting involved in the first place!

On the day of the auction, the team took over like the professionals they had become. Additional volunteers came out of the woodwork to decorate while a small army busied themselves transporting donated items. The team had tripled in size since the beginning.

"We can control it from here, Ana," they assured me.

"Get your hair done with my hairdresser, Ana. My treat. Rest up and look beautiful." Vickie was not one to argue with, so I acquiesced, relinquishing the final hours to my team of enthusiastic volunteers.

At this point I didn't think I could stand the suspense. The day literally dragged by as I waited nervously for the magic hour of reckoning.

At seven o'clock that night, my husband and I arrived at the civic center. Streams of formally attired people, buzzing with anticipation, surged through the front doors. We followed the crowd upstairs to our designated function room. Twinkling lights, candelabras, and tiered tables boasting a festive feast enticed us as we entered. Smiling chefs positioned at different stations prepared pasta, sliced roast beef, and tossed salad. Tall ice sculptures glistened in the candlelight while a tiered table beckoned guests to taste its chocolate delicacies. A crowd of animated people poured over the long rows of tables filled with displays of silent auction packages. One hundred and eleven items, twenty-seven combination packages, and fifteen deluxe items for the live auction flirted with the bidders. Not bad for a small church's first effort.

Soon the well-dressed guests claimed their tables, and settled in for the live auction and entertainment. Max, in a tuxedo borrowed from his father-in-law and secured with safety pins, charmed the audience as our emcee. Our church musicians showed off their flair for hot, Saturday night jazz. The pianist, drummer, guitarist, and our beautiful soloist cut loose for the appreciative audience. The professional auctioneer lost no time in exciting the crowd with his runaway monotone chatter, rising in inflection, pausing only for a new price. Bidding galloped at a fast and furious pace. Pretty soon, new owners claimed every item. The musicians cranked back up and we filled the dance floor, laughing with the giddiness brought on by success.

The next day, Sunday, the anticipation felt thick enough to cut with a knife as the congregation anxiously awaited our results. The minister called me to the dais for my much-awaited announcement.

"Ladies and Gentlemen," I began in a low voice, "I promised you we would raise $30,000 with our auction. But we didn't do that."

I paused, looking downcast. Silence settled like a ton of bricks over the audience. Their disappointment weighed heavy in the room.

I paused one more moment for effect, then announced, "We made $40,000!"

The room exploded with whoops and clapping—a joyful noise! Pride flowed like a river through the church that day, starting with me and spilling over each and every member who had contributed to this valiant effort.

The lessons from that experience provide rich insights in any team endeavor:

Take your inner voice seriously.

Ideas will follow commitment.

Never underestimate team members no matter how different they are from you.

A team needs a shared vision, which you sometimes must provide for them.

People need the freedom to utilize their own ways of working.

People come through at different times, though not necessarily on your schedule.

The climate must at all times remain positive; avoid complaining, backbiting, or gossiping.

Stay focused on the vision; it is easy to lose sight of that vision through the course of working together.

One person's success can spring the whole team to action.

Team synergy can achieve miracles.

One little church, a handful of state workers, a few professional women, and some stay at-home mothers purchased a magnificent education building that year. Small, compared to the mega churches that exist today, but magnificent just the same, surrounded by a beautiful deck and flowering shrubs. The pride of pulling together to realize a community dream energized us, enriched us, and bonded us with a deep sense of shared history. What if I hadn't listened to that nagging little voice?

Dinner Questions

❑ When have you been energized by a team dream?

❑ How have you misjudged a group of people who proceeded to pull off a miracle?

A Treasure Map of Fame

*Often the search proves more
profitable than the goal.*

— E.L. KONINGSBURG, *FROM THE MIXED–UP
FILES OF MRS. BASIL E.
FRANKWEILER*

"I want to be like you, Mom. I want to be famous!"

Eleven-year-old Simone looked at me longingly, her face full of hope, her eyes full of stars. I hardly considered myself famous, I was still establishing my reputation and confidence. I considered myself a struggling artist/business woman. To my daughter, the news clippings and videotapes of local and national media events of twenty years ago convinced her that I was someone worthy of the media's attention and therefore, by default, famous.

"Sweetheart, you must do something very original or help someone in an outstanding way. Maybe you can think of a way to stop pollution," I added, hoping to steer her away from some of my more bizarre methods of gaining attention, such as swinging from a crane over Winston-Salem, one of my clandestine adventures that happened to gain me a moment of fame in Tampa, Florida.

"Pollution?" she had sighed, disappointed. "Oh, Mom." She wanted fame and she wanted it NOW.

"Okay, Simone, you want to be famous? First, you picture it. Make a treasure map," I suggested. Her eyes lit up; there was something concrete she could do.

Treasure-mapping enables one to visualize future goals. I have taught workshops to help people visualize lifestyles of balance, healthy relationships, and successful career paths. Always one to practice what I preach, I employ some of the same techniques with myself as well as my family. Every January, we sit down with old magazines and search for pictures that depict personal goals, dreams, and aspirations, such as where to go on family vacations. Having seen this exercise work for so many people, myself included, I wanted my children to use this method for realizing their goals.

The following month, I invited my daughter to accompany me to a business exposition sponsored by the Chamber of Commerce. Simone received permission from her school to attend the event as part of "Take Your Daughter to Work Day." Her budding interest as an entrepreneur had manifested a sporadic pet sitting business, an occasional car wash, and a magic show where a neighbor bought two tickets.

Dressed in her best jeans, Simone carefully took notes as she interviewed the marketing reps working at the business booths. She seemed stimulated by the abundance of high energy present in the convention center that day. Her goodie bag quickly grew heavy from promotional freebies presented by the salespeople impressed by her interviews. I scouted the area for other ways she could interact with business owners.

I spied a digital portrait business. "Look, Simone! You can get your picture taken." Seated behind a computer monitor, the owner took instant photographs of willing subjects, then, for a small fee, printed them on a mock cover that emulated *Time Magazine*.

"Simone! That can be part of your treasure map for being famous!" I exclaimed, and offered to pay for her sitting.

Simone jumped into the seat and smiled for the camera.

"We need a caption on here," advised the cameraman. "What will be your claim to fame?"

"Top cookie seller," quipped Simone without hesitation.

Simone sold Girl Scout cookies every year and anticipated the upcoming sale with great eagerness. The businessman typed it in, clicked a button, and waited for Simone's magazine cover to print.

"Cool," Simone smiled with approval.

She slipped the magazine cover into her goodie bag and forgot about it. When we came home that evening, I carefully retrieved the magazine cover, knowing the uncanny results from treasure-mapping. We didn't have a clue, however, that the cover would be a harbinger of things to come.

Six months passed, the Business Expo long forgotten, and the cover languished on a shelf in Simone's room. Simone busied herself in school and Girl Scouts. December brought the beginning of order-taking for the annual cookie sale. Every afternoon, Simone put on her vest laden with badges and waited for her father to come home. Robert provided the support behind Simone's cookie sales since I was the troop leader and had the whole troop to motivate. A former Army recruiter, Robert knew the value of persistence and goal setting. He would drive Simone door to door from one neighborhood to another. At the end of each evening, Robert treated Simone to a milk shake, knowing that a child needed immediate gratification for such hard work. He also knew that Simone's cookie sales would earn her an entire summer at Girl Scout camp, her all-time favorite summer activity. Robert carefully recorded Simone's achievement, keeping the totals from year to year.

A month-and-a-half later, the cookies arrived. We cleared room in our garage as thousands of boxes created formidable mountains of cookies waiting to be delivered. Robert and Simone began the tedious task of delivering after supper every night. In addition, they set up cookie booths outside of grocery, home improvement, and department stores on weekends. Meanwhile, I left town for a weekend convention, relieved to escape cookie mania for a brief period.

The night after my departure, Simone would sell her 10,000th box of cookies, her cumulative total from years of hawking the tasty treats. Robert, determined not to miss a marketing opportunity, calculated the event to happen between seven and eight o'clock. The local paper agreed to capture the momentous occasion. When I returned home from Atlanta, Simone waited for me in the garage, the front page of the weekend newspaper in her hands and a huge grin on her face. There, over the masthead of the front page, a color photo of Simone teased readers with her story. I gasped to discover a half-page article in the local section, with three more color photographs. Simone beamed with pride. Her fifteen minutes of fame, I thought.

The following weekday, we received a call from the local affiliate of a major television broadcasting station. Would Simone agree to an interview in our home? With bright lights set up in the living room, Simone calmly listed her keys to success in selling cookies for the cameraman, her uniform boasting her active Girl Scout involvement with all its badges, patches, and other official insignia.

"Make eye contact," she advised with the easy assurance of an old pro. "Thank everybody even if they don't buy. Don't quit. Just take a break, get a treat, and keep on going. Be sure to dress professionally."

Two days later, we received another phone call, from a radio station.

"Could we interview your daughter about her Girl Scout cookie sales?" the DJ asked. "We're from a station in Burlington."

I was familiar with the small town in North Carolina about an hour from our home in Winston-Salem. My husband had frequently commuted there for business.

"Sure," I replied, knowing my daughter would be pleased to oblige.

The morning of the radio interview, I answered the phone and quizzed the DJ.

"We wanted to listen to the interview on the radio, but I don't recognize your call numbers," I explained. "Where did you say you were located?"

"Burlington," the DJ patiently reminded me. "Burlington, Vermont!"

My mouth dropped open. A radio station from another state wanted to interview my daughter! Simone grabbed the phone and adroitly took over with confidence.

"Hi, I'm Simone ! Do you want to hear about the greatest cookies in the world?" Simone gave her pitch, even hitting up the DJ's for a sale on the air.

She added five more boxes to her growing total. The following night, we received a call from another DJ in Jacksonville, Florida, then others in Chicago and Milwaukee. A friend across the state sent us a news release touting Simone's accomplishment, a story sent by Associated Press wire. Customers at the shopping centers started to recognize her. Little girls from other troops pointed at her excitedly.

"That's her! The girl in the paper!"

Simone had realized her treasure map. She had stated her goal, worked towards her goal, and achieved her goal. Fame belonged to her.

Simone's success reminded me to reflect on my own goals. How many opportunities are simply waiting for us to merely visualize them first? How much easier life would be if we identified our major goals then rewarded ourselves for achieving small increments on the way to that goal! If we kept track of our little successes and reviewed them from time to time, we would feel a sense of accomplishment sooner. Simone's lesson is not about fame, it's about recognizing life goals and going after them. We all need to step back from our lives, give ourselves permission to dream, and start treasure-mapping our goals.

Dinner Question

❑ What dream would you like to nurture with a treasure-map?
❑ How do you teach your children life skills?

The Blue Funk Swamp

If you feel depressed you shouldn't go out on the street because it will show on your face and you'll give it to others. Misery is a communicable disease.

— MARTHA GRAHAM

Most people describe me as an enthusiastic optimist. Every day offers me opportunities to encounter new people and new experiences. But every so often I find myself trudging through what I affectionately call "The Blue Funk Swamp." Every step seems laborious and heavy, like the time I found my shoes caked with six inches of sticky black gumbo mud when I lived in Arkansas. The good news is that, for me, the Blue Funk Swamp is a temporary condition, not a true depression, caused by a normal emotional downswing that occasionally slows me to a crawl. I have found that the best approach to the Blue Funk is not to resist it. Just wallow in it for a day or two, then drag yourself out and get on with your life.

Women deal with the Blue Funk in different ways. My friend Sara puts on her bathrobe and holes herself up in her house with three old movies, junk food, and chocolate-covered raisins. Jana flees to a beach house with an armful of good novels. Florence found that, for years, an escape to her mom's provided just the thing: good old-fashioned nurturing with hot homemade soup. Comfort foods, empathy, and a mother who doesn't care what you look like on these down-home retreats can pull you out of the Blue Funk Swamp.

Why do we suddenly find ourselves wallowing in the Blue Funk Swamp? The Blue Funk can be caused by burnout, overextending one's boundaries, or sometimes even a let down from a wonderful vacation or motivational convention. A major disappointment demands time for licking wounds. For some of us, physical conditions, like menstrual cramps or migraines, require a time out.

Here are some ways you can get over the Blue Funk and actually use the mood to move you forward:

Write about it. Write down every single negative thought, every worry, every fear, and every disapproving judgmental opinion rendered to you that haunts you now.

Sort out what you know is untrue, and write down the facts that prove this.

Write affirmations, which are positive thoughts in present tense, to address each of the negative fears, worries, and judgments. I wrote my affirmations throughout one of my most difficult times in a journal. I put them to music and made a tape of my most powerful ones to listen to before I go to sleep, when I drive, and when I perform mindless activities.

Write down as many of your negative thoughts as possible, and conduct a mental "housecleaning" so that the positive affirmations can replace the prevailing negativity. Fears and worries are future based. For the present, they are only thoughts but these thoughts are capable of absorbing our energy if we keep them in their negative form.

Visit a friend who is facing a major challenge herself. Or volunteer to help people who have crises to combat. Usually, a Blue Funk happens because we focus on our own problems, so reaching out to others in need can dramatically change our focus to a more optimistic outlook concerning our own life. Have you ever found someone who has problems you would rather have? Of course not.

Discover that a person who we think of as less fortunate than ourselves truly has a deep well of faith that can inspire us out of our own personal Blue Funk days. These individuals, despite their misfortunes, are very fortunate indeed. One such person is Debbie, a victim of muscular dystrophy. In spite of her progressive disease, Debbie is committed to letting her inner light shine through her unfortunate circumstance. From her wheelchair, she contributes hours of volunteer time to her church and to the Girl Scouts. Her courage and determination inspires everyone who knows her.

Do something. I find the best way to shake off the Blue Funk is to get active doing something you like. Exercise to happy music. Sing. Play upbeat records.

Find a new look. It helps me to change my persona by altering my outward appearance. I cut my hair, wear a soft, plush robe, or don an exotic dress from my costume closet. Another friend I know wore a crown while recovering at home from a hysterectomy. She laughingly recalls the day the postman caught her sunbathing in the front yard with it on.

Try something new, or try something old again. Paint. On a camping trip with my nieces, I took out the children's set of watercolors, markers, colored pencils, and pastels. As I encouraged my nieces to experiment, I layered blues, reds, and purples, enjoying the vibrations of the colors against each other. My enjoyment turned into exhilaration! I realized that I don't even have to know how to draw to enjoy the undulating effects of color, the sensual diversity of different media together, and the soulful expressions that color can create.

Read through old journals; creatively express feelings in new journals. They document prayers, blue funks, goals, and other highs and lows of life's journey. Paste pictures in them. Write with colored pens. Scribble. Draw arrows and highlighted exclamation points. List all of the alligators you can't cope with at the time. With journaling, you will begin to see reminders of your inner strength, the love of supportive friends, the grace of God, and the transitions of life.

Finally, pray specifically for encouragement, and then take time to listen. God listens and responds in the perfect way, though not always in the way we expect. Although I've listed this suggestion last, do it first.

Ironically, I have composed this page during a Blue Funk Swamp Day. I needed to remember what I know to be true. As I have written these thoughts, I realized a nap is calling me. Pardon me, while I indulge. This is, after all, what I do when I find myself in my Blue Funk Swamp.

Dinner
Questions

❑ How do you enjoy a Blue Funk Swamp Day?

❑ When has a depression led to creativity?

Chocolate

*Chocolate is no ordinary food. It is not
something you can take or leave, something you
like only moderately. You don't like chocolate. You
don't even love chocolate. Chocolate is
something you have an affair with.*

— GENEEN ROTH, *FEEDING
THE HUNGRY HEART*

Chocolate delays reality. When I am eating chocolate, everything is on hold: anxiety, panic, frustrations, and insecurity. Chocolate offers a profound richness, a sweetness of life, a euphoric sensation of luxury. I love chocolate in any form, from M&M's to imported Lindt balls; from dark fudge frosting in a pop-top can to truffles in a golden Godiva box.

It is difficult to eat only a little chocolate. I cheat myself when I chew it up quickly and swallow it like other food. To eat chocolate correctly, one must let it melt in the mouth with eyes closed, feeling the delectable thick smooth velvet coat the tongue. It is also difficult to eat really good chocolate silently. I usually purr a long ummmmmmm of feminine satisfaction when enjoying such a pleasure.

I have strategies to keep from eating chocolate. Targeting the times during the day when chocolate holds its strongest allure for me and identifying why I am most likely to cheat, I try to restructure my life to avoid my sweet nemesis. I meditate after lunch, enjoying the sweetness of life without calories, I brush my teeth after drinking my afternoon coffee, and I give any chocolate that finds its way to my doorstep away to my mother so that it's not tempting me in the house. But it comes back as gifts from other sources, knowing that it is loved and cherished in my presence.

My daughter loves chocolate, too, a hereditary trait, I guess. Sometimes my mother, my daughter, and I enjoy reveling in our chocolate ecstasy together, a female bonding of sensuous gratification. We give each other gifts of chocolate Easter Bunnies, chocolate Christmas balls, and chocolate Valentine confections, gleefully sharing our blessed bounty with each other. We hide it from other family members, and never apologize for succumbing to such greedy decadence. We have trained the men in our lives to buy it for us by expressing our enjoyment and satisfaction with lip-smacking, vocalized bliss. We permit our chocolate gift givers to be voyeurs of our pleasure, and they seem aptly rewarded.

I have a girlfriend that refers to chocolate as the fourth basic food group. She brazenly consumes it publicly, in front of people, instead of holding private chocolate sessions where no one can count bites or pieces or calories. The self-righteous judges who indignantly reprimand us for our sin of chocolate do not sway her. Sometimes this guilt for indulging is brought on by ourselves, our split personalities simultaneously loving and hating our obsession. My sister-in-law denies her children chocolate's evil influence, but personally yields to its entrapment. Chocolate calls her name, beckoning her in a trance-like state to follow its seductive aroma to the kitchen. I know that aroma well; it cannot be contained in a cardboard box, a foil wrapper, or an insulated refrigerator.

I like to tell myself that chocolate is really good for me. I eat chocolate to wake me up. At three o'clock in the afternoon when I want to stop and take a nap I bribe myself with chocolate to keep on working. Much preferred as my personal carrot-on-a-stick, chocolate is a self-imposed bribe to keep me pushing on. Of course, this bribe has negative consequences when my jeans don't fasten. I then must deny this temptation, giving in to the nap instead.

I suppose the alligator here is the addiction, but addiction to what? Chocolate? Or pushing to achieve? What a shame that my obsessions are activities that don't burn calories, but none of these do—striving, planning, dreaming, persisting, setting boundaries, checking off chores, reviewing goals, paying bills.

The bottom line is that I refuse to give up chocolate. I know women who have—women committed to thinness. I'm personally committed to enjoying my life, which would simply not be possible without chocolate. I have willingly accepted other dietary limitations, and I can readily refuse other desserts, bread, and wine during the week. But chocolate is a whole different matter, never to be confused with mundane, commonplace food.

They say that chocolate actually releases chemicals in a woman's body making her feel better. I am positive this is true. There have been two times in my life when women friends eased my unbearable pain with gifts of chocolate. Chocolate was, without a doubt, a salve for my emotional wounds.

A miscarriage devastates women with loss—loss of a child, a dream of family, of the marvelous feeling of life growing within her own body. A miscarriage can happen so quickly. One minute you are carrying a precious baby, the next minute you are not. For me, a night of torturous contractions abruptly ended my pregnancy, leaving me to grieve in the empty calm of my bedroom. After the emergency D and C in the doctor's office, I returned home to ponder my misfortune, taking the rest of the day off before returning to the office. Alone in my house, my sorrow numbed my thoughts, which was fine with me.

The phone rang, and an angry male voice from a volunteer organization I was working with barked at me from the other end.

"Why haven't you worked harder in my campaign?"

"Frank, I can't talk now. I'm sick."

The man became angrier. "This is critical," he protested.

"Not now." I hung up and returned to bed.

More phone calls followed. A co-worker, uninformed of my situation, called to discuss a project. She needed answers right then.

The morning dragged on, without any glimmer of sympathy. My husband came home at lunchtime to warm up some soup for me. The doorbell rang, and he went to answer it. I could hear voices in the house. Who on earth would be coming over in the middle of the day?

"Ana, someone's here to see you," Robert smiled.

"Vickie!" My best friend from work entered the bedroom.

In her easygoing, nonchalant manner, she said, "Just thought I'd come and check on you."

Her very presence comforted me. We hugged without saying anything.

"I brought a little something to cheer you up, when you feel like it," Vickie added.

She set a clear plastic container on the bed, a take-out box. I recognized the label from my favorite creative caterer. Inside, an enormous slice of three-layer triple chocolate cake with fudge frosting waited for my consumption. I gasped at the sheer decadence of it.

Vickie smiled knowingly and left. There are times when calories don't count. The chocolate extravagance communicated empathy, compassion, and reassurance. It was Vickie's way of saying to me "you deserve the best, not the worst." I loved her for that.

The second occasion of chocolate comfort came later, this time with a successful pregnancy. Every mother knows the challenge of the last week before birth. We are tired, swollen, heavy, and vulnerable to a roller coaster of emotions. For some unexplainable reason, women often have the misfortune of experiencing a major change at this inauspicious time: moving to a new house; wrecking the car; dealing with a family crisis; or suffering a natural disaster.

My unfortunate challenge during those last few weeks of pregnancy came in the form of a confused, rebellious stepson. This angry teenager had set fire to a house in the neighborhood, and apparently excelled at stealing from our neighbors. Our entire neighborhood felt stressed by his appearance, to say the least.

Meanwhile, my baby didn't want to come out. He enjoyed kicking my ribs and stretching my enormous belly, but he was clearly in no hurry to make an appearance. I waddled throughout the neighborhood, stopping for mild contractions. Nights I worked jigsaw puzzles and waited. My dear elderly friend, Garnet, came to stay and help out, sleeping on a mattress in my daughter's room. Our resident burglar recognized an easy victim.

"Has anyone seen my purse?" asked Garnet, wringing her hands with anxiety.

My heart sank, as I feared the worst. After taking her money to treat his friends to breakfast, our son hid the purse and its remaining contents in the woods. The purse contained Garnet's insurance cards, medical information, and driver's license. I felt so responsible for the loss.

I sat propped up with pillows and stared out the window. Anger, frustration, and feelings of helplessness added weight to my heaviness. The sky reflected my mood, black clouds threatening imminent rain. A car, pulling to a stop in front of our house, interrupted my glum depression. It was my friend, Clarissa, a nurse by vocation but an artist by avocation. I shuffled to the door to greet her.

"Ana, I thought you could use a little cheering up," she smiled warmly.

Little did she know! Divine intervention. An angel must have whispered in her ear to go minister to an overly pregnant woman with way too much on her mind.

Sensing my melancholy mood, she opened the grocery bag she had brought in with her. "Sometimes we all need a special treat."

She offered not one but two containers of gourmet ice cream, filled with macadamia nuts, ribbons of dark chocolate, and slivers of fruit. Never had ice cream tasted so good! Clarissa hugged me and went on her way, leaving me with a heavenly assurance that everything would be all right because I had chocolate in my belly and a friend who cared enough to bring it to me.

This is not about chocolate, really. Chocolate, for me, is a forgivable transgression, and we all must allow ourselves to be absolved from guilt for the parts of our lives that we need to hold on to for sanity, whatever they may be. Chocolate, or whatever brings us pleasure, can release us temporarily from our pain and despair. We must, sometimes, seek this pleasure in order to go on with our lives. Without guilt. This is also about the kindness of dear friends, who care enough about us in our darkest hour to reach out with that which brings us pleasure, easing our pain and enabling the euphoric glimmer of hope to come back into our lives.

No, I will not give up chocolate.

Dinner Questions

❑ How do you give yourself pleasure?
❑ What do you indulge in?

Alligators in My Closet:
Ghosts of Failed Romances

*The time you spend grieving over a
man should never exceed the amount of
time you actually spent with him.*

— RITA RUDNER, *NAKED BENEATH
MY CLOTHES*

What can be more wonderful than being in love? Romance brings
out the best in a person, doesn't it? Yet we often face our darkest selves
while involved in a relationship, looking into the reflection of our own
criticism, fearing rejection, feeling the bitterness of jealousy. For me,
the chasm of failure runs deep. Ghosts of old relationships haunt my
closets—intimate memories that instantly bring with them feelings of
inadequacy and shame. I remember the men who told me during an
embrace that I wasn't thin enough, or the one that used me to make a
girlfriend jealous. I recall the hurt I felt when men promised to call and
then didn't. One man wondered why I didn't eagerly respond to his
desire to tie me up with rope. Another ordered that I get on my knees
and beg forgiveness. Still another seemed shocked when I refused to live
as his mistress.

Why do we continue to do all the wrong things when it comes to
men? It takes us so long to learn about love and respect for ourselves.
We are so desperate to be loved and are so convinced that a woman
requires a man to be whole. We lower our standards, easily falling for a
man convinced of his own superiority. Attitudes have not changed as

much as we might think. I listen to my daughter's teenaged friends who verbalize the exact same relationship conflicts that we experienced when we were young and are still experiencing now that we are grown. We constantly try to please other people, avoid the disapproval of our family and friends, or maintain appearances of a relationship acceptable to society.

At first I blamed men. After all, they failed to rescue, protect, honor, and admire me. They tricked me, seduced me, rejected me, raped me, and used me. I began to hate them all, losing any shred of respect for these creatures who were only driven by their sexual needs. Where is my Prince Charming? What about my soul mate, the kind and generous partner who will love my mind and my inner being as well as make passionate love to my body? But the actual alligator I had to wrestle was not the men I knew but something that still lived inside of me—the alligator of inferiority. What if I was unlovable and unwanted for the rest of my life, an unsuitable partner for a man?

Driven by my fear of being inferior, I, in turn, tricked, seduced, rejected, and used men as well. Another alligator followed—the alligator of shame. I hid, pretending it didn't happen. I put on a costume with a mask, relegating another ghost to hang in my closet. They haunt my closets still, faint wisps of dead weight, invisible yet prickly to the touch. I wish I had realized in my earlier days how vulnerable intimacy is for women. These ghosts from past lives, skeletons from past eras, are secrets I still guard from my mother and my daughter.

Since I was no longer a princess or a Southern Belle, I protected my past. I was a woman of the world now, with all the baggage that came with that designation. I was scared and alone, divorced and vulnerable. I had developed an eating disorder—bulimia. I was still convinced that I had the wrong face, wrong hair, and wrong body. Although religions promise forgiveness, the healing love did not come until I learned to sit in the silence and experience God inside of me. The wonderful Divine Love engulfing me, bathing me with its light, loving all of me, precisely the way I was at that moment. With the silence, and the love, came a still, small voice inside of me, a voice of absolute Truth. The voice began as little whispers from my heart, a reassurance that somehow, someday, it would all work out.

As I stopped to listen to the little whispers, I grew stronger. My wrestling style began to change slowly, evolving through processes. First came forgiveness. I forgave men for being sexual creatures, for thinking they knew it all, and for being so greedy as well as needy. I forgave women for setting me up, for gossiping, for being critical. The most difficult one to forgive was myself. I forgave myself for being afraid, naïve, and vulnerable.

Next, came the process of acceptance. I accepted my mother's purity and her limited ability to understand me. I accepted the humanness of men, and I accepted the lost little child in each of us. Finally came the process of understanding that I had choice. I began to make lists of what I wanted in a relationship. I found pictures of how I wanted my life to look. I began to seek groups of people who supported those same values. To my surprise, I found my voice. A calm, steady voice. A voice that cared.

Though I often felt I had no choice in the direction my relationships would go, times have changed. Today women freely choose to live alone. Many women prefer single life, some even adopting children but opting to live husband-free. When I see a single woman enjoying the beauty of her home and the pleasure of her freedom, I celebrate her commitment to her choice and her strength to carry it out. I want my daughter to know that she has choices within the boundaries of her own humanity, and can experience a complete life regardless of her marital status. She does not have to impress anyone, cook for anyone, or beg from anyone. She will be able to support herself independently and enjoy her choices because she alone made them. My voice encourages her to find her own.

The following stories happened during the miserable time of my life when my relationships hurt. Disappointment from dates that never became relationships, self-destruction amidst promiscuity, and the deep hurt from disappointing others who had high expectations of my life wrote these chapters of my life. All of these stories spring from permanent scars on my heart.

The failures of my past relationships have led me to the joy of my present life. My marriage continues to grow, and I follow my own path, enjoying the beautiful love that engulfs me whenever I sit in the silence.

Sometimes, these haunting ghosts of the past offer connecting points with other women, women who have suffered the same aching fear, who have shared a deep connection in sisterhood because of this over-whelming angst, and who have developed an understanding as well as a support system that enables us to move on.

Dinner Questions

❑ What types of past experiences still haunt you?

❑ How do clean out your emotional closets (release old memories and self defeating judgments)?

Front Row Seats

*The good-looking boy may be
just good in the face.*

— APACHE PROVERB

Girlfriends tell me that love can be found anywhere, even in a grocery store. I was a believer, once. The handsome produce manager handled peaches with such strong yet gentle hands that conspicuously did not bear a wedding band. His eyes flirted with mine over the lettuce. When he smiled, I forgot my grocery list. Shy men attracted me for some reason and I knew if I didn't ask for a date, I might wait forever for him to make the first move. Until now I never had the nerve to initiate dates with men. Taking a deep breath, I blurted out the invitation.

"Hi. My name is Ana. We sort of know each other so I was wondering if you would like an edible adventure?"

An edible adventure. What man could say no to a date with food and a surprise? It was also the name of my business, a theatrical catering service that I invented to make the best use of my talents. Convinced I lacked the idyllic beauty desired by men, I depended on my creativity to provide allure and intrigue. I almost swallowed my tongue when this conservative fellow accepted.

Since I marketed my business on a shoestring, I resorted to cheap sensationalism for ongoing publicity. I wore costumes everywhere—bizarre hats, flashy rhinestone necklaces, fluorescent-colored dresses. It

151

worked. My reputation grew quickly. Word of mouth and monthly newspaper photos brought business from people looking for the unusual. However, for the quiet produce manager, spending time with a woman like me would be on his list of high-risk activities, next to public speaking at The Kennedy Center. He probably won't show up, I thought to myself as I left him standing in the produce department.

But he did, promptly at five-thirty that evening. I took it as a good sign. Maybe, just maybe, he appreciated unique and stimulating women. He showed no expression of approval or disapproval for my ensemble. I had selected for my date my favorite, red sarong. I had embellished the hibiscus print with garnet-colored jewels purchased from Billy Rogers, vendor of exotic costumes for circus people. After a brief exchange of polite conversation, I grabbed my heavy picnic basket. Our dinner, prepared with extra care, emanated a warm aroma of melted cheese and cooked shrimp—a seafood quiche. As we climbed into the cab of his blue truck, I wondered if my date had grown up on a farm, which would explain the truck and his career choice in produce.

I directed my handsome escort to drive toward the Florida causeway. We didn't talk much. A good thing since the electricity I felt between us would have made me stutter. At last we reached the long stretch of Florida beach where the highway connected Tampa and St. Petersburg. Only seagulls, pelicans, and an occasional fish jumping out of the sparkling water broke the solitude. We looked odd together, me in my sarong and he in a plaid shirt and jeans. In this setting for lovers, we seemed more like two mismatched socks trying on shoes.

We plodded across the sand to the lifeguard's wooden platform mounted seven feet high over the beach. I led the way, scrambling up the scaffolding to perch in the seat just wide enough for the picnic basket and the two of us. He still said nothing.

"Would you like dinner?" I asked.

"Sure," he responded politely.

I unwrapped the hot, savory quiche and poured wine into crystal stemware, grateful to have a task at hand. We dined in silence. Intelligent questions refused to come to mind. Should I ask for cooking suggestions regarding Brussels sprouts? Or whether all mushrooms are grown in manure? My mind futilely searched for conversation topics. He didn't seem to be searching at all.

The ocean took over, as if keeping its agreement with me to provide headliner entertainment for our front row seats. Endless waves like white ribbons joined together and disappeared into the sand—rolling hushes—frothy fingers massaging the shore and seducing us with its continuous rhythm. An occasional pelican hurried home in the salty sea breeze. Then nature's conductor answered my request with impeccable timing. With the slow intensity of an orchestra building to a climax, the sky filled with veils of magnificent fiery red-orange sunset, as if Tchaikovsky's "1812 Overture" had exploded into color. Cannons firing red balls reverberated in bright streaks of yellow, horns heralding vivid pinks, and woodwinds wafting soft violets. I sat captivated in my front row seat as the moment of insatiable beauty engulfed all our senses and left us mesmerized by the astounding finish. I knew that, as far as dates go, I had achieved near perfection

He drove me home, still silent. We said goodbye, and I never saw him again. He never called, or spoke to me in the grocery store—another disappointing date. I remember the hurt I felt from that experience as if it had happened only yesterday.

There were other times as well that I had my heart broken because I had high expectations of men, only to be disillusioned by the outcome. I had negotiated with a restaurant client who agreed to pay me part of a fee he owed me with a wonderful Christmas dinner. My date stood me up. I cooked Thanksgiving turkey for another man, and got stood up again. Naturally I blamed myself. I was at a place in my life that made it impossible to consider that it might have been the *men* I was dating, but, at the time, I was convinced that something was wrong with *me*. Maybe I just couldn't entice a man, any man, to be with me.

It never occurred to me until years later that my produce manager probably had his own hidden reasons for responding to me, reasons having nothing to do with what I did or said or was. He might have had another girlfriend, or even a fiancée. But at the time, I could only focus on what I didn't have to offer, what I didn't cook, or what I lacked to his liking. In fact, if he had any sexual expectations of me that night, I had left him dissatisfied in that department as well. I was, to myself at least, an all-around loser.

I never think those thoughts any more because I now know there is a divine order in life that is not influenced by what you wear, what you cook, or what you do or don't say. I learned, after many painful lessons, that sometimes relationships don't click or things don't work out for a reason beyond our comprehension. I never feel alone now, even in my solitude; I no longer look to people to complete me. Walks on the beach are my time with God. I find I enjoy gourmet dinners the most with female friends, not male dates.

I did experience another enthralling sunset performance some years later. This time, my partner and I knew we wanted to share a lifetime of sunsets. I still do.

Dinner Questions

❑ What old regrets can you laugh about now?

❑ What would your life be like if you had taken the plunge with a relationship mistake?

Hitting the Bottom

*Tears are a river that takes you somewhere....Tears
lift your boat off the rocks, off dry ground, carrying it
downriver to someplace new, someplace better.*

— CLARISSA PINKOLA ESTÉS, *WOMEN WHO
RUN WITH THE WOLVES*

Sometimes life hurts so much it threatens to get the best of us. Without foreseeable solutions, relief from despair, or humane support systems, fear becomes a vicious alligator that can effortlessly maul us to death. I have been there. I hit a bottom so low that my tears ran like an endless river that flowed for days on end. I cried on the phone, I cried to my mother, I cried myself to sleep at night. The alligator had taken a powerful hold of my body and spirit and had dragged me to the bottom of the river for a final death roll. I nearly drowned.

How could I become so lost and downtrodden after growing up in such a healthy, stable home? Yet, that lonely, destructive time led to the miraculous discovery of a reliable source of strength that was accessible at any time I needed it. It was also a time of finding myself, both the good and bad of me.

I stuck religiously to the rules as a "good girl" growing up, but when I didn't win the promised prize, the rules seemed meaningless. Throughout high school and college, I had saved my virginity for my future husband, as the good girl rules had stated. Although I dated very little, this goal was sabotaged by date rape. Still, I accepted my script, as dic-

155

tated by my mother, for a girl's success: attend the family college, meet a nice boy there, get married, and live happily every after. I set off for college, threw myself into organizing campus events, and never dated. Sometimes I forgot classes altogether, I was so busy with my new life. I remember panicking my freshman year when I woke up one day to realize that I would have to take a major chemistry test in one hour and I had no clue what the test would even cover. That moment still occurs in my dreams, waking me up in a sweat.

That same panic overwhelmed me my senior year when suddenly I realized that I would graduate in two months and had no idea of what would come next. I felt completely unprepared. My only career goals consisted of glamorous but hazy dreams of becoming a flight attendant or a portrait artist. My one boyfriend, also unprepared, convinced me that I could find a teaching job, though I had no teaching certificate. So we married, became teachers in a small country school, and shared a turbulent life together.

Divorce seemed inevitable, as this marriage did not fit any of my mental storybook pictures. I wanted out. Since we owned very little, divorce was easy, a quick meeting in a judge's office. Now what?

Unprepared to support myself, I opted for graduate school. My first act of self-reliance consisted of obtaining a school loan. "I'm on a roll," I thought to myself. After securing a job as a church secretary, I bought a book entitled *Typing Made Easy*. My employer, The First Presbyterian Church in Tallahassee, became my emotional anchor. I loved the church families, the bustling energy generated by the congregation, and even the dear cleaning lady who shared her wisdom with me as she dusted. I looked for ways to contribute to this wonderful community. I made banners to hang on the walls, and organized a social group for adults.

I performed for the church preschool. When it became evident that secretarial work was not my forte (in fact, I was terrible at it), the church actually created a position for my creative talents. Other church ladies obtained a scholarship for me. The cleaning lady took me to visit her African American Church and the preschool director's family adopted me as a relative. Why couldn't I recognize that the divine order in my life was already putting things in place for me? Good things would have happened to me then, if I had just had faith in the plan God had made for me. But at the time, I was clueless about my unique plan. In fact, I assumed that there was no plan at all for me, and that is why I felt, and acted upon, fear.

Suddenly, panic hit again. Graduation approached with the speed of a moving train threatening to crash into an abyss, which loomed large on the horizon, disguised as the rest of my life. Once more, I had failed to prepare for the next transition. What would I do and where would I go? Again, in desperation, I turned to a man for the answer. This hopeless rebound marriage lasted less than a year, for it was once again built on little more than distrust and fear.

The failures of two marriages brought a profound sense of shame into my life. I began to distance myself from church and from my parents. The loss of these two critical support structures had severe repercussions to my health and sanity. I particularly mourned that I had drifted from the community of the church. I could no longer face the church ladies in my hometown, or the people from the church that supported me in Tallahassee. It embarrassed me to visit the church where I attended with my second husband, and I had severed ties with friends from my first marriage. I felt everyone was labeling me as incompetent, unworthy, and unlovable.

I tried to get back into the saddle by starting new relationships. Dating among divorced singles automatically assumed sexual relationships and, with my limited sexual experience, I didn't know how to handle that either. My own sexuality terrified me, filling me with more shame. Handsome men pursued me with gifts and dinners in fancy restaurants. At the beginning of the relationship, I had no clue whether or not the men were even single. But then, after the second or third date, the hard luck stories of why they were dating me began to surface. They excused their infidelity because of a cold wife or her overwhelming commitment to the children. My shame deepened as I recognized myself as "the other woman," potentially breaking the heart of another hapless woman who waited at home.

The relationship arena was not the only troublesome area of my post-graduate life. I was still unclear as to exactly what I wanted to be when I grew up. With little more than intestinal fortitude and ideas, I decided to start a catering business. It never occurred to me at the time to learn about the nuts and bolts of running a business. Naively I forged ahead, distributing flyers proclaiming my services. Marketing came naturally but I couldn't balance a checkbook. I was so incompetent in that regard that I accidentally threw away a refund check for $200. Dealing with customers petrified me because I felt I couldn't trust anyone to actually pay me for my services.

The "personal growth" seminar frenzy of the seventies gave me another carrot to chase after. I hoped that by attending and following the suggestions espoused during these meetings I would be able to "fix" my defects. They all promised, "If you just take this seminar, you can have the life you want." I tried to be an ideal follower of the seminar gurus. I gave up personal possessions, and "trusted the universe." I lived from moment-to-moment, relying again on my instincts, my wits, and emergency checks from my parents. The "personal growth" seminars taught me unconditional acceptance but not prosperity.

Meanwhile, the success of my creative business resulted in fame, locally and nationally. People imitated me at parties, men called me from around the country, and the local artists and writers crowned me the queen of their ball. But, despite the notoriety, the phone call from a stalker caught me off guard.

"I followed you down Franklin Street yesterday," he began in an agitated voice, "I know where you live … and I want to fuck you."

My heart stopped. I took a deep breath, my hands shaking, and spoke slowly and calmly in a low voice.

"I would like to talk with you," I lied, "but you must respect my feelings first." I hung up and waited. I had no one to call for help. No friend to run to, and no one to comfort me. I busied myself with preparations for another performance.

The following night, the stalker called again, his voice distinctly different without the agitation. "I'm sorry I said those things last night," he apologized. "I'm going through a divorce, I was on drugs, and I'm in a lot of pain."

I felt sincere compassion. " I'm sorry. Do you have children?"

"Yes," he continued, "a five year old son. I miss him so much." He wept openly on the phone.

Empathizing with his pain, I began to ask gentle questions, listening to his heartbreak. His name was Bob. Struggling through a new divorce, he found his anguish unbearable. Two days later, I received a small envelope in the mail. It was a thank-you note from Bob, with a crisp one hundred dollar bill, just for listening.

Although my encounter with Bob turned out to be innocuous, it brought an indisputable fact to my attention. Because of the flamboyant way I dressed and the extravagant way I acted in public, I began to be afraid that people would start taking me wrong and perhaps expect certain things from me that I was not willing to offer. I decided to run from my outrageous reputation in Tampa to Orlando, thinking that a move to a bigger city and getting a real job would improve my life immensely.

Fear motivated me to leave, but I did not leave fear behind. It accompanied me to the big city and inside a Fortune 500 company. I discovered that the corporate world operated on a different set of rules, with hidden agendas, blatant double standards, and an invisible hierarchy. I had absolutely no clue as to how to navigate this new unfamiliar territory to find support, learn the ropes, and make a career path. Unclear about my job, untrained to function in the corporate culture, I left the company, disillusioned, to flounder in a strange city where I had no job, no friends, and no plan. I felt set adrift in a foreign land with no anchor.

My loneliness grew intensely. The big empty house I rented quickly depleted my savings. "Plenty of space to rehearse," I had told myself when I rented it. Ideas for a convention entertainment business had floated optimistically around in my head, but they remained only that— ideas. I lacked business savvy and money. In Florida, when a person has no money, that means one can't afford pest control. Without pest control, the palmetto bugs move in and reproduce at an amazing rate of speed. For those of you who are not familiar with these creatures, palmetto bugs are giant roach-like creatures that make loud, annoying clicking noises as they walk across the floor, up the wall, or on the ceiling. Lying in bed listening to their footsteps and hoping they wouldn't drop on me resulted in many nights without sleep.

I was finally forced by my poverty to advertise for a roommate. A young woman, employed by the same company I had left, agreed to split expenses and moved in. It never occurred to me to interview her for suitability or check her out in any way. Since we never saw each other, friendship was out of the question. After all, we both occupied our time with boyfriends. She went her way and I went mine. It still came as a shock when I found her note:

"Moving out. Sorry."

She left without paying her half of the rent, and would never be able to help me pay for the house again. I walked into her bedroom, stunned by its emptiness, then walked into her bathroom. The entire bathroom wall had been crushed and knocked in from a forceful blow. My roommate and her boyfriend, both secret drug users, left me with the aftermath of an incredibly violent fight.

About this time, I began going to a downtown church. It had been years since I last attended a church. Here, in a new town, no one knew about my failures in marriage. At first, I considered churches as fertile ground for dating opportunities for single, divorced people.

This church offered new territory for me, but the men seemed no different than anywhere else—confused, lonely, with sexual relationships as their priority. I started dating a man thirty years my senior, but soon grew tired of his jealousy. I considered possibilities outside the church. Acquaintances from my old job set me up with weird blind dates. The roller coaster ride of the singles scene continued to drain me emotionally, and, outside of church, married men continued to pursue me.

My relationship with my body fared no better. Eating disorders had haunted me since college. Ten years of battling my secret nemesis, bulimia, had now escalated to an all-consuming obsession.

I blamed my weight for all my failures. "If I were just thin enough," I told myself, "everything would be all right."

Frantic with fear and starving from emptiness, I ate away the lonely hours. During the daytime, I worked with an incessant drive. At night, I ate to assure myself of survival, I ate to comfort myself, and I ate to deaden my feelings. For me, binge eating felt like I was entering a trance, and it was becoming an addiction that helped me avoid the pain of my shame, my fear, and my feelings of failure as a person.

Every morning I woke up with feelings of self-loathing and guilt. I swore that today would be different. I would put on my running shoes and shorts and then hit the pavement, running for miles, trying to undo the damage I had done the night before. One eating binge led to another, and another, numbing my feelings, helping me pass the time in a mental stupor, a lot like an alcoholic. I accepted strenuous exercise and harmful purging as necessary retribution for being a failure. I required gum surgery, which was another fitting punishment for my lifestyle. Bulimics frequently require surgery to repair the serious physical damage inflicted on their teeth and gums each time they throw up.

I knew I had hit bottom. I lived in such isolated loneliness that it seemed as if my cries for help echoed from a vast canyon. I felt that no one for miles around could help me in my desolation. My rented house, lacking furniture other than a desk, a bed, and a borrowed sofa, even seemed like an empty cavern to me. My savings had dwindled to almost nothing, with barely enough to buy a pair of stockings for a job interview. Depleted of self-respect, self-control, and money, I called home and cried, pathetically lost, hopelessly helpless.

"Mother, I don't know what I'm going to do. I can't make it." I wailed.

I waited for the expected response: the comforting reassurance, the spirit-building pep talk, the morality-boosting lecture. This time, it never came. Instead of sympathetically asking how much money I needed, she merely said, "Honey, I know you can work things out."

The door I had always counted on shut in my face. Instead of warmth, I got ice. I hung up the phone and sat down hard, paralyzed with the fear of being utterly alone in the world, without a soul, not even my mother, who cared for me. But that thought quickly fleeted through my mind, and another, much stronger thought took hold.

The impact of her refusal to help incongruously made me feel better. Her words had stunned me but they hadn't hurt. With her refusal to help, Mother had empowered me. She let me know, in no uncertain terms, that she still had faith in me to succeed with my life. She still believed in my ability to solve problems in spite of all my failures, real and imagined. Her faith in me, not her money, fueled my confidence. I'm sure she prayed for me a lot during those bleak times, and maybe it was her small, quiet inner voice that told her to refuse to help.

Fortunately, the church I attended offered me something besides dates. Different from the traditional church I grew up in, this church offered the message I hungered for: I was God's Child, loved, cared for, and cherished. God had given me the ability to create what I wanted in my life. Just as I often created relationships that didn't work, I could also create relationships that did. Instead of listening to my blaring thoughts of fear and failure, I could choose to sit in quiet stillness and listen to God's wisdom.

At last I found another way to fill my loneliness. I began to make friends with other women, with couples, and with families. At this church, people supported each other, hugged each other, and attended workshops on positive thinking. I learned to meditate. Playing a tape of Pachelbel's "Canon in D Minor", I sat on the floor visualizing God's arms rocking me like a baby. I learned to write affirmations.

"I am a child of God. I deserve to be loved. I am loveable, and capable. Life is good to me."

Pasting the affirmations on my cabinets, in my bathroom, and on the refrigerator, I yearned for the good results they would bring me. I practiced them daily, believing fiercely in each one.

Fear did not disappear instantly. Eating binges still controlled my life, leaving me to wake up each morning with the familiar dread and self-loathing. Downing a low-calorie liquid diet drink only made it worse. I had to take a serious step to regain control of my illness. I was beginning to feel more confident in my ability to change. I bought a notebook to keep a journal. Remaining very conscious while I ate, I documented every painful feeling of anger, hatred, and fear. I wrote with emotional fury in red, scrawling all over the lines in big, erratic scribbles.

The journal was a startling glimpse at my raging misery, so much misery that I couldn't get it all out by merely writing words. I looked for ways to express my depression through a stronger medium. My words lacked the color and intensity of my soul. I needed pictures. Scanning the pages of a discarded magazine, I searched for visuals to supplement my words. The picture literally jumped out at me, a photograph of a despondent woman, lying motionless in an empty room, distorted by an eerie blue light, her face without expression. She had covered her nude body with a sheet and had wrapped her hair in a white towel. An unnatural light bathed the room. It was a sad and lonely light. Gluing the picture in my journal, I scribbled over it, reiterating the dark torment that I felt.

Taking a sales job, I moved into a smaller apartment and threw myself into a new challenge. My problems continued, however, following me around like an iron ball chained to my leg. I felt driven to chase success, working harder, to reach for higher goals each day. I ate and exercised fanatically, and clung, out of habit, to a dead-end relationship. My financial problems hung over my head like a cloud, and my new bosses applied more pressure for me to produce sales.

Suddenly my world, as bad as it was, got worse. Doctors diagnosed a tumor in my abdomen. I would need immediate surgery.

When life seems to be falling apart, it is really clearing away the old to make way for the new. Maybe the tumor was God's way of hitting me on the head with a two-by-four in order to get me to turn my life around before it was too late. This time, with the seriousness of the situation in my mind, I stopped and listened, not to the fear, but to the still quiet voice inside. Instead of frantically jumping into surgery with my impatience to "get on with it," I cancelled the procedure. I called a woman I had heard speak on fruit and vegetable fasting as a cure for various diseases and asked her to send me her plan. I then phoned my minister.

"Bill," I began. "This is Ana. I'm going on a healing fast to heal my tumor and I need your help."

Bill paused. "I'll support you if you make this a spiritual fast first and a food fast second," he negotiated.

Without hesitation, I agreed. A journey I would never regret began that very moment.

I learned to sit in silence.

How could such a simple task require so much discipline? I learned to be still, to focus on my breath, to listen to my heart. For the first time in my life, I felt calm, at peace. I treasured my meditation time, making it the primary function of my morning, afternoon, and evening. I quit my job, feeling immediate relief from the pressure and anxiety. I ate one kind of fruit each week, as much as I wanted. I lost weight, reaching my ideal weight within a short period of time, and maintained that weight. More importantly, I began to experience miracles.

Whenever I felt fear, I stopped whatever I was doing. I sat in the silence, surrendering my fear, my ego, my anxiety to the silence. I listened. During one of these struggles to surrender, the phone broke the silence.

"I heard about your healing challenge," a friend said over the receiver. "I want to support you by loaning you the money to pay for your rent this month." I was astounded.

Wonderful people meditated with me. Sometimes we played music, sometimes we prayed, and sometimes we just sat in the silence, feeling God's presence together. The minister made a tape for me to listen to, and lent me books on meditation, which I read voraciously. One day, while sitting in my peacefulness, I noticed a strange sensation in my mouth. A sweet taste, like honey, flooded my taste buds, although I had eaten nothing. Serious meditators often have this experience.

Other miracles happened. I had become a distributor for a natural vitamin company, and, without making any sales calls, I generated a sales volume of $4,000 that month. Not bad for sitting in silence! I also received a call from a small town in south Florida who was seeking my services as an entertainer. This job led to the meeting of my future husband, a relationship totally unlike my past dating disasters. I reconnected with my parents, and began selecting values, many of them the values they had taught me. I had struggles ahead, but a clear direction began to take shape.

Finally, my bulimia disappeared, never to bother me again. The affirmations became my way of thinking, and meditation a constant comfort. With my refreshed, optimistic outlook on life, I enjoyed a flow of ideas, reassurance, and insight. The tumor? I resorted to surgery, knowing that the real healing I sought had already taken place. Since I had quit my stressful job, I no longer had health insurance. I paid many years for my lifesaving surgery, but with gratitude and no regrets.

A spiritual journey changes lives. I'm no longer afraid to confront a crisis time. I've even accompanied a dear friend on her journey as she faced a health challenge far more daunting than mine. Again, it brought love, peace, and fulfillment to my life, as well as hers.

As I look back on life, the painful times are not for naught. The mistakes of my college years and first marriages provide the guiding light for me as a parent, determined to prepare my children with clear career goals and tools for meaningful relationships. God's Divine Order runs through life like a ribbon; it always has, even when I couldn't see it for my fear. In spite of growing up in the church, experiencing real faith required desperation, demanding that I seek a source far greater than myself. A man was not the answer, nor was money or a slim body. Only God's love can provide real security that never runs out.

Stepping from fear to silence, I listened as a voice of love spoke with wisdom and assurance. Peace came, not alligators.

Remember the stalker? Seventeen years later, he located me on the Internet and called again.

"Ana," he exclaimed, "I wanted you to know that I'm happily married with two beautiful children. I've found the Lord!"

Life has its pain but it is often from that pain we find our greatest gifts and His supreme wisdom.

Dinner Questions

❏ When have you felt destitute?
❏ How did a bad situation lead you to a good one?

Disappointing the Fairy Godmother

Remorse is the poison of life.

— CHARLOTTE BRONTË, *JANE EYRE*

The story of Cinderella left out some important details. Do poor housemaids such as Cinderella know how to act at a royal ball? Surely she felt scared to death of protocol, manners, and royal speech, a culture foreign to her simple life. In reality, she probably bumbled through the night, a total embarrassment if it weren't for her beauty (beautiful women can get away with anything, right?). And what about Cinderella's character flaws? There's never any mention of those. She disobeyed her stepmother, as well as the Fairy Godmother (she stayed out too late, remember?). One would deduct that she would disobey her husband as well. We could label her a "Royal Disappointment."

What about disillusioned Fairy Godmothers? Do they get angry? Do they punish a wayward maiden or reject her with icy reproach? Are they forgiving? Do they look for another Cinderella to promote?

Fairy Godmothers are real—women with big hearts, magic wands, and a desire to make a difference in a young girl's life. The godchild of a fairy godmother knows what the requirements are: she must work hard, express gratitude, demonstrate obedience, and be home by midnight. Speaking from experience, I have broken a few pumpkins along the road to finding my Prince Charming.

The Junior Year Abroad study program realized a dream come true for me. I thirsted for the adventure of exploring a new culture, acquiring a second language, and seeing the world. Energy, curiosity, and ambition motivated me to select a church-related program that provided logistical support for a year of study in Belgium. My parents supported my dreams, determined to squeeze turnips if necessary to provide a once-in-a-lifetime opportunity for their daughter. I tackled the required reading, packed my bags, and flew to New York.

Bound for Europe, I sailed aboard a charter ocean liner designated for students only. Feelings of intimidation overwhelmed me as I observed the decadent behavior of the American youth traveling on the ship with me. Foreign to my own experience, these students flagrantly used drugs, flaunted nudity, and engaged in sexual displays of affection, reflecting the defiant attitude already prevalent on larger campuses. My small-town Arkansas childhood and conservative Presbyterian campus life neglected to prepare me for that aspect of world discovery. I retreated to the safety and familiarity of my sketchpad, and spent the cruise time drawing portraits of the Italian crew, who eagerly posed for free souvenirs to take home.

On my twentieth birthday, homesickness and apprehension gripped me as I stepped off the train in Belgium. Clutching the address of my American advisor, I negotiated with a taxi driver who deposited me at a busy intersection on the bustling boulevard that encircled downtown Brussels. Sophisticated shoppers strolled arm-in-arm while Belgian children chattered in rapid syllables, reminding me of my inability to speak or comprehend fluent French. I quickly found the right building and took the elevator to the American office, anticipating warm hospitality. The Belgian secretary smiled courteously, gestured to a sofa, and then left me alone in the reception room. I sat down with my suitcases at my feet and waited. My growing anxiety competed with growls from my hungry stomach, worrying that I had been forgotten.

Sudden sounds from a back office grabbed my attention. The Happy Birthday Song in English! Tears welled up in my eyes as I sat alone in the reception room. After twenty minutes, a man in a brown suit emerged from the back office.

"You must be our new American student!" he greeted me. "Sorry I'm late, our secretary is celebrating her birthday today!"

"Me, too!" I lit up. Maybe they would offer me a piece of cake and let me share in the birthday revelry.

The American ignored my hint and continued.

"Glad you made it. Unfortunately, I'm leaving with my family on sabbatical, so you're on your own. You can rent a little room on the top floor until you get your feet on the ground."

Panic gripped my heart. My advisor? Leaving?

Since the little room on the top floor offered an immediate bed to cry on, I accepted it. A dark cage of an elevator creaked up to the top floor opening onto a hall with my room located at the end. Unlocking the door, I walked into a minuscule cell with a sink and a bed under the window overlooking the noisy street corner. A communal bathroom down the hall contained a WC (water closet) or toilet, which flushed by pulling a handle on a long chain suspended from the water tank mounted high on the wall. The hall light worked on a timer, compelling me to scurry in the dark from the bathroom to my little bedroom at night. Living out of my suitcase, I began the task of learning French, studying street maps, and getting my bearings around the ancient European city. I never saw my hosting sponsor again.

Fortunately, my cautious father back in America had anticipated potential problems. He quietly concocted a Plan B backup system, just in case. How one's gratitude for parents grows with age! It must have been a courageous sacrifice not only to scrape together money for such an adventure on a tight family budget, but also to encourage a teenage daughter to sail away, unchaperoned, to another continent. Since Daddy belonged to Rotary International, he had alerted the Belgian Rotary Club of his concerns. My first letter from home included the phone number of a Monsieur Albert Willenz who graciously invited me to his home to dinner.

Monsieur Willenz spoke perfect English and managed a successful business in international financing. He and his wife, Yvette, lived with their two grown children in an apartment filled with antiques, Oriental carpets, and art. He had invited two Belgian Rotarians and their wives, as well as the official Rotary Scholarship student to dinner. Sensitive to the upper class etiquette of the evening, I spoke slow, careful French and studied the manners of the Belgian guests.

Little did I know that the dinner party served as an informal interview for adoption! Monsieur Willenz had schemed on my father's behalf to locate a couple that could provide supportive contacts for me. Monsieur and Madame Opsomer, in their sixties, had reluctantly accepted Monsieur Willenz's invitation, their calendar already filled with cultural and social obligations. Madame Opsomer organized fundraisers and charity projects for Her Majesty the Queen. She had no need for another charity. Fortunately for me, however, Madame Opsomer loved to give advice.

"Madame," I ventured in my painstaking French, " where might I find a store with art supplies?"

Madame responded enthusiastically. "Ma Cherie! I know just the place to find the best price!"

I continued with my next question, "Madame, could you tell me what to do when offered an aperitif? I am not used to drinking."

Madame Opsomer insisted on sitting next to me throughout the evening, answering my questions, correcting my French, and pointing out small details of etiquette from how to eat snails to how to slice cheese.

Two days later, I received an invitation to lunch with Madame Opsomer in her spacious, continental home. Taking me under her wing, she supervised my living arrangements, studies, and cultural opportunities. She regarded me as her American Eliza Doolittle. I thrived in her praise and advice, and she relished the stories of my Belgian adventures over our Tuesday lunches.

Tuesdays became a regular highlight of my week. Madame greeted me with the three traditional Belgian kisses on the cheek and expressed her pleasure whenever I presented her with a humble box of her favorite chocolates. She planned the lunch menus to expand my knowledge of French cuisine and took me for walks in the nearby park, correcting my French with great care. Monsieur Opsomer would join us for lunch, entertaining me in his impeccable English with witty little jokes. My love for the Opsomers grew as they opened their home and their hearts to me.

One day, in a spontaneous moment of affection for this gracious lady, I timidly requested permission to call her Aunt Simone. Holding my breath, I studied her face as she pondered my request. Had I overstepped boundaries in this society of proper manners?

"Ma Cherie," exploded Madame, "Absolutement! That would be wonderful!"

Adopted relatives! Madame and Monsieur became Tante Simone and Uncle Henri from then on, and our relationship deepened.

The Opsomers invited me to dinner parties and occasional soirées in elegant restaurants. Monsieur Opsomer, retired from the linen industry, served in a position similar to that of our Supreme Court judge. He continually spoke to me in English in spite of his wife's insistence that he contribute to my increasing competency in French. A balding man with a cheerful, ruddy face, Monsieur Opsomer adored his large-boned, tall wife and referred to her as "Ma Petite Chou," or his Little Sprout.

Madame Opsomer wore thick glasses that magnified her soft, generous eyes. Her gray hair, coifed in waves, found frequent refuge under a small, cloche hat that matched her Parisian-style coat. She followed modern conservative fashion closely, and maintained a supply of fine fabrics for her dressmaker to adapt to Paris styles. She busied herself with her projects and the maintenance of her household, which consisted of an Italian servant, Guisseppe, his wife Conchita, and their ten-year-old daughter. Guisseppe cleaned the house, gardened, and served the meals. His wife, Conchita cooked. Every lunch began with a thick soup of oxtail, endive, or mushroom. Sometimes Conchita served pasta she had made by hand, cranking long strips of dough into a machine that turned out spaghetti.

The Opsomer household also included Quitto, a silver-haired Belgian sheepdog that behaved in chic French restaurants and understood French, Flemish, and Italian commands. Quitto enjoyed chunks of steak slipped without discretion from the dinner table and a daily chocolate bonbon given with affection by Madame Opsomer after lunch. He relished the life of a pampered blueblood, transgressing only when guests arrived. Quitto could not resist sniffing the crotch of a well-dressed lady. Usually kept downstairs when the Opsomers entertained, he frequently managed to escape to the living room and embarrassed many dignified matrons.

Tante Simone located a pleasant room for me in the apartment of a widow not far from the university. She arranged for art lessons at the Royal School of the Arts, and insisted that I study with her own painting teacher, an award-winning impressionist named Madam Barbé. Their invitations seemed endless. With the Opsomers as my hosts, I enjoyed being the guest of honor at a Russian banquet and attending a formal soirée at an international floral festival in Ostende.

Tante Simone recounted stories of her youth, and her French upbringing. We discussed the "royals," the European nobility. When I inquired about the Belgian queen's ties to the Italian mafia, she reproached me quickly.

"Out of respect for the Queen, we do not discuss her brother," she whispered. End of subject.

When spring came, Tante Simone whisked me away to enjoy a week at her mountain retreat with Uncle Henri and Quitto. There, the Opsomers enjoyed a simpler country life, where Quitto could splash in mud puddles while his masters sipped café au lait from bowls like the country folk. As we strolled through the lush forests of the Ardennes Mountains, the Opsomers pointed out old war trenches from World War II, monuments on their property to the Nazi terror that had gripped their lives. They drove me to nearby Luxembourg, and walked with me through a sea of white crosses. Graves of American soldiers, their American names ringing with familiarity miles away from their hometowns and mine. For the first time, I felt the abysmal consequences of a world war touch my heart in a personal way.

As my return to America drew near, Tante Simone supervised my final wardrobe purchases while the heaviness in my heart became unbearable. Henri selected a prize bottle of wine from his wine cellar for my father, though I knew my non-drinking father would not fully appreciate it. I presented Tante Simone a new tape recorder, thrilling her with the prospect of helping me to maintain my French after I left Belgium. The Opsomers drove me to the airport, and as my plane took off, Simone dabbed at her eyes with Henri's handkerchief while I cried inconsolably.

At first we fervently stayed in touch. Madame Opsomer wrote faithfully and made tapes on the tape recorder. She and Henri flew to America for my wedding after graduation, and presented me with a beautiful gold necklace bearing a twenty dollar gold piece, American money from the nineteenth century. Their generous gift touched me deeply. Within a few months, my new husband insisted that we hitchhike through Europe, using his dad's Air Force connection to get us there. My husband's eagerness to be their guest and take advantage of their hospitality embarrassed me. Our differences in values had already begun to strain our marriage.

Feelings of loneliness threatened to engulf me in my new marriage. My husband worked nights in the summer, leaving his young bride alone for long hours. Our communication skills were lacking. The happily-ever-after part of life I had longed for since childhood had ended as the marriage crumbled.

My friends, all a part of the early women's movement, offered enticing options in the name of women's rights and liberal behavior.

"You deserve better!"

"Take care of your needs if he won't."

"Have an affair!"

Acquiescing to this last suggestion is not something I'm proud of, even now. My husband could never forgive me. We sought therapy, but that didn't promise immediate change. Negative feelings festered.

I could not discuss my failed marriage with Tante Simone. I harbored my dark secret and my shame within myself. Devoted and faithful to her husband, she would never understand. I even felt unworthy to wear the beautiful necklace that she had given me, a precious gift for a marriage that didn't last. Tante Simone knew me in my innocence and now that innocence was gone.

With so much to hide, my letters grew further apart, then ceased completely. I'm sure my lack of correspondence hurt Tante Simone, but I couldn't bear the thought of disappointing her with the miserable details of my life.

"She wouldn't love me anymore," I convinced myself. "She would find me despicable."

Maybe she would think that I was just a lousy letter writer. My cowardice filled me with more shame. My fluent French became less fluent. The tapes sat, unopened, never listened to. Still I couldn't forget the loving woman whose approval I valued so highly.

Time passed. I entered graduate school, attempted a second marriage, which failed again. For seven painful years, I floundered, confused and lonely. For seven years, I searched for love and strength. Life became a journey with no map to follow, no clear destination, and no traveling companion. I wandered, burdened by extra baggage, with no money, no advisor, and no support system. This personal sojourn required more courage than traveling through any foreign country.

When I found my faith, and met Robert, my life finally stabilized. With new spiritual strength, I needed to heal the broken relationships in my life. I assessed the damage I had inflicted on others as one surveys a landscape after a war. Bridges to build and fences to mend. With the help of a French woman who attended our church, I wrote an honest letter to Tante Simone. I confessed my continuing love for her, and asked for her forgiveness. I expressed my deep sadness and regret at my long silence. I mailed the letter with a prayer.

Would my letter speak to her heart, permitting her to let me back in? Had she already dismissed me from her thoughts? I waited for weeks, praying for her acceptance of my apology and forgiveness. At last, a letter arrived. Trembling, I read Uncle Henri's careful printing in English:

"Simone died last year . . . "

Stunned, my guilt overwhelmed any expression of grief.

How many times in life do we put off our amends? We procrastinate from fear of disappointing our loved ones. We are apprehensive of our failure to meet their expectations. We dread their disapproval. Instead of taking the risk for understanding and forgiveness, we choose, instead, to drag our suitcases around, heavy with unresolved relationships. Without the courage of the Prodigal Son, we miss the opportunity to say "goodbye," "thank you," "I love you," "forgive me..." With those important words spoken, peace can descend on the relationship. Without them, there is little chance for healing except by time. I missed my chance with Tante Simone. The massive burden in my heart felt like a mountain as I tried to dismiss her death as a closed chapter in my life, another failure to add to the pile mounting in my mental closet.

But Tante Simone could not be easily dismissed. A strong woman with a determined will, she had firmly implanted her influence in my life, leaving an imprint on my heart that could not be erased. During a special meditative experience, I strongly sensed her presence. A process of holotropic, or circular breathing, sometimes referred to as rebirthing, resulted in a healing release. As I lay relaxed in the energizing yet calm peace of this process, I felt Tante Simone near me. Suddenly, deep sobs of remorse and loss gushed from my heart and choked in my throat.

Concentrating on my breath, I experienced a cathartic release. What happened next can only be explained as a spiritual phenomenon. A bright flash of light and wisdom filled my body. A profound insight entered my mind, and with it a message of Truth. Tante Simone embodied pure love when she died. Any disappointments she harbored melted away, leaving her with understanding. In her death, she had loved me and had forgiven me. I know that now beyond a shadow of doubt.

Sometimes I regress. I still hurt inside when I feel that I have disappointed someone. Asking for forgiveness and forgiving myself remains a challenge. I am envious of people who shrug off the day knowing they did the best they could. With affirmations, I work toward that ideal of achieving peace in myself.

Tante Simone left a legacy for me. She has guided me to nurture other young women. She opened her doors to me, lavished gifts upon me, and bestowed advice; she was my fairy godmother. Simone Opsomer lives in my memory as a real woman filled with a loving Spirit, blessing my life with her presence. I remember her generosity daily, for I have named my daughter Simone.

Dinner Questions

❑ Have you made amends with your past?

❑ When have you handled loose ends that dangle, draining your emotional energy?

Nurturing the Women Who Wrestle with Alligators:
Stories of Sisterhood

*Female friendships that work
are relationships in which women help
each other belong to themselves.*

— LOUISE BERNIKOW, *AMONG WOMEN*

A woman must have courage to become a mother, whether by natural means or through adoption. A woman who gives birth requires a copious amount of courage in order to get that big creature out of a womb through such a tiny tunnel and into the world. It seems strange that we give medals for the courage to kill but not for the courage to give life. In addition to not being able to give birth, a man cannot nurse a child. Nor can he tell a woman's story.

Women's storytelling intrigues me the most when women share the humor of their mistakes, the witty resolution of their conflicts, the harrowing tales of their crises. An evening in the company of life-loving women equips me with surplus energy while renewing my own outlook on life.

Write down your stories. Keep a diary or a journal. Jot down events of your day, feelings aroused by life's surprises, and lessons learned from encounters with fellow travelers. List the unforgettable moments in your past when you made key decisions about life or when you discovered your future survival tools. Save the humorous gifts that flavor your days.

175

Record it all, the good and the bad, the happy and the sad—all have value. Your past pain might provide comfort for others, encouragement to continue. Your insights bloom into a legacy to pass on to daughters, sisters, and mothers who follow. You can leave your legacy of humor and survival even to the fathers, husbands, sons, and brothers who have been touched by your own special music.

This next section presents for you five stories from very innovative, strong women who have survived and learned from their own personal turning points. Within each of you are similar stories of love and loss, waiting to be shared with a friend, a mother, a sister, a daughter, or your future self through your journal.

Dinner Questions

❑ How do you create regular time to rejuvenate yourself with energy from positive women?

❑ What women would you like to validate?

The Coalminer's Sweetheart

Stories are medicine

— CLARISSA PINKOLA ESTÉS, *WOMEN WHO RUN WITH THE WOLVES*

I never met a woman who didn't possess her own collection of stories about her childhood, her lovers, her husbands, her babies, and her aspirations. Usually one good story leads to another, leading her listeners down a path of unbelievable tales of courage, fate, and suspense; of rescue, romance, and revolution; of heroes, healers, and hypocrites. Stories told from one generation to another pass on sage advice concerning human relationships in all its forms. Even the oft-times volatile ones with the opposite sex were not off limits, confirming our eternal drive to love and to be loved that has stimulated flirtation and seduction from the dark ages.

A gift of such intergenerational advice became mine at the age of twenty-four when I was a patient in a strange hospital. I was petrified and totally unprepared for the painful recovery that followed my surgery. My abdomen was swollen with an enormous dressing and every movement caused excruciating pain. A middle-aged patient from down the hall obviously needed someone to talk to, so she appeared at my doorway one day.

"Hi, my name's Mable," she introduced herself in her homey West Virginia accent. "Why don't you come down to my room? I've got some real tasty pecans. Do you like pecans? They've got chocolate on them."

She linked her arm in mine and together we shuffled down the hall to her room.

A kindly widow with short, wavy hair, she brought out a hidden stash of edible goodies not found on any hospital tray. As I encased myself in a knitted afghan and munched on chocolate pecans, we began to swap stories. Mable fixed hair in Beckley, West Virginia. Her profession enabled her to hear the community's juiciest gossip and the mini-dramas of the people who lived there. I listened intently as she described dramatic kidnappings, tragic fires, and wayward lovers. She told of a billboard that advertised six brothers and sisters, missing for several decades. Then, Mable took her turn listening as I recounted my adventures while a student in Europe. Every day we continued our story sessions, stopping only for a nurse's request to chart vital signs.

Mabel's romantic antics with her late husband entertained me the most. A West Virginia coalminer, he adored his young wife, loving her faithfully until he died of black lung disease.

"He was a lot older than me," reminisced Mable, "and, honey, he spoiled me something awful. Why, I was all the time gettin' presents."

"He bought me ruffled nightgowns that looked like can-can dresses! And the fanciest lace negligee from Paris. He bought me all kinds of jewelry, the kind made for movie stars."

"What for?" I pried.

"For no reason!" Mabel sat back and looked at me. "He just loved me like a crazy fool."

"So, what did you do?" I wanted more.

"Oh my," Mable chuckled. "Why I dreamed up surprises. I would dye my hair and pretend like I was another woman! Then I would flirt like mad."

"One time, I left little love notes, hidden all over town. Each one had a clue where to find the next one. Of course, the last one told him where I was.

"Yessir. He loved the treasure hunts when I was the treasure. One time I wrapped myself up in saran wrap and waited until he found me. I liked to sweated to death!"

Laughing with tears running down my face, I had to wrap my arms around the enormous dressing covering my abdomen, holding the stitches in place lest I pop them apart.

Mabel found in me a willing protégée for her worldly advice and lovelorn secrets. I suppose we were an unlikely pair of friends, she being a fifty-something widow and me a naïve, young schoolteacher struggling in a first marriage. But, like two butterflies who had the misfortune to be caught in a jar, we enjoyed each other's free spirit. After our hospital sojourn, we stayed in touch. She returned to West Virginia and I resumed my life as a schoolteacher. Mabel sent me pictures of her daughter, a teenager with Down's syndrome. I poured my heart out in letters contemplating divorce from my first husband.

Mable became my confidante. A willing listener, she comforted my troubled heart and encouraged me to think more clearly. She understood and empathized about the painful issues I couldn't discuss with my mother. We called each other and exchanged photos, sharing our worlds miles apart in cultures and distance. I wrote letters about graduate school and my newfound freedom. Mable kept me updated on her brain tumor, and the antics of her daughter. She sensed that her life might not last much longer.

A year later, an enormous package arrived at the little house I rented while attending graduate school. Eagerly, I read the return address, recognizing Mabel's big scrawling handwriting and the familiar address from Beckley, West Virginia. My curiosity mounting, I tore off the brown paper and cut through the thick layers of tape. The contents of the box had been carefully wrapped in tissue paper. I gasped as I explored the treasures.

Ruffled nightgowns that looked like can-can dresses, a fancy negligee made in Paris, and jewelry made for Hollywood stars. A legacy for new love.

Dinner Questions

❑ When have you found a most unusual person with whom you connected immediately from your heart?

❑ How did this new friend meet a special need for you?

full Circle

*Spiritual love is a position of standing with
one hand extended into the universe and one hand
extended into the world, letting ourselves
be a conduit for passing energy.*

— CHRISTINA BALDWIN, *LIFE'S COMPANION*

Jana pinched herself. It's working out, she thought to herself. At twenty-one I'm living the life of my dreams. Jana didn't mind the tiny, bare apartment or working long hours. You just have to do what you have to do, she told herself. She smiled. Her life, along with her husband's, was serving a much bigger purpose, just as she had always hoped for when she was growing up. Everything had gone right for her, especially finding her husband.

Jana and Gary knew without a doubt that they were meant to be soul mates. It had nothing to do with outward appearance, although everyone said they made the perfect couple. It was true that Jana had been a pretty, perky cheerleader and class officer in a big, Orlando high school. And girls swooned over Gary, the handsome blond quarterback, who starred in every high school football game in Pulatka County, Florida. But this was not what mattered to either of them when they first met. It was a sense of mission that magnetically attracted the two teenagers to each other, and a shared vision that was more mature than their years.

"Jana, I need help with the bus ministry. Do you think you could meet me on your lunch break and explore some ideas?" Gary's blue eyes had gazed steadily into Jana's green ones.

Home for the summer from his freshman year at college, Gary lost no time in tackling the top two priorities on his list. He activated a ministry for the poor rundown community in Orlando's industrial area and contacted Jana. Although he had written the lively auburn-haired high school senior, their relationship had been limited to activities with the church youth group. Much to her delight, he asked her to lunch.

"Your family has helped with the bus ministry before," Gary began, ignoring his hamburger, "So you know what the need is. There are hungry children to feed, lonely people to visit, and, if we hold Sunday School, I just know we'll pull in a full house."

Jana's mind had already been investigating possibilities. "I've been thinking, Gary. Here's what we can do." She loved to jump into projects with both feet and take off running, especially with a project like this that called to her heart. Pushing their lunches aside, the two teenagers planned an extensive outreach program that would fill their summer with both rewarding work and exhaustion.

Looking at her watch, Jana suddenly sat up and moaned. "Oh, no! We've been talking for three hours! And this is my first week on my job." Jana grabbed her purse and ran.

Sure enough, Jana lost her job. But that didn't seem to matter. She had also lost her heart. Two weeks flew by, Gary and Jana worked side by side as a well-coordinated team. Gary's charisma, drive, and outgoing nature attracted a small congregation in spite of his youth and inexperience. Full of ideas, Jana preferred working behind the scenes, teaching Sunday School and feeding the children, while dreaming of becoming a missionary.

"Colonel," Gary approached Jana's father with an outstretched hand, "I'm going to marry your daughter."

Jana's father, a hardworking man prominent in the political scene in Orlando, stepped back in amazement. Who was this outspoken young man from Palatka County and what could he possibly provide for his daughter? Two weeks of working on a summer project together hardly constituted a courtship.

"We'll see about that, young man," the tall businessman replied with a twinkle in his eye. "Right now, Jana will attend the Bible College we've picked out for her and that's that," he added firmly. Jana's father laid down the law in the family, as did most Southern fathers.

Love has a way of overcoming obstacles. Not even six hundred miles between campuses could keep the teenagers apart. A homemade Christmas wedding ended Jana's sophomore year in December. The couple decided to spend the rest of the school year settling into their marriage. Getting a job as a photographer's assistant, Jana spent evenings and weekends helping Gary with the outreach ministry, which was now official. The Orlando Baptist Church agreed to pay Gary an associates' salary. At the end of the following summer, Gary returned to the seminary, while his bride worked in a music store, waiting her turn to complete her education.

At the end of two years, Gary came home with an enthusiastic announcement. "Jana ! They selected me! The Home Missions Board has chosen us to go to Columbus, Georgia, and start a church!"

"That's wonderful, Gary!" Jana basked in the warmth as her husband's passion caught fire. "When do we go?"

"But your education, Jana," Gary faltered. "I know it's your turn. It will be hard for a while. We have to make presentations in churches to get them to support us. My salary will hardly be anything!"

Gary waited anxiously for Jana's response. She did not enjoy being in the public eye as much as he did. She would have to keep working at dull jobs.

"Let's do it, Gary," Jana threw her arms around him. "This is our calling. We both know that. I will support you no matter what. My turn will come."

He kissed her. "The Lord blessed me when He gave me you, Jana. A kind, beautiful wife who helps me serve His people. I love you, sweetheart." He stroked her hair in gratitude.

Their young marriage had already survived difficult trials. Living in a student apartment hadn't been easy. Even though Jana took birth control pills, their first year of marriage resulted in a painful miscarriage. It had been rough for Jana, hemorrhaging in the middle of the night, being so far away from her home and family. The next morning in the

hospital, a callous nurse walked in and causally asked the young, grieving wife, "What do you want us to do with the body of your baby boy?"

Devastated, Jana cried for days.

"Don't cry, sweetheart," Gary crooned, reassuring her. "Things will
get better. I'll find a way."

Columbus, Georgia, needed Gary. Servicemen and their families
stationed nearby at Fort Benning, weary from endless moving, welcomed
the young man who knocked on their doors. "We're starting a church!"
he announced. "We'll have Sunday School, too! Your own church!"

In the meantime, the young couple struggled financially.

"Honey," Gary would say in a meek voice, "This congregation just
barely makes ends meet. There's only fifty dollars in the collection plate
today. But it's more than last week when we only had twenty-six dollars!"

"This is our calling," Jana would say, pouring Kool-Aid into the
champagne glasses from their wedding. "We'll make it."

The young outreach minister and his wife barely kept their heads
above poverty level. Jana spent her days filing endless piles of thin car-
bon copies for an insurance office in a tiny hot room that contained
wall-to-wall filing cabinets. A sponsoring church gave the struggling
ministry a few hundred dollars consistently, but Gary had to scramble
for the rest. The couple decided to let Gary's insurance policy go for one
year, until their little church offered a more stable income. A difficult
decision, since Gary himself knew the hardships his mother had experienced. His dad died when Gary was fourteen, leaving him and his mother
without insurance. They both worked to pay for Gary's college expenses
and, sometimes, even for bare necessities.

Jana and Gary focused on their ministry, never once jealous of their
Florida friends who were having babies and building careers. Their spirits soared with love and devotion to each other and to their mission.
Jana spread blankets on the floor for candlelight picnics, while Gary hid
love notes all over the house.

One day, Gary entered the apartment to find Jana especially excited, in spite of the flu-like symptoms that had kept her home from
work.

"Gary! It's not the flu! I'm going to have a baby!" She handed him a
champagne glass with cherry Kool-Aid.

"That's wonderful!" Gary's eyes lit up and a grin spread across his face. "I know without a doubt that it's a boy!"

They stayed awake until midnight, dreaming together, laughing at the funny names Gary proposed for his son. "How about Mergatroid?" Jana giggled.

"Or Linberry? No, Dr. Livingston! Yeah, We'll give him a head start on a degree!" Gary hugged his wife, content to be holding her, hearing her laughter, and knowing she was carrying his child.

A new atmosphere of anticipation took over the apartment. Gary came home early the rest of the week. The couple strolled through the mall looking at maternity clothes, baby shoes, and nursery items. All too soon, the mission work demanded that the daydreaming couple return to the present.

"Jana! A farmer committed suicide. His wife has no family, nobody. And talk about depressed! Please make some food for her. I'll take it over tonight." Gary's voice sounded urgent over the phone.

"Gary, we're all out of food ourselves!" pleaded Jana. "We only have a bag of rice and a can of mushroom soup!"

"Look in the pocket of my jacket in the closet," Gary instructed. "There's two dollars in there. Please get some chicken pieces for a casserole. We'll just take a little off the top of the widow's pot for ourselves, and give her the rest."

Gary's inner fire blazed brighter than ever as people responded to his tireless work. Leaving home at six in the morning, he would knock on doors, street after street. At eight o'clock in the evening, Gary would come home to the little apartment, exhausted. After supper, he would collapse into bed, setting his alarm clock for two in the morning.

"Gary, living with you is like being married to Moses!" Jana declared. "How can you put in a fourteen-hour day, then get up in the middle of the night for Bible reading?"

"I just can," Gary maintained. "How can I preach His word if I also don't listen to what He has to say to me?" He treasured his early morning meditations, personal prayer time, and beloved scriptures, especially since he was anticipating becoming a father.

The following week, Gary did not wake up for meditation and Bible study. It was Jana who awoke. Her husband's body jerked in the bed as he yelled football plays.

"Over here! Throw it! I'm ready! They've got it, block it! Do it! Five yards to go!" He's dreaming, Jana thought.

Gary tossed, screaming to a fellow football player. Suddenly he sang at the top of his lungs, "Rock of ages, cleft for me, let me hide my soul in thee. Throw it here, I'll catch it!"

Singing hymns, yelling football plays, Jana wondered what was going on. She shook him by the shoulders.

"Gary, Gary, wake up!"

No response. Jana turned on the small lamp beside her bed. Gary's pajamas clung to his body with sweat. His eyes were open, and though he was looking at Jana, he was not seeing her. He continued to toss and yell. He doesn't even know who I am, Jana realized with horror. He's delirious. She put her hand on his forehead, which was burning with fever. Inexperience caused instant panic, and Jana immediately called her mom in Florida.

"Get his fever down, Jana. Put him in the shower," her mother insisted.

Jana half dragged, half carried her husband to the bathroom and turned on the water, reducing his fever as her mother had instructed. The next day, the fever had returned to 104 degrees. Calling her one friend in the apartment building, Jana obtained the name of a doctor, an internist that was reputedly the best in Columbus.

The doctor dismissed Jana's alarm. "It's nothing. I've checked him out, and it's just a flu or something. Here's a prescription for antibiotics. He should be fine by the end of the week. Go home and put him to bed."

Jana took her patient home, calling work and pleading for another day off.

"You had better come in tomorrow," the office manager spat her words out in warning. "First morning sickness, now your husband is sick. Excuses, excuses."

Gary seemed worse on the antibiotics. By evening, the thermometer still read 104 degrees. Jana called the doctor's office again.

"Calm down," the doctor chastised her. "You're making a big deal over nothing. Give the medicine some time."

Jana returned to her husband. It was only two days before Christmas, and three days before their third anniversary. Surely Gary would feel better for their special day. Jana looked at the tiny artificial tree that twinkled merrily from their kitchen table. She wanted Gary to feel well enough to get genuinely excited about opening her present. For six months she labored over her gift for Gary, making her first quilt. Calling her grandmother for directions, Jana had patiently cut the small pieces and sewed them each night before Gary came home for dinner. The quilt waited in its box, wrapped with care and tied with a big silver bow.

Jana slept little that night, listening as the rattle in Gary's chest grew louder. She wrapped him in blankets on the sofa, and camped out beside him on the floor. She missed their personal time together, and she cherished the moments when he seemed to be coherent. They talked about the baby, and stared at the lights on the tiny tree. After a few minutes, Gary would slip back into his incoherent state, which was more of a stupor than restful sleep. When, at last, the sun came up, Jana seized the phone.

The insurance office manager showed no empathy. "Don't bother coming in. Ever!"

Jana dialed the doctor's office next. The answering service picked up after two rings.

"Tell Dr. Adams to meet me in the emergency room of the hospital," Jana stated firmly. "I'm taking Gary in right now. His chest doesn't sound right and he still has a high fever."

As Jana opened the apartment door to maneuver her husband to the car, he whimpered. Looking down, she realized that he had no bladder control. Her stomach sank as she assessed the seriousness of Gary's disease. Jana changed his clothes, and then called his family.

"Gary's really sick. I'm taking him to the hospital. The doctor says he'll be all right but I wanted you to know. Could you call my mother for me?" Jana knew she couldn't afford two long distance calls to Florida.

As soon as she put the receiver in the cradle, the phone rang. It was the doctor's office. "Calm down," ordered the brusque Dr. Adams. "It's Christmas Eve. This can wait a few days. You are over reacting." The phone clicked.

Jana pulled Gary's arm over her shoulder and dragged him out the building to her car.

Although the emergency room doctor couldn't identify Gary's specific disease, he immediately suspected a severe illness. In spite of a skeleton crew for the holidays, he ordered an x-ray of Gary's chest.

"We need a pulmonary specialist," he announced. "I'm putting him in intensive care."

Two hours later, Jana looked at Gary, amidst IV's and tubes. The hospital had cut off his wedding ring; Jana held his hand praying that he would know she stood near. A knock on the door interrupted her silent communion with her husband. Looking up, Jana recognized Dr. Adams, the doctor who had repeatedly reprimanded her for overreacting to her husband's symptoms.

Standing in the doorway in a new buttery-soft, black leather coat, the doctor barely met Jana's eyes. He hung his head. "I'm sorry," he said barely audibly. "I'm really sorry."

He waited in the doorway like a small child, as if he needed Jana to tell him everything would be all right. Jana looked at him in disbelief. With her precious young husband fighting to live, a respirator clamped over his face, and ulcers burning his lips, how could this doctor deserve a reputation as one of Georgia's finest internists? She glared at him coldly, her stare conveying the clear message of disdain she felt for him.

At that very moment, as if on cue, Gary opened his eyes. Recognizing the doctor despite his casual clothes, Gary smiled and blinked his eyes. It's okay, his body seemed to say. I forgive you. His message delivered, he lapsed back into unconsciousness.

The hospital permitted patient visitation for fifteen minutes at ten o'clock, two and eight in the evening. Jana camped out in the waiting room, praying incessantly. By the third day, Gary turned yellow. He was experiencing kidney failure, his systems were shutting down, and blood was seeping through his skin. The waiting room filled with an ominous foreboding for Jana, though she no longer waited alone. Gary's mother and sisters arrived from Florida, followed by Jana's mother and sister.

"I'm taking you back to your apartment, honey," Jana's mother took her by the arm. "They'll call us if there is any change."

It suddenly felt good to be taken care of for a change. Jana returned to the apartment, where she and her mother collapsed on the bed.

At two in the morning, Jana sat straight up, fully alert.

"What is it? Jana?" her mother groggily inquired.

"Something's wrong. I just know it," Jana helplessly covered her face with her hands.

As if in response, the phone rang. It was a nurse from the hospital.

"Gary's heart stopped, but we resuscitated him," assured the nurse. "We'll see you at ten in the morning."

Gary died before the ten o'clock visitation time. The doctor gently conveyed the news to the family, then a nurse handed Jana the plastic bag of his personal effects. No one knew for certain what had killed him. Gary was dead, leaving a stunned pregnant wife to cope with the aftermath of his demise.

"You don't want to see him, do you?" the nurse inquired. "Not like this! Take my advice and remember him the way he used to be. You don't want to see him with all the tubes and stuff." She added as an aside, "Oh, by the way, the doctor took some samples to send to the Center for Disease Control in Atlanta."

She turned Jana toward the waiting room exit, encouraging a decision Jana would regret for the rest of her life. For twenty years, Jana would be seeking closure. As a young wife and mother-to-be, the fast, secretive treatment of her husband's sudden death offered no time for goodbyes.

"Let's go home, Jana. We'll pick out his funeral clothes and later we'll pack up your stuff and bring it to you." Jana's mother took charge, her daughter overcome by grief that settled in a fog of depression over her mind, her only way of coping with the harsh reality life had just thrust upon her.

Jana and her mother flew home to Orlando, beginning preparations for Gary's immediate funeral. With barely time to mourn her husband's death, Jana submitted herself to a thorough physical the following day.

"Just to make sure," the nurse had cautioned. "We don't want you or the baby to get sick, too." Three months later the Center for Disease Control confirmed the cause of Gary's death: Legionnaire's Disease.

As if losing her husband and the father of her unborn child were not enough, the harsh reality of their impoverished life together quickly came to haunt Jana.

"You can't get a job so soon, Jana," her mother consoled the young widow. "You do have a lot of debts, but your dad and I will cover them for you. Didn't Gary have insurance?"

"We had to let it go," Jana held her head.

"But honey, there's a grace period, it might still cover things." Her mother had more experience at these things.

Gary's insurance did, indeed, have a grace period. The policy would provide $30,000, exactly the amount needed to cover Gary's medical bills, funeral, and Jana's upcoming maternity expenses. However, the grace period expired eight days before Gary's death.

Jana felt determined to assert her independence and resourcefulness. It would be too easy to succumb to her mother's desire to manage her life. Within a week of the funeral, Jana put an ad in the paper for a yard sale. The few pieces of furniture, her dishes, and the wedding gifts paid for most of the funeral costs. The family put the word out amongst friends and business contacts. Within a few days, Jana secured an interview with a dynamic man who served as senior pastor of a large metropolitan church and executive director of an international outreach program.

"You'll be my personal assistant," said Dr. Ware following the lengthy interview. "That includes lining up international plane flights, scheduling all appointments and personal appearances, coordinating conferences, and contacting the media. Oh, and I need you to oversee the weddings and funerals I perform. After you catch on to the basics, we'll work out the details for the school's fund-raising campaign. Can you start tomorrow?"

Jana nodded her head. Somehow, she would find the strength to sort out the details. She buried her loneliness inside of her next to the baby growing in her womb. She stumbled through the motions of living. She retreated to her small bedroom early each night, to lie in her bed, numb, praying for sleep to rescue her from thoughts of Gary and her desperately solitary life without him. The unborn baby forced her to eat, although she had no appetite. While the pregnancy and her career flourished, Jana's spirit continued to wither and fade.

Seven months later, Jana experienced three days of strenuous labor, followed by a Cesarean birth.

"He's named Gary, of course." Jana managed a small smile. She held her new baby close, feeling a confusing mixture of relief, joy, and pain while cradling the tiny creature who bore a striking resemblance to his father.

A busy nurse interrupted Jana's reverie. "You don't want to breast-fed, do you? Trust me, it's so much easier to give him formula. Especially with you working and all. Let me just give you a shot to dry up your milk. How about it?"

Brought up to obey authority, Jana relented, feeling little confidence in herself, especially her ability to mother this small person without Gary. Another decision she would regret for the rest of her life. She allowed her milk to dry up, severing one of the most critical ties a mother can have with her newborn. Shortly after coming home, the baby failed to thrive because of severe allergies and asthma—both potentially preventable had she breast-fed. The baby could tolerate little but Gatorade, and Jana feared she would lose him, too.

Although the baby required constant attention, and Jana's love for him poured from the very depths of her soul, he did not take away her loneliness. Jana was consumed with her depression, swallowing large helpings of guilt for not breast-feeding and for her inability to be happy for her baby son. She dreaded each morning, each day, and each night.

As soon as the baby gained weight, Jana resumed her job. The church maintained a nursery, so Jana brought the baby with her. Once she arrived in the office, she lost herself in a sea of errands, phone calls, and appointments. No one would have guessed that the pleasant, efficient executive assistant felt hopelessly stranded and depressed, alone on an island of despair.

No one, except Mrs. Birch.

Members of the same church, Mrs. Birch knew Jana's family for years. Mrs. Birch's son, Jake, had briefly dated Jana in high school. A matronly woman in her fifties, Mrs. Birch's gentle, pale blue eyes were framed by short dark hair. Wearing no makeup and simple dresses, Mrs. Birch exuded sweetness. Never a leader, she remained in the background of the church community, baking casseroles for families in need and holding babies in the nursery. Parents considered it an honor to have Mrs. Birch hold their babies. She, herself, had nurtured her own four children who had since blossomed into young adulthood.

The Birch family was considered part of the church's faithful following. Sitting in their regular pew, Mrs. Birch would quietly pat her eyes during the prayer concerns, with her lace handkerchief dabbing at the tears she would shed when hearing of another's hardships. Like her husband, Mrs. Birch never had much to say, keeping her thoughts private through the years.

"Jana," Mrs. Birch shyly addressed the young widow after church, "I must talk with you. May I take you to lunch this week?"

"Sure," Jana nodded. Adjusting the baby on her hip, she fished in her purse for her calendar. "How's Thursday?"

The date set, Jana left the church with a growing curiosity. Mrs. Birch had rarely spoken to her before.

While the waitress served the food, Mrs. Birch dished out stilted small talk punctuated by awkward pauses. Fidgeting in her seat, her gaze darted nervously around the restaurant as if she were looking for someone to come rescue her.

"Jana," she stammered, "I'm going to get right down to business. This is not easy for me, but God told me to call you. I think you need to hear something."

Jana swallowed a bite of salad, more interested in the strange lady in front of her than in eating.

"I don't go around telling people my personal information. But like I said, I think God wants me to tell you this." She took a deep breath, as if she were about to take a plunge from a diving board sixty feet in the air.

"Twenty-four years ago, I was the happiest woman in the world. My husband and I lived in the country in our first little house. Jake was two and I was pregnant with Mary Ann. We didn't have a lot of money, but we had a little garden, and my husband had his small business. We had everything we needed. My husband and I were so in love. We had big plans for a business and for the children. Everything seemed perfect."

"After work, my husband loved to fish more than anything. Several times a week, he took his boat out on the lake and fished in the moonlight. I waited up, knitting baby clothes in my rocking chair and watching the road for the headlights of his truck. I always recognized those lights as they turned onto the road to our house. Then, he'd come in and kiss me. I even loved the way he smelled, like bug spray and fish. We would go to bed and celebrate his good luck."

Mrs. Birch's chin quivered and her eyes filled with tears. She reached for her handkerchief and began patting her eyes, just like in church.

"One night, those headlights didn't come down the road. I rocked and rocked, waiting for those lights. Pretty soon, the sun came up. I knew I wouldn't be seeing those headlights ever again."

Jana reached across the table and touched Mrs. Birch's arm as she continued her story.

"I called my husband's brother, who lived nearby. They found the empty boat on the lake. Had to drag the lake for five hours before they found his body." Mrs. Birch paused, pressing her handkerchief to first one eye than the other. The tears refused to stop.

"I wanted to die. How would I live with out him? I didn't know how to do anything. I wasn't prepared to work, and I was four months pregnant. We didn't have much money saved up. I didn't know how to sell the business, or how I was going to pay the rent."

She paused, catching her breath, and gathering the strength to continue her tragic tale.

"I didn't feel like eating or even living, but I had to take care of the children. I sold everything we had to pay for the funeral."

Jana nodded her head at the all-too-familiar story, remembering her life after her own husband's death.

"I found a factory job and a neighbor to keep the children. It was hard. Sometimes I was so tired, I couldn't even get supper ready." Mrs. Birch's voice grew stronger as she recalled her determination. "But every day, my husband's brother would stop by and take care of things. He brought me groceries, fixed things, kept the truck running. He was so kind, just being there."

"Three years later, he asked me to marry him," Mrs. Birch spoke slowly, watching Jana's face as she divulged her secret. "He knew I could never love anyone like his brother. But we've been happy. It's been a good life. He has raised Jake and Mary Ann like they were his own, and we had two more children. The family stayed intact."

Mrs. Birch stopped and smiled, looking into Jana's eyes to see if the meaning of her story had been understood by the young widow sitting across from her. Tears streamed down Jana's own face, confirming that the message had been received.

"You're the only person who truly comprehends what I've been through!" Jana whispered.

Mrs. Birch reached for the young woman's hand. "Honey, I knew you needed this story. It's hard, but you'll make it. Life gets better. It just takes time."

Jana smiled and said nothing. The two women gathered their things and left the restaurant. Approaching the parking lot, they embraced, as a mother and daughter sharing a personal sorrow. Jana fought to maintain her composure. Mrs. Birch nodded, patting Jana gently on the back. Words were no longer necessary. The icy loneliness around Jana's heart melted from the healing power of a woman's story. Mrs. Birch's love and understanding wrapped Jana in a blanket of compassion, soothing the deep hurt that had cut her so deeply for so long.

The soul-to-soul connection of Mrs. Birch's story ignited a flame in Jana. Within a few months, Jana, herself, waited after church to set a luncheon date. Perceiving a foreboding mood in a pregnant church member, Jana again took out her calendar, ready to shine an empathetic light of compassion and understanding into the obviously dark depression of another troubled woman.

Even without a tragedy, pregnancy presents challenges. Donna's pregnancy had threatened disaster from the beginning. A petite woman in her forties, Donna's closet boasted of Ellen Tracy designer suits in size six; the wardrobe of another life for her. Now Donna struggled with severe toxemia, causing extreme bloating of her body and feet. The once svelte executive expanded to a girth equal to her height and condescended to shuffling around the office in bedroom slippers. Each day Donna's morale diminished and her anxiety burgeoned. Jana easily read Donna's apprehension in her face and in her body.

"It's time for a shower for you and your baby," exclaimed Jana, figuratively rolling up her sleeves. Sending out an alert to every woman in their church, Jana organized a party.

Donna balked at the idea of a shower. "I have nothing to wear. I look terrible!" she wailed.

"Be there!" Jana commanded. Jana recruited Donna's husband as a chauffeur to guarantee her attendance.

Reluctantly, Donna showed up, outfitted in her latest barn-sized maternity dress and quilted pink slippers, the puffiness of her face evident despite the careful makeup. Surveying the empty room with its long table decorated with food and flowers, and the circle of sixty chairs that encompassed the room, Donna looked puzzled as Jana pinned on a corsage.

"Where is everybody?" she asked, a look of disappointment filling her face. Her pregnancy was going so badly thus far that she immediately assumed the worse—no one was coming to her shower.

"They'll be arriving any minute," reassured Jana.

A ruckus in the foyer announced the arrival of guests, who filled the hall with laughter, whooping, and guffawing. It sounded more like a Mardi Gras party than a shower. The door to the hall opened and in trooped the guests. Sixty women, ages fourteen to ninety-three, each dressed to appear to be in a full-term pregnancy. With arms bracing arched backs, the women waddled to the circle and carefully lowered themselves into chairs. Setting their presents nearby, they smoothed their dresses over their big, stuffed bosoms and giant bellies. Donna was reduced to endless giggles as the months of anxiety and depression disappeared from her tired face.

Every chair overflowing with mock motherhood, Jana commenced with the entertainment portion of the shower.

"Donna, we didn't want to have a baby shower where we play those stupid games…like guessing the circumference of a pregnant mother. Nothing makes a woman feel worse than to have everybody guess her size!"

A chorus of "Amen's" acknowledged the truth experienced by various new mothers.

"We thought you would like some company. Those of us who have been through this remember how it feels!" Jana exclaimed as heads nodded in agreement all around the circle.

"Honey, I carried twins to term. Talk about swallowing a watermelon!" The organist patted the enormous padded stomach under her muumuu. "This is how I looked at two months!"

The women laughed.

"That's right. We need to hear some stories." Jana smiled at the party guests. "Who wants to go first?" She scanned the room of eager faces as arms shot up ready to share their stories of pregnancy, birth, and babies.

That day sixty women reached out and nurtured their sister with love and humor, offering personal tales of unbelievable catastrophes and maternal miseries, archival memories of the price they paid for their treasured children. Some had borne twins, others had breech births, and still others delivered in incredible locations such as elevators, cars, and a grocery store. With each story, Donna felt the strength of love and motherhood. With each story, Donna's flame of resilience grew brighter. Jana had come full circle.

Dinner Questions

❑ How have you experienced the spiritual support women provide each other at births and deaths?

❑ How have you passed on positive uplifting support from another woman?

Best Friends

Friends are the family we choose for ourselves.

— EDNA BUCHANAN, *SUITABLE FOR FRAMING*

"Shirley, I have a delicate problem. Could you come over right away?" Mom needed our neighbor.

We lived next door to the Methodist manse. Ministers and their families moved in and out, most of them busy with their own lives. Polite yet transient. We unanimously deemed the Burlesons our favorites. Clint and Shirley, an upbeat, loveable couple, were well-suited to each other. Their eyes twinkled while ready chuckles sprinkled their conversations. They also had children, three precocious, creative yet well-behaved children younger than, though compatible with, our family. We all enjoyed living next to each other, but most of all, Mother had a best friend for a while.

Mother's predicament, indeed, required a best friend. While pulling weeds in a squatting position mother lost her balance and fell backwards, sitting down hard on a clump of small cacti. A human pincushion. She could not drive herself to the medical clinic nor could she sit in a car for someone else to drive her. We kids were in school and Mom would never call my father at work for assistance.

So Shirley hastened over with magnifying glass and tweezers. In order for Shirley to have easy access to remove these nasty intrusions, Mother bent bare-bottomed across her lap. This position provided little in the way of steadiness, however, for the two women shook with laughter at their plight. Shirley worked diligently for an hour, freeing Mom of the painful spines.

When I came home from school that day, I was told the hilarious tale of my mother being rescued by her best friend and neighbor in a most delicate manner. I distinctly remember feeling awe for these women, thinking how important it is to have a friend who could pull cactus spines from your bottom. That story became one of the landmarks in Mother and Shirley's mutual history, a history filled with memories they shared through the trials and successes of motherhood. These women still share their lives today, in long distance phone calls or their annual Christmas letters.

My daughter Simone formed a "best friendship" at the age of three when we moved next door to Hannah in Tallahassee. For six-and-a-half years, Simone and Hannah swam together, spent the night back and forth, and guarded thousands of secrets. They grieved over dead hamsters, licked the frosting off just-iced birthday cakes, and played dress-up in my wigs and costumes. They spun endless tales of make-believe, choosing parts for themselves as bunnies, kittens, or pirates, and savoring the ongoing adventure that continued with the next visit.

True friendship is a bond that goes beyond the social interaction it appears to be. Like a marriage, it includes the emotions, which in turn affects the physical well-being of both parties involved. Sometimes friends can hurt each other emotionally. Others actually hurt each other physically, even though it might be an accident, like the time when, in a moment of rough tumbling at school, Simone grabbed Hannah by her knees, causing a fall on the hard cement. Hannah broke a permanent front tooth, an event that caused extreme grief for both sets of parents. Pain always comes when best friends are separated. Both girls' families left Tallahassee to relocate in different states, causing Simone to experience endless stomachaches. After blood tests, x-rays, and multiple exams, a specialist confirmed that the pain was a result of serious stress—stress from being separated from her best friend.

Simone and Hannah have managed several reunions in the five years since then. Each time, they reconnect where they left off, sharing more secrets and living more adventures. Every visit results in a tearful goodbye, a long embrace reminding them of their continued acceptance and appreciation of each other that has grown up with them. I keep a picture on my dresser of one of those embraces. Eight-year-old girls in love with life together.

I can't imagine life without best friends. Friends you can trust with your deepest secrets, your hearts' regrets, and your soul's desires. Friends who can laugh with you at your follies and hold you in your pain. Friends who enjoy your pride for your children and can commiserate with your disappointment in them. Friends who empathize with your frustration with growing older and who can see your beauty without makeup. Friends who keep in touch, refusing to let years or miles be an obstacle to your relationship.

Now, in the middle of my life, I realize that best friends also share a spiritual dimension. My friend, Ann, and I began our friendship at that dimension. Our lives differ since Ann is childless and married to a physics professor. Together they are introverts, lovers of nature and each other. Ann and Bob enjoy long, romantic summers at their beach house, and weekend music jams on their back porch, singing Country Western music to the trees. Ann's career has been on the community college campus, where she attends endless meetings, arranges campus-wide events, and organizes international opportunities for faculty and staff. A high goal setter, she has earned a Ph.D., authored two books, supported countless entrepreneurs in starting their businesses, and delivered professional speeches around the country.

In contrast, I am a working mother juggling career with children. My husband and I are extroverts, our calendars filled to the brim with community service and kids' events. While Ann glides from one conference to another in vivid purple silk pantsuits, I plant trees with Girl Scouts while wearing blue jeans and a sweatshirt. Ann and her husband enjoy a quiet New Year's Eve for two; Robert and I endure the noise at an alcohol-free family fun night at the fairgrounds. Although I, too, prepare for speeches and travel, I do so amidst laundry, dogs, and science projects under foot. Ann luxuriates in her beautiful office, perfectly appointed with a teal computer on her desk and a breath-taking view of the city from her long, glass windows.

But despite the differences in our outward appearances and our circumstances, a spiritual like-mindedness and a flair for the outrageous attract us to each other like magnets. We admire each other's pluck and believe in each other's potential. We both practice affirmations—positive statements charged with spiritual energy that uplift our thoughts and frame of mind. We decided from the beginning to be prayer-partners for each other. For several years, we began the day with a phone call, sharing our anxieties with each other in exchange for an affirmation.

"Ann," I lamented, "I feel overwhelmed and frustrated. There's no way I can get everything done. My computer is on the blink, the kids have dental appointments, my speaking engagement is tomorrow, and I have nothing to wear."

"Take a deep breath," Ann advised me. "You have handled worse situations than this. Wear your turquoise suit, it looks great."

"I need an affirmation, Ann, I feel frazzled," I begged.

"Try this one." Ann paused, and then continued with an air of assurance. "I take time to connect with Spirit, knowing that necessary details will be handled, children nurtured, and my audience inspired."

Ann repeated the affirmation while I wrote it down, cementing it to my mind to get me through the day.

"OK, now it's my turn," Ann continued. "Help me adjust my frame of mind for my upcoming trip. You know how I dread airplanes."

We became indispensable to each other, offering quick enlightenment or a sympathetic ear for complicated problem solving. When Ann applied for a new position, I mailed daily affirmations on postcards with stars and colored glitter. Or I would call when wallowing in discouragement, losing steam as I plotted my career path amidst sick children, school volunteer hours, and soccer games.

"Ana, you're living your dreams! Right now!" Ann pointed out to me.

"You're right!" I agreed. She usually was. "I'd rather have my problems than someone else's."

One day Ann called needing more than an affirmation. Her voice seemed lower than usual, her tone of delivery for a devastating message.

"Ana, my breast cancer has recurred. I have to get a bone marrow transplant!"

Her announcement hit me in the chest, an emotional wallop. I could hear the tears threatening to take over our conversation.

"It's going to be in November," she continued. "I'll miss all the Christmas parties."

Ann loved the endless whirl of holiday festivities and floated from one event to another in her glittering holiday finery. I remembered having lunch together and laughing at the Christmas lights swinging merrily from her ears.

Hearing her desperation, I prayed for guidance and began talking, having faith that God would supply the right words.

"Take it as a spiritual journey. I'll go on it with you." We made a pact right then. I hung up, stunned. Prayer was my only recourse.

For Ann, a private person, the inclusion of an outsider in her healing process required a new risk. She usually coped alone, nursing her vulnerabilities exclusively with her immediate family. I felt honored that she let me in. We each committed to meditation and spiritual reading, then shared passages on the phone.

"That's a great one. Read it again," Ann requested. I read to her from Jim Rosemergy's book, *A Daily Guide to Spiritual Living*. We both enjoyed the inspiration so readily available. We soared on this spiritual journey, then remembered our fears and cried some more. I didn't want Ann to sense my panic.

Another phone call presented a new challenge.

"Help me prepare for the hospital," Ann requested as her admittance date approached.

"Do you want to borrow my feather boa or Bob Mackie negligee with feather trim?" I knew how she loved to be glamorous and in control.

"Yes!" she said to both suggestions.

Ann's delight ended the next day. "They don't permit feather boas in the hospital," she reported drably. "Germs."

I grasped for ideas. "Why don't you gather up peaceful music tapes, and buy little treats to give your favorite nurses?"

I accompanied Ann to the wig store as she anticipated her hair loss. The day she checked into the hospital, my phone rang, her voice frantic on the other end.

"Ana! It's gray! My room! They gave me a gray room! Everything else is stark white! It will make me sicker!"

I thought of Ann's love for color, exemplified by her teal-colored living room, her purple silk suit and her office filled with bright flowers, colorful batiks, and the picture window where she watches the birds. Sharing my penchant for vivid hues, she felt trapped in a colorless prison.

"The colors are in your mind, Ann," I responded feebly. "You can see them anytime."

That night I shared my sadness for Ann with my children.

"Can we go see her?" They asked with sincere compassion.

"No, she can't have visitors, but we can light a candle and draw pictures to cheer her up," I suggested, knowing the power of children's art and what their handmade pictures could mean to a woman stuck in a lifeless gray hospital room.

We spread out art supplies on the kitchen table. Ann's plight had captured their determination to help. Simone sat down with her crayons and wrote her get-well wishes. John simply began cutting strips of colored paper.

"John, don't you want to draw a picture for Ann?" I asked, disappointed with his refusal to follow my suggestion.

"Mom, I'm making a paper chain of colors. She needs colors!"

He knew better than I.

We lit our candle and wrote prayers. I packaged up our humble offerings and sent them to the hospital with a neighbor who volunteers there. Our gift received rave reviews. Ann kept John's desire to send her colors close to her heart.

The bone marrow transplant process can only be described as intensely brutal. Ann sacrificed weight, hair, muscle mass, and anything that could be lost. The chemicals caused a tormenting rash on her skin. Known all her life as gorgeous, Ann no longer attempted to maintain her usual beauty routines but focused on her basic desire to survive. This is when I witnessed an amazing transformation. Without her flawless makeup, glamorous jewelry, and vibrant colors, Ann's inner beauty glowed brighter than ever. Even without her athletic energy, Ann's spiritual energy replaced all her physical losses with a most incredibly relentless power.

During the most intense part of Ann's treatment, she shared with me the devoted tenderness expressed by her husband. She appreciated the compassionate sensitivity of her male hospital attendant, and expressed her heart-felt gratitude by presenting little angel gifts to the tireless nurses in the cancer ward. Ann turned her role as a cancer patient into a conduit for loving others.

In spite of a low blood count, she came home for Christmas. This event deserved a party. Filling my picnic basket with dips, vegetables, cookies, and exotic treats, I packed my car with a "Christmas-to-go" care package. To guarantee a memorable celebration, I donned my platinum wig, and opulent fairy costume, stuffing the voluminous tulle overskirt into my car for later attachment. I felt a little silly parading around as a forty-seven-year-old fairy catering a Christmas party for two, but I was dedicated to my mission to bring a little holiday joy to my best friend. Bob and Ann awaited my surprise, and gasped with delight at my grand entrance. It was magical to hear Ann laugh again.

Ann's recovery became a miraculous time of self-discovery for both of us. A professional speaker's coach named Juanelle Teague had created an intense workshop for exploring personal values and life missions. The workshop required the participant to work with a partner. Since Juanelle sought volunteers to test market her product, I received a copy and brought it to Ann proposing that we do this together. Ann loves opportunities for personal growth and jumped at the prospect. Every week I commuted to Ann's house in the country, where we dictated stories of early family values to each other. We explored our passions, cried about our losses, and confided our deepest yearnings. We took turns fixing lunch for each other, and as Ann's strength and appetite returned, so did her flair for cooking. The favorite part of our "workshop" occurred after lunch, when we shared adventures from our past. Lost loves, outrageous risks, and scandalous capers. We laughed and hugged, taking new insights home to study and perfect.

A cancer survivor, Ann's life grows busier than ever as she flies around the globe and contemplates new opportunities. Our daily phone calls are a luxury of the past, and our personal workshop became the emotional anchor for our current life pursuits. We remain close in spirit, available to each other in crisis, and committed to supporting each other's dreams. Ann reads my stories and encourages me to continue writing and speaking. Her encouragement has kept me going many days when my goals seemed unreachable.

The rich rewards of having a best friend come with a dear price. Ann and I learned to share time for nurture and play when life seemed most fragile. We hurt with the pain of helplessness and we shared our faith together when we needed strength. We took risks as we opened the closets of our guarded pasts to each other. Hannah and Simone also trusted each other with confidential safekeeping. Expressing their love for each other, they experienced the heartbreak that comes with separation. Mother and Shirley risked being vulnerable together as well. They wrapped a moment of crisis in laughter, bonded with the glue of lasting friendship. A best friend, I'm sure, is an example of God's grace.

Dinner Questions

❑ When have you allowed a friend to see your most vulnerable self?

❑ When have you been involved with a best friend during illness?

❑ What did you gain?

Rites of Passage

*Rituals are the formulas by which
harmony is restored.*

— TERRY TEMPEST WILLIAMS, *PIECES
OF WHITE SHELL*

Women friends are the treasures of my life, whether they are best friends, adopted sisters, older mentors, friends from work, babysitters, church friends, Girl Scout leaders, or favorite authors. The camaraderie found in a group of women offers laughter to release pent up anger, comfort for difficult journeys, and compassion for the raw wounds still healing. There is nothing like it in any other gathering of humans on earth.

Groups of women birth a source of power, like waterfalls feeding the river of life as it flows toward the ocean, gathering momentum and maturity. The celebrations with these women's groups have been rites of passage for me as I negotiated the challenges of each particular phase of my life.

The Presbyterian Church women provided a support group for the women in my family for several generations. My mother never missed her monthly circle meeting. When I was a senior in high school, these churchwomen organized a brunch to entertain the twelve graduating teenagers. We received engraved invitations implying Sunday dress and our best manners.

The brunch itself dazzled us, a presentation fit for royalty. We stared in amazement at the starched, embroidered tablecloths, polished silverware, and flowers from the florist. Impeccable placards, with our names written in calligraphy, honored us. Crystal glasses sparkled with cold orange juice as hot quiche, colorful fruit, and buttered biscuits arrived on beautiful china. A small gift for each graduating senior adorned every place. These kind women made us feel so important and grown up.

Other churchwomen sent presents to our homes. Reflecting on each gift and giver, I took great pains in writing my thank-you notes. These ladies had become our personal cheerleaders. They collectively rooted for our success as we ventured into college and the unknown future. I can still picture the women's faces, middle-aged to elderly, smiling with kindness, hope, and faith in us to do well out in the world.

The next significant gathering of women in my life consisted of my first consciousness-raising group in the seventies. Sitting in a circle, we brazenly talked about subjects that were taboo in our upbringing. I listened nervously as a more outspoken young woman described her sexual fantasies in great detail. Another suggested we take off our shirts and appreciate our diverse breasts. This suggestion paralyzed me with fear. Fortunately, we moved on to other topics such as our desire to know more about our bodies, our need for women gynecologists in a male-dominated field, and how to use vibrators.

We questioned our recent marriages to men who didn't understand us. We laughed at the old-fashioned values our mothers had taught us with such naïveté. Behind those defiant conversations, we hid our true fears and insecurities about who we really were as women. We encouraged each other to be freer yet we had no idea what that actually meant. Most of the women in my group divorced their husbands within two years, which was a far cry from my mother's conservative Bible study circle.

The number of single and divorced women increased in the early eighties. My group of women friends struggled to nurture children, express themselves as artists, and survive on meager incomes. We found creative ways to explore our womanhood. We dressed as our grandmothers in their youth, sharing their stories of survival. We invented our own rituals and ceremonies, finding a way to nurture each other without words but rather with symbolic gifts of incense and aromatic teas. We danced in fringed shawls and colorful bangles. One such event occurred in a Florida forest, where eighty women formed temporary tribes, exploring together the dynamics and nuances of being female. We brushed each other's hair, nursed our heartaches, and celebrated our exotic natures. We completed our magical day by "tying our loose ends," knotting purple ribbons into a lovely web between the pine trees.

Women in Augusta, Georgia, provided my rite of passage into motherhood some years later. With infants strapped to their chests and toddlers nearby on the floor, they gently encouraged me to relax into the world of babies.

"Your only goal as the mother of a newborn is to drink water, get rest, and nurse your child," they assured me at my first La Leche meeting before the birth of my daughter. It promised a drastic change of pace for me, a working woman with my lists of goals, a packed schedule, and a determination to "do it all."

When the baby came, these wonderful mothers I barely knew filled my refrigerator with casseroles, the nursery with diapers, and our dining room with baby equipment. Nursing did not come easy. My baby couldn't latch on to my nipple correctly. She cried nonstop and wore us both out. As little Simone lost weight and her parents lost sleep, La Leche League mothers continued to come. Some were women I didn't even know! Bringing more food, they took turns in the rocking chair, calmly suggesting better positions for holding the infant, encouraging me not to give up. Finally, the "football hold" worked. The baby latched on, gained weight, and our new family became part of La Leche community that was dedicated to loving and caring for children.

"How can I possibly pay you back?" I asked these women in my gratitude.

"Just pass it on," they replied. "Pass on a mother-to-mother understanding, encouragement, and compassion." And I have.

The new millennium has brought a richer treasure chest than ever before as I contemplate the vast diversity of incredible women interacting together. Women focused on personal missions and global visions determined to improve the quality of life for their community, their family, and themselves. Female executive directors negotiate with city leaders and inspire scores of employees to achieve new successes. Professionals with calendars full of meetings, their plane tickets carefully organized in plastic pockets, schedule nannies and family trips as well. Women doctors listen to patients with a sensitivity and competence that might never before have been experienced in the medical profession.

Personal connection with a women's group replenishes our spirits. The more diverse the group, the more delightful it is to swap stories and lives. We dance to throbbing music and cheer each other on with "You go, girl!" We applaud our successes, past and present. Our diverse gathering includes women of different ethnic groups and sexual orientations; grandmothers and new mothers; women avoiding life and women facing death. We hug each other, feed each other, and cry for each other.

Because of this incredible legacy, I planned the rite of passage for my daughter when she celebrated her thirteenth birthday. Even as a young, single woman, I knew someday I would prepare a rite of passage for my daughter, validating her gender, and welcoming her to the responsibilities of adulthood. It would have to be something more than presenting her with a box of Kotex and a book on sex education. What symbolic, meaningful gesture could I offer to enable her to embrace the joy and responsibility of being a woman? I thought of her crammed schedule, the stress of school, and the pressure she put on herself to excel. What does she have to look forward to? More stress from school, then later from work? More pressure to perform? I wanted to assure her and affirm her on this significant day. I devised the perfect ritual for her rite of passage.

Four friends of Simone's provided the ideal participants for this sacred event. A few mothers and a friend offered to help create the ultimate celebration to mark this momentous transition in my daughter's life.

"Shall I blindfold you?" I asked at the beginning of our adventure.

"Yes!" they squealed in high-pitched voices, wiggling in joyful anticipation.

For four years, these girls had participated in service projects, leadership development, and goal setting together in their Girl Scout troop, preparing for their own futures as activists and leaders. Hailing from different cultures and schools, the blindfolded girls giggled together excitedly as I drove them on a mystery tour. Our first stop was for fast food favorites. Never again will I serve Mexican tacos to blindfolded teenagers in my car.

We took off for the next activity. The suspense of the girls intensified when I stopped the car. "Get out!" I ordered in a mock stern voice, "and hold on to each other."

With arms outstretched and attached to the shoulders of the girl in front, the blind train followed me cautiously as I led them through a building and down the stairs, ending up in the locker room of the YWCA swimming pool.

"Guess what? I happen to have your swim suits!"

They shrieked with delight. After an hour of swimming and splashing, we piled into my car and headed for another mysterious stop.

"What's next?" the girls pried, their wet hair wrapped in towel turbans.

"A fancy restaurant," I teased, "for dinner."

The girls gasped.

"Don't worry, nobody will know you there," I smiled, knowing full well what each girl was so concerned about. After our swim, they wore no makeup, their hair was wet and in a towel, no less, and they were not appropriately attired to be seen in a fancy restaurant. To a thirteen-year-old girl, it would have been kinder to shoot her.

The girls watched in disbelief as I turned into the parking lot of a well-known ritzy steakhouse. I could feel the panic mount as the girls anticipated an embarrassing entrance.

"Wait here a minute," I said, pretending not to notice them whispering to each other in a moment of frantic problem solving.

I popped out of the car, flipped up the trunk, and pulled out sack suppers.

"Here you are!" I called out, tossing a bag to each girl. "Enjoy your supper at the expensive restaurant!"

The girls laughed together in relief and devoured their sandwiches and chips.

"One more stop!" I announced, "Our last destination! The ultimate finale!"

The girls couldn't wait.

My friend, Jana, had transformed her house into an elegant spa. Two other friends awaited our arrival, eager to contribute to this evening of female fun. As the girls entered the darkened living room, glowing in candlelight, Jana reviewed the evenings' offerings.

"There are four centers of relaxation in my spa," Jana spoke with an affected accent, giving a little European flair to the drama dripping in the atmosphere. "One for the back, one for the face, two for the feet, and another for the hands. Now, who wants to start with the back?"

After assigning the girls to the different stations, Jana filled the footbath with warm scented water and floating orange peel curls. The women went to work. Jamina, a friend and assistant leader to my Girl Scout troop, massaged the back of a girl luxuriating on a nest of comforters piled in the corner. Virneva, another mom, pampered young faces with a facial, applying an organic mask to combat the mischief done by teenage oil glands. I massaged each girl's feet, soft from soaking in the fragrant water. Jana gave hand massages with a rich lotion. The girls rotated station to station for feminine indulgence, accepting our attention with unabashed delight.

At last we lined our young charges up on the couch, each mellow in a dreamy state of relaxation.

"For your last sensation, we need you to put your blindfolds back on." I instructed.

The girls obliged eagerly. This would be like the grand finale of a fireworks display. There, in the dark living room lit by soft candles, with Joni Mitchell crooning in the background, four women gave five girls a gift from their hearts. Spraying a light mist of aromatherapy around them, tickling them softly with feathers, and offering treats of mint creams to melt in their mouths, we women knew that this experience would remain forever in the memory of our young charges.

"You are a priority," I pronounced in my most official high priestess voice. "Remember to take care of yourselves, to treat your senses to simple pleasures when your minds seem burdened with stress. Being in the moment of such peace will renew your desire to give to others. Even though you may dedicate yourself to service, learn to give to yourself as well as to receive from others. May you always find Sisters to help you celebrate life together."

The women nodded their heads approvingly. The four women presented an age span of twenty years, two cultures, and a diversity of lifestyles. Single, divorced, and married; a professional, an entrepreneur, and a student, we bonded in our mission for the evening. In two magical hours, we taught five girls a lesson in life balance. Even more importantly, we introduced them to Sisterhood.

Dinner Questions

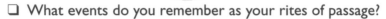

❑ What events do you remember as your rites of passage?

❑ What legacy do you wish to leave to each of your children to help them deal with adulthood?

Sacred Rituals for a Fiftieth Birthday

*Most women still need a room of their
own and the only way to find it may be
outside their own homes.*

— GERMAIN GREER, *THE FEMALE EUNUCH*

Some places have a mysterious aura where ghosts of historical grandeur seem to linger. Settings like these beg for unusual events, celebrations of great importance. In Winston-Salem, there is a house that exudes that spirit. A visionary, Mary Jamis, renovated an old two-story house with a rambling front porch expressly for nurturing the souls of women. She named the house Whistling Women. This sacred space promised intimate splendor for my fiftieth birthday celebration.

The house provided the framework; I called upon a friend to transform it. Jana, once a professional hostess for a corporation, creates a unique ambience wherever she goes. Even when Jana camps in the mountains, she takes a small table and three large candles for atmosphere outside her tent. I explained my objectives and chosen themes to Jana. Whistling Women offered us a variety of rooms, each one sparsely furnished yet elegant with high ceilings and majestic fireplaces. I designated a theme and a ritual or activity for each: a Feasting Room, a Chocolate Room, a Tribute Room, a Maiden's Room, and the Grand Salon. My treasured costumes from past performance art days could provide decadent décor. My own retrospective art show!

A tour of Whistling Women ignited the fire of Jana's inspiration. "I see Oriental rugs and the painting of Sleeping Women in this room….lots of throw pillows on the floor, and Hot Mama red lamps in this room…" Jana's eyes danced.

The day before the event, Jana loaded her van with choice items from her personal collection then spent two days transforming the house. Large paintings of women in sensuous backgrounds, her treasured rugs, and oversized tasseled pillows added royal magic to the Grand Salon. Upstairs, hurricane lamps reflected dancing lights on my red feather boa gracing the mantel as a red sequined gown glittering on the wall enticed women to the chocolate room. Framed photographs of softly lit nudes underscored the sensuality for such epicurean pleasure. Outside, luminaries with cutouts of stars invited guests up the steps to the front porch covered with tiny white lights, promising excitement and fantasy. Jana's touch created the enchanting environment for secrets, dreams, and shared moments of discovery.

Animated and resplendent, my guests arrived at Whistling Women anticipating the evening's surprises. Jeanne, my goddaughter, and her college roommate posed angelically on the porch, barefoot in their prom dresses, to greet the guests. Inside the front door, two giant, laminated posters promised an unusual evening. They featured characters from my past performances: me as a Mermaid with a Lobster and as a Strutting Peacock.

From the vestibule, a wall displayed more vintage pictures and costumes. Gauzy Arabian bloomers danced on the wall. Rhinestones shimmered from a black satin gown, and a waterfall of silk azaleas cascaded from a pink and white lace frock. Handwritten bits of trivia, snippets of memoirs, accompanied the aging frocks of gossamer and sequins; a fairyland of past decadence. Trappings of fantasy disguised both bathrooms: feather boas, glittered hats, huge six-inch rhinestone shoe clips, candy dishes filled with gold beads, and a diaphanous ball gown glowing with lights.

The guests arrived bedecked in sensational attire. An African dress in copper tones with its regal head wrap, an authentic Japanese kimono, a blue Indian sari sparkling with spangles, sequined multi-colored cocktail dresses, and a homemade Spanish mantilla diversified the apparel. Another woman wore an eclectic jacket adorned with black feathers.

Two young women proudly boasted pregnant bellies, luscious round shapes under black satin dresses.

My women friends brought savory gifts from their kitchens: dips and spreads, tasty nuts and fruit breads, meatballs, and exotic, pita sandwiches loaded with colorful ingredients. Tyra cooked a delectable vegetable curry that made one's taste buds celebrate. The wonderful array of entrées was complimented by an astounding variety of wines.

The room designated for chocolate filled quickly; expensive Belgian chocolates, chocolate Kahlúa cheesecake, brownies, and rich, chocolate cake with decadent fudge sauce. Women hovered over one table then another, their plates filling with temptations. It's no wonder I heard heavy breathing and moans of pleasure as women indulged in chocolate delight.

The Maidens' Room buzzed with activity. The two college girls who greeted my guests on the front porch reined supreme in this room dedicated to preening and pampering. Jana's large ornamental cushions encouraged floor lounging while a red velvet chaise invited royal reclining. Miniature lights winked magically in the dusk while soft rock music proclaimed the generation of these contemporary damsels. A low table in the center of the room offered cosmetic adventures: copious bottles of nail polish in a multitude of outrageous colors, body glitter, elaborate temporary tattoos, and henna for making mendhi, a decorative design worn by Indian women on the palms of their hands and soles of their feet. The girls basked in their element, nibbling pizza while adorning themselves and any woman who ventured in for a peek.

"Would you like a tattoo? Look, I have this pretty butterfly. We can give you nail polish to match. And a little glitter for your face."

They enticed women into their lair, filling the room with oooh's and aahhh's of admiration for their handiwork.

The Tribute Room maintained the air of a hallowed museum. Guests brought precious pictures, artifacts, and objects of art to honor women who had been an inspiration in their lives. The small room, outlined in tables, overflowed with carefully placed treasures and cherished photographs. My mother displayed a picture of her mother's wedding day, while my tributes included a trophy representing the champion speaker in Florida who had coached me and the pictures of the brazen performance artist in Georgia who gives me courage. Jana tenderly arranged her grandmother's quilt beside her picture with a carefully composed inscription. One guest brought a sizeable statue of the Virgin Mary accompanied by two banners of multi-colored Hail Mary's. My friend, Ann, exhibited a charcoal portrait she had drawn of her mother and aunt, women no longer living in the physical world but who continued to provide wisdom and reassurance from their spiritual realm.

The Grand Salon rendered a women's sanctuary for celebration. Jana draped a large overstuffed sofa in rich fabrics of royal red, purple, and gold. Placed at the head of the room and defined by Jana's Oriental rug, this throne seated three queen mothers, the "Royal Wise Women" who held court. Two Ladies-in-Waiting invited individual guests to seek audience with these Royal Wise Women. Kneeling on giant, tasseled pillows, the younger women disclosed the fabric of their life stories to our three matriarchs, who listened before offering blessings or advice, pressing small mementos into the hands of the recipients. These rituals were taken seriously as we remembered close ties of women's ancestral heritage of empathy and encouragement.

The Royal Wise Women reigned supreme in their roles. I discovered a closet actress in Bonnie, the local Executive Director of the March of Dimes. She arrived dramatically attired in her red velvet robe and an imposing feather mask. The second Wise Woman, a girlfriend from my life fifteen years ago in south Florida, brought the distinction of "foreign" royalty and emanated glamour in her sequined raiment, contrasted by the tender warmth of her smile. The third Wise Woman, my mother, was plainly dressed. She had been so caught up in arranging flowers from her garden for the party that she forgot her queenly apparel.

"Mother, you have forgotten that you are a Queen Bee, not a Worker Bee!" I had admonished her, laughing at my mother's love for getting involved in preparations to the detriment of getting herself ready.

Never lacking in imagination, however, she threw herself whole-heartedly into her role, taking breaks to visit the Chocolate Room.

Chairs lined the walls of the Grand Salon, and extravagant framed prints of serene women echoed the intimate bonding of sisterhood. Guests, gathering in animated clusters, exchanged stories of how they knew me, discovering new points of connection and shared interests. By eight o'clock, we assembled from the various rooms and activities, sixty women anticipating the culmination of our magical evening.

I passed a bronze planter bearing slips of paper, prompts for stories.

"Tell about the time a major personal challenge turned out to be a blessing in disguise" one slip read. "Tell about the time you got in really big trouble" read another.

The stories tumbled forth. As soon as one storyteller finished, another would volunteer, "That reminds me of the time when . . ."

The stories ranged from funny and whimsical to painful and poignant. Tales of a child's close encounter with death, of a woman's wild scheme to impersonate the press at a rock concert, another's attempt to foil a bank robbery. Together we laughed, cried, and applauded each other. For an hour and a half we celebrated our lives with our stories, cognizant of the growing strength in the web of sisterhood that enveloped us.

The occasion called for special closure. Terry, an instructor of women's studies at a local college, led us in a women's chant. "Woman am I, Spirit am I.... I have no beginning and I have no end . . ."

Grasping each other's hands we performed a spiral dance, our energy radiating from face to face, as we savored our expression of power. The spiral complete, my composure melted like a candle as they sang the birthday song. I felt so much love emanating from these women. It took the depth of my fifty years to truly appreciate the full meaning of this experience. These women, so blessed in spirit, shared a history even though they didn't all know each other. A history of personal milestones, of maternal legacies, and individual triumphs, all treasured by each other. For an instant we felt like a family. After a flurry of hugs, everyone dissipated, each carrying the glow of the evening out the door with them. The experience exists now as a precious memory, a cherished jewel in each guest's treasure chest of life.

Dinner Questions

- ❑ How would you incorporate your life's joys into the ultimate celebration with your friends?
- ❑ When can you do this and who will help you make it happen?

Enjoying the Life of an Alligator Wrestler
Increasing the Pleasure

Too many people, too many demands,
too much to do; competent, busy, hurrying
people-it just isn't living at all.

— ANNE MORROW LINDBERGH, *BRING*
ME A UNICORN

"I'm frustrated again," I wailed to my friend Ann. Running a business from my home seemed like an endless string of stressful situations, multiple battles fought in order to win an unspecified war.

"I can't find anything. I put in my high-tech computerized filing system wrong, my computer keeps freezing up, Simone has a doctor's appointment, I have a huge presentation next week…" the list of my complaints went on and on.

"Ana, everyday you tell me you are frustrated and overwhelmed. When are you going to do something about it?" Ann always knew how to target the exact problem, no matter how much it might hurt me to hear it.

A coherent response to her question evaded me. I sat in dumbfounded silence for a moment, then grumbled, "I'll think about it."

She was right. I did need to stop whining and start doing something about it. Remembering an article for women on time management, I created a chart to assess my time and activities. For every activity that I monitored, I assessed the efficiency of that activity and how I felt about it. The results demanded careful consideration. While I adored preparing and presenting programs, most of my time was consumed by the drudgery work behind the scenes. Spinning my wheels in organizations that weren't in my target market drained even more time. Driving to and from these engagements, plus my usual chauffeur responsibilities, ate up a big portion of my day as well. If I was ever going to stop feeling frustrated and overwhelmed I needed to make major changes.

After contacting a business consultant, I drastically changed my career strategy. Since I valued my involvement with my children, I relaxed my professional goals, focusing on jobs that directly generated immediate income. I chose to concentrate on writing, allowing me to be more available to my children during these challenging years. I also decided to try and balance the daily feelings of frustration with feelings of pleasure. I started to list my pleasurable moments each day to make sure I was indeed achieving a reasonable balance. Putting my journal on my desk, I wrote down any experience that brought me even a fleeting moment's pleasure.

The first day of pleasure consisted of one item. I had taken a break and nuzzled my big, floppy dog.

The second day, I paid more attention and sought pleasurable moments I could write down. I picked a flawless yellow blossom from my rose bush and placed the vase next to my computer monitor. Smelling the intoxicating fragrance brought a divine sense of sweetness, reminding me of fragrant roses in my past. Next, instead of my usual coffee, I fixed a cup of hot Earl Grey tea during another break. Ahhh…another sensory pleasure associated with a vivid memory. My list of pleasurable moments began to grow. Tackling the problem of wasted time during driving, I played tapes of inspiring or informative speakers that transformed my driving time into an uplifting and productive event. Irish dulcimer music soothed my ears while writing at the computer, engulfing me in a euphorically cheerful mood. I prepared an enjoyable lunch for myself—hot soup with an English muffin. As I smeared blackberry jam on the muffin, I recalled yet another pleasant recollection from my past. At the end of the day, my journal page listed moment after moment of delightful sensations. Three of my favorites—the roses, the tea, and the blackberries, flooded me with lovely remembrances to savor in detail. Another pleasure to indulge in! True wealth is a state of mind.

Dinner Questions

❑ Do you permit yourself to indulge in memories of past satisfactions?

❑ Have you surrounded yourself with serene beauty or do you wade through clutter?

The Fragrance of Love

*Smell is a potent wizard that
transports us across thousands of miles
and all the years we have lived.*

— HELEN KELLER

My mother never cried. She took everything in stride and solved each problem as it arose. When I walked into the kitchen at the age of five and found my mother sitting at the table sobbing, I knew something terrible had happened.

"What's wrong, Mama?" I ventured.

Mother broke the news to me gently. "Grandpa died, honey."

Retreating to my room, I sat on my bed, trying to sort out what had happened. How could my grandpa go away and never come back? He loves me and treats me special, I thought, feeling immensely sad that I would never again hear his voice, see his smile, or know his love for me. Gradually, at the ripe old age of five, I came to understand that life had cheated me of my grandfather.

There couldn't be a more ideal grandpa than my maternal grandfather. He gave us horsy rides on his back, and he made things for us. Once he carved a rocking horse just my size in his little shop. Painted bright red, it provided hours of imaginary travel for cowgirl play. He would hug me, hold me on his lap, and laugh a lot when we talked. No other man in my life provided such warm and unconditional affection.

219

Both my father and my other grandfather maintained a respectable distance from me, but not the man who had just died. How unfair!

My grandpa died just after my fifth birthday. We had celebrated my special day at his house, an hour away in Munford, Tennessee. He and my grandmother lived in a small manse near the Presbyterian Church where he served as minister. As we left their home that day, after what was to be my last visit with my grandpa, I clutched my new straw purse with a pink flower decorating the front by its handle. Inside the purse lay the rose stone he had given me. Looking like an oblong peach pit, the rose stone smelled wonderful.

"You could put it in your clothes drawer," Mother suggested.

After hearing of my grandfather's death, I found my rose stone in my drawer. Clutching it to my nose, its familiar fragrance comforted me like nothing else could. The sense of smell, more than any other sense, triggers strong memories with amazing clarity. I associated the rose stone and its smell with my grandpa's love. As I grew older, the rose stone found a safe home in my treasure box. I have it to this day.

Thirty years passed. Robert and I found a church to attend in Fort Lauderdale where we lived as newlyweds. We invited church members to dinner, building friendships. Lyall and Norma attracted us immediately. Young and vibrant in spirit, if not in body, Lyall and Norma led active lives for most of their seventy years. Lyall amused us with his mischievous humor. Norma dressed beautifully, her petite figure complimenting her modest but well-kept wardrobe. She took great pains to apply her makeup, amusing me by drawing little black eyelashes on her upper eyelids. And, she always smelled of tea roses.

Lyall and Norma treated us to their favorite meal, a champagne breakfast. We felt like close friends, holding hands with our spouses and walking together near the peaceful beach at sunrise in Fort Lauderdale. Two couples madly in love, one newly married and the other celebrating their fiftieth anniversary. We continued to maintain a close relationship with the older couple, attending the *Course in Miracles* together and hugging each other every Sunday after church. Robert's transfer came through, relocating us to Georgia, but we still visited Lyall and Norma after they moved to an assisted-living residence. We kept in touch through letters. Then, almost overnight, Norma's letters became uncharacteristically accusatory and bitter. A letter from Lyall followed, informing us of Norma's Alzheimer's disease and her subsequent death. We would miss her.

Thirteen years later, we moved to North Carolina, and spent considerable time searching for the perfect house. We recognized it immediately when we at last found it. It had such a feeling of openness inside, and was surrounded by beautiful trees outside. Directly behind the house, a lovely rose garden awaited its new owner.

Armfuls of roses filled my house that first year, delighting me with their wonderful fragrance, reminding me both of my precious rose stone from my grandfather and Norma's tea rose perfume.

The rose on my desk is regarding me now, its lovely yellow head tinged in pink. From time to time, I lean close and breathe deeply, breathing the memories of my grandfather and Norma. I know now that life doesn't cheat us out of special people, we carry them in our hearts always. We have been blessed with the gift of their presence, regardless of how short a time we have known them. We assimilate their loving impressions and kind energy into our beings. How sad that we stay so busy that we deny ourselves the gift of remembering. Because of these two rose-scented memories, I know the importance of loving a grandchild with endless affection, and of walking in the sunrise, holding hands with my sweetheart. Maybe someday, a rose will remind someone of me.

Dinner Questions

❑ What smells evoke strong feelings from your childhood?
❑ When has another couple nurtured your ideal of relationships?

Madame Goffin's Cup of Tea

*How we remember, what we
remember, and why we remember form the
most personal map in our individuality.*

— CHRISTINA BADWIN, *ONE TO ONE*

She had short, tousled red hair, green eyes, and an exuberant personality that literally exploded from her body. Madame Denise Goffin loved brilliant color layered on with a palette knife. Whenever I drink Earl Grey tea with milk and sugar, I am immediately transported back to her Brussels studio flat for painting lessons. Denise Goffin, robust and sexy at fifty, always welcomed me with open arms. Her studio was a haven for the serious art student, providing the perfect atmosphere for unleashing one's creativity and artistic talent. Her energy filled every nook and cranny with her radiant warmth and passionate devotion to her art.

Certain rituals of Belgian hospitality at Madame Goffin's studio demanded observation whenever one entered the room, which included making the rounds and visiting the station of every student with a cheerful "Bonjour, comment ça va?"

One was required to greet Madame herself with three kisses, first one cheek, then the other, then back to the first, a typical Belgian greeting for fond friends. The next expected step in the greeting ritual included shaking hands with one of the two nude models Madame Goffin hired for the class, Pierre, a tall lanky man who wore makeup and Mariel, a distinguished looking blonde who maintained her well-kept body in spite of her just over-the-hill age. Mariel had a particularly keen knowledge of the art world herself. Her air of dignity enhanced her natural beauty, which I greatly respected and admired.

At four o'clock, Madame Goffin served us Earl Grey tea with cream and sugar. We art students would leave our paintings-in-progress, the model would put on a robe, and we would sit down to tea. We swapped gossip about the small art circle found in Brussels, discussed plans for holidays, or contemplated the upcoming exhibition of Madame Goffin's paintings. At every lesson, without exception, we stopped for tea and cookies.

Madame Goffin encouraged my soul to sing in paint. She also opened the door for an experience I will never forget—a visit to another culture. Madame Goffin invited me to visit the mountain cabin where she and her husband skied in the winter. A Southern girl from flat Arkansas, I couldn't wait to experience the legendary mountains covered with snow. Together we drove one weekend in the couple's Renault to the snow-topped Ardennes and the little cabin where we played in the snow. Early in the weekend, I sensed the couple's need for time alone and asked Madame Goffin where I might explore. She pointed up the road to a large farmhouse. "Go visit the farm," she replied with her usual gusto. "There's a nice family living there and they would love to meet you."

Trudging up the road blanketed by snow, I spied an old, brick farm building. A slight figure bundled up in a dark blue jacket with a thick scarf and soft red knit hat waved at me.

"Bonjour!" A ruddy-faced old man, his eyes rimmed in red, smiled at me and waited.

"Bonjour!" I shouted back.

His accent differed from Madame Goffin's, and from the guttural Belgian accent of the blue-collar workers in Brussels.

"Where are you from?" the friendly man asked, his rosy face glowing.

"America," I replied. "I'm a friend of Madame Goffin. She owns that little bungalow over there," I pointed. "She's my art teacher."

"Ahhhhh!" the old man's face lit up. "An American! I've never met an American! Come in, come in. Meet the family! You must be cold."

My new acquaintance opened the door for me and I entered his home, stepping through the entrance and into a simple room with a hard dirt floor. The family of five adults sat around a table drinking wine, a fireplace providing warmth nearby. His wife rose to greet me, a toothless grin spreading across her face. Next to the table, the family cow chewed its cud contentedly, providing as much heat as the fireplace. My host fondly patted her on the rump.

"This is Yvette," he introduced the bovine family member.

"Bonjour, Yvette," I greeted the cow tenuously.

"Have a bite to eat," the mother stood up, smoothing her apron.

The family leaned toward me expectantly. A bottle of red wine sat on the table, with a long loaf of crisp bread, a dish of butter, and a slab of cheese. The adults huddled together on their bench, making room as I climbed over the bench to the table. After pouring me a glass of wine, the questions tumbled forth, slowly at first, then with mounting enthusiasm.

"Do you like Belgium? What did you think of the food? Really something, huh? Have you ever seen houses this old?" They grinned as they anticipated my accolades for their country.

Whenever I met Europeans away from the tourist areas, I found myself bombarded with questions, not about my culture, but about my opinions of *their* culture.

"I love Belgium, " I assured them, "but I sure do miss eating popcorn."

"Pop *corn?*" Their eyes opened wide and their mouths dropped in surprise.

Belgians grow corn purely for animal consumption. I always elicited a shocked expression as I described the favorite American movie snack. The farm family expressed equal amazement. We bantered for a good hour, comparing the laid back lifestyle of the simple Belgian country living with the hasty American fast-paced world of plastics and instant food.

I couldn't wait to tell Madam Goffin about the cow in the living room and the farm family. She nodded her head, delighted with herself for instigating my adventure.

"You made their day," she informed me. "They will tell the entire village about their American friend."

Now, many years later, these scenes come back to me in a flood of memories whenever I drink Earl Grey tea with milk. I love those moments when a taste, a scent of perfume, or a specific sound triggers far away, long ago memories. They are the gifts in life that we are privileged to revisit, paying homage to the person who made an impact on our lives at the time. Here's to you, Madame Goffin!

Dinner Questions

❑ When have you ventured into another world?

❑ When have others been shocked by your food preferences or lifestyle?

The Blackberry Summer

*I sharpen more and more to your
likeness every year.*

— MICHELE WOLF, *WHEN I AM AN OLD WOMAN
I SHALL WEAR PURPLE*

In the annals of every family history, there are defining moments which showcase a person's character, shining brightly amidst an unexpected crisis, a holiday tradition, or a historical event. During my thirteenth year, a blackberry summer revealed the spirit I share with my mother, the very force that propels us both into action as motivated women.

My grandfather, an electrical engineer with peculiar habits, married my grandmother in one of his more inspired moments. Her talents included impeccable housekeeping in their heirloom home, cooking in the Southern tradition, and providing conservative Baptist parenting for their two sons. She also put up with Granddaddy's strange ways. Granddaddy rolled his own cigarettes, rarely expressed affection, and taught his dog to sit on a saucepan.

Granddaddy built a small, cinderblock cabin on a wooded property that accessed a lake close to Watts Bar Dam, about thirty miles from their home in Sweetwater, Tennessee. This cinderblock cabin provided a summer retreat for our family's vacation. While Grandmother looked forward to our annual summer visits, my grandfather enjoyed us children best in small distant doses.

Every summer featured unique amusements at our little cabin on the lake. One summer, we had a marvelous time with an old parachute, retired from providing backup safety for a pilot friend. With this huge expanse of silk and our imaginations, we had created a tent for secret club meetings and overnight sleeping. We couldn't get enough of that parachute until a June thunderstorm foiled our night of camping and our fun with the parachute. Three wet, wild-eyed urchins ran screaming to my parents' bedroom that night, abruptly ending hope for an evening's romance without kids.

Another summer, Granddaddy brought his electrical worm-dancing machine to supply bait for our fishing attempts. After sticking wires in the ground, he connected them to a battery, and worms were supposed to come up out of their dirt dwelling dancing. Actually, they never did come up, dancing or otherwise, but the concept impressed us. The following summer we found Harry the Mole, naturally blind, with two front feet turned sideways. Harry rooted persistently with these little digging flapper feet, even when we held him up in the air. It was the summer of the blackberries, however, when my mother and I left the rest of the family to amuse themselves while we discovered our shared destiny as focused, fanatical achievers.

By chance, our vacation that year occurred during the peak of the blackberry season. We had never noticed the bushes before, covered with stickers to protect their black seedy treasures. The fruit-laden shrubs grew to eye level and thrived prolifically in the woods. The area, just developing at that time, consisted solely of dirt roads and a few cabins. In spite of the ninety-plus degree heat, the annoying existence of mosquitoes, and the rumored presence of snakes, we couldn't wait to begin our blackberry-picking venture.

Being a member of the Girl Scouts had trained my mother well. As my leader, she had often camped with me in primitive settings. We lashed our tables, rigged up latrines, and fended off chiggers at day camp. We learned how to find water in grapevines and where to pick edible wild salad. In short, we knew how to deal with nature's discomforts. We sprinkled a foul smelling sulfur powder in our underwear and around our socks to ward off the chiggers, and doused ourselves in 6/12 mosquito repellant as well. We wore our long pants even though we knew we would soak them with sweat from the sweltering heat. Straw hats topped off our ensemble as we set out for our day, two determined women on a mission.

We selected containers for our pickings, a saucepan and a plastic pitcher from the little cabin's kitchen. Entering the brush down the road from our cabin, we didn't hesitate to negotiate the prickly thorns to capture our prize. We picked diligently, focused on our task, calling each other when locating new bushes heavy with blackberries. We learned tricks for accessing those delectable fruits, carefully manipulating the branches with their vicious stickers. We discovered a bigger, juicier version of blackberries, locally called "dewberries." These weren't seedy and offered a juice so sweet we couldn't wait to sample them; we delighted in tasting the fruits of our labor as we went. When our saucepan and pitcher overflowed with the red-black berries, we hurried back to the cabin to empty them into a dishpan. We couldn't wait to return to the blackberry patch for more. All day, we picked the fat juicy berries, making trip after trip to our little kitchen, filling the dishpan, then the mixing bowl, even the coffee pot with blackberries.

After hot showers and clean clothes, we drove into town with the family for supper at Grandmother's house, anxious to show off our achievement and wash our stinky clothes. "Oh, my goodness!" exclaimed Grandmother. "What beautiful blackberries!" She knew exactly what to do with them.

"Francis, find some buckets for Margaret and Ethel Ann to take back to the lake house." Normally obedient and submissive to her husband, Grandmother didn't hesitate to order Granddaddy around when it came to her territory—the kitchen. Armed with gallon buckets, we couldn't wait to begin our compulsive routine the next day, sprinkling more sulfur in our clean clothes, and lathering on our arms and faces more 6/12 mosquito repellant. We had busied ourselves in the scratchy bushes before Daddy and the boys had even decided where to fish. By this time, we had gained speed and had become much more efficient in our task. We were experienced pickers. Steadily, relentlessly, we picked and picked. Our enthusiasm for our mission never waned.

"Oh, Mom! Over here, there are tons of them. Big ones!" I would cry.

"OK, let me finish this patch first," she would say. "These are too good to pass up."

We picked our way deeper into the brush, trespassing on properties without cabins, innocently winding our way down the road, across a ditch, and over a fence. We emptied our buckets and resumed our jobs after a hasty lunch. Like some obsessed automaton, we couldn't stop.

I'm sure our respective motivations for such impassioned picking differed. Mother loves a bargain. Passing up free food would be considered a heinous crime. Thoughts of blackberry syrup on ice cream urged my fingers to reach even further into the prickly bushes. Meanwhile, we both underestimated my grandmother. Our trip into town that night rewarded our efforts beyond expectations. Grandmother's screened-in porch accommodated two tables for six, both set for dinner. We consumed big juicy tomato sandwiches, with purple onions and cucumbers. Hot corn on the cob dripped with butter, while Grandmother's deviled eggs excelled the best ones at church suppers. But when it came time for dessert, Grandmother brought out the biggest blackberry pies I had ever seen, with vanilla ice cream waiting to crown our pie wedges à la mode. Not only had she made pies, but a whole kitchen full of blackberry jam.

Needless to say, the next day Mother and I hit the blackberry patch again. The more we picked, the more Grandmother cooked—blackberry cobbler, blackberry jelly, and blackberry syrup.

Our vacation week ended too soon, and we had to go home, our fingers stained purple, our arms tanned, the smell of sulfur still lingering in our noses and in our underwear. We grieved to imagine the acres of blackberry patches unpicked, left for the birds or rotting on the ground. But we returned home to Arkansas with several jars of Grandmother's delicious jam, and hopeful expectations of such luck in future summers.

Sadly, we never experienced another blackberry summer. We overshot the berry season the following year. Soon the area transformed with resorts and cottages, while our blackberry patches disappeared forever. I went off to college, dreaming of a career instead of blackberries and ice cream. Mother herself returned to school and began her own career as a schoolteacher. Our worlds separated for a while as I searched for myself, made my mistakes, and discovered my path. Mother still had three boys to raise, a husband to retire, and a household to manage through life's many transitions. We lived miles apart and visited only on holidays.

Three decades later, we relocated to be near each other. Mom stays close to home, caring for my dad while maintaining a prolific garden, serving on her church board, and tutoring Hispanic children in reading. I follow a career path strewn with creative projects, community service, and out-of-town speaking engagements, while raising two children. Mother and I serve as each other's best support system. Although we reflect different personalities with contrasting interests, we understand each other. We share a passion for learning and adventure. We each strive for high goals while delivering a personal message. Focused on our personal life missions, we persist. Unstoppable. For us, life is a blackberry patch ready for picking.

Dinner Questions

- ❑ What traits do you share with your mother?
- ❑ How are you different and how are you alike?

Retreating for More

If one is out of touch with oneself,
then one cannot touch others.

— ANNE MORROW LINDBERGH,
GIFT FROM THE SEA

I love long journeys. I pack my gear, load the car, turn on the tape player, and drive. My car becomes my sanctuary, a venue to explore the inner recesses of my mind and to, ultimately, rediscover and reinvent myself. This is when I have time to connect with God, fill my spiritual reservoir, and experience the beauty of the world around me. When I get to my journey's end, I lovingly give of myself and receive lavish, heartfelt gratitude when I do. My destination is almost always a retreat with women—a rich experience of love, energy, and laughter.

There are logistical obstacles to overcome, of course. Blocking out time on the calendar, fixing casseroles for the family knowing full well that they will eat pizza for every meal except breakfast, and then returning to children who cling to me like little octopi, sucking out what is left of my energy. But the rewards far outlast the obstacles. These journeys and retreats are the emotional support systems that rally around me in crisis, that celebrate my life achievements, and that enable me to see progress when it isn't apparent on a daily basis. On these sojourns away from my home and family I find sisters of my soul who sustain me even in their absence.

Many memories in life become a blur. Christmases run together; birthday celebrations have faded from mind; arguments no longer exist in my memory. Gone, like leaves that have fallen from a tree in winter. Yet I can recall all of my retreats with women with vivid clarity. Long walks with Renate in Augusta, listening with utter amazement to her accounts of extraordinary bicycle treks at the age of sixty; hot tub soaking with Kathy, comparing our spiritual journeys while slurping juicy ripe mangoes; an Orlando slumber party with Maxine, Gail, and Elizabeth, our exhilaration in being together eliciting a rush of pleasure that reduced us to a gaggle of giggling girls.

Sometimes the retreat reunites old friends, eliminating twenty years of separation as we share our most intense experiences. Births and adoptions, fights with cancer, and family deaths evoke compassionate connections while pictures of children and stories of dreams fulfilled inspire and touch us. Many retreats result in new friends, discoveries of precious jewels to add to my emotional treasure box. I cherish the recent addition of Susan, one of my brightest gems.

Like all retreats out of town, the drive itself helps me gain a new perspective on my life. I shared this particular trip with a fascinating fellow speaker, a self-made man whose life experience knew peaks and valleys totally foreign to my own existence. Our destination was the National Speakers' Association East Coast Workshop. We both anticipated with some trepidation sharing rooms with strangers in the expensive Atlanta hotel. Our weekend would bustle with workshops and networking with some of the most renown speakers in the country. Little did I know that my stranger roommate herself would provide the most awesome experience of the conference.

"Would you like some cheese?" Tall and gracious in a flowing caftan, her southern drawl reflecting her Georgia roots, Susan offered me a snack as I unpacked and started to recover from my trip.

"Sure," I accepted, smiling at the woman. I thought she must be about ten years older than I; she could be my older sister. Although I never had a sister, I find myself adopting women throughout life—older sisters, younger sisters, and now even daughters.

Susan arranged crackers and cheese on a small tray with fruit, an unexpected bit of hospitality in our hotel room.

"What do you speak on?" I asked. Susan had been referred to me by a mutual acquaintance. The only thing that I knew about her was that she didn't smoke.

"I'm a performance artist," Susan began.

"No! A performance artist? Why, performance art is my media, too!" I gasped.

What an incredible coincidence! Once considered preposterous within the art world, performance artists create theatrical performances that don't have dramatic plots; sometimes they are bizarre visual statements with political intent. Performance artists rarely surface as respectable women attending conventions for professional speakers, especially from southern communities. I studied this woman with her short, dark hair and six-foot frame, thinking she was an unlikely person to be a performance artist. Surely she has grandchildren.

The story swapping commenced. Susan, a feminist full of spunky wit, mesmerized me with her tales of costumed performances at national monuments. We discovered overlapping themes in our exorbitant antics. While I sported bright yellow butterfly wings, Susan fluttered about in lavender gossamer as a lunatic moth. My turquoise tail feathers fanned behind me as a peacock while Susan's ten-foot wingspan enabled her to dance the Dotty Matrix of the Dotty Birds. We both had served a version of "Breakfast in Bed." Our performances often explored our feelings about life's commonly accepted yet unjust rituals. Susan researched gynecological atrocities while I explored the painful loneliness of suicide victims. Our lighter performances involved children. We both collected hats.

As this particular convention continued, I found myself looking forward more to the breaks, times when I could rush back to the room and rest in another one of Susan's magical stories. Our sharing grew deeper as we described our joys and successes, the support from our logical husbands, and the expectations we have for our daughters.

Susan touched me with her spiritual search for a certain relative. "I retraced the footsteps of my aunt who studied in Paris in the nineteenth century," she began. "I found the school where she studied. I located the hotel where she stayed, and the very room where she lived. I even felt her presence."

Susan produced a set of brown postcards, recreations of ancient journal entries, with drawings of women dancing in their long skirts during an afternoon outing. Another postcard duplicated the ornate menu from an elegant cruise ship in 1824, and the graceful, spidery handwriting of a letter to her aunt. Packaged together in a black envelope, a rust-colored seal with gold letters implied the importance of such mementos.

"I produced these cards as a tribute to my Aunt Anna," explained Susan. "Would you like to have them?"

Honored, I accepted the treasure, tucking her stories permanently into my heart.

Susan sent me a photo collage for my birthday. She smiles at me from a place of honor over my computer printer, reminding me to be true to my artist nucleus. Someday, we will enjoy another retreat.

My most recent retreat took place in Highlands, North Carolina, with a friend from my old Florida life. As Jeanie and I rocked in caneback rockers on the mountaintop, we took in the sunset and caught up with each other's lives. Delighted to have a whole day together, we hiked a shady mountain trail, exploring our life histories while looking for wildlife. We discerned patterns in relationships as well as fresh bear tracks by the creek. We questioned the dangers faced by today's teenagers and cautiously tiptoed past a black snake coiled on a nearby branch. Inspired by Jeanie's willingness to try any new experience, I cooked for her, relishing her compliments as we dined on chicken marinated in fresh ginger and salad dressing, with mushrooms, peppers, and onions washed down with a cool Chardonnay. Jeanie urged me to read my stories to her and shared my dreams of facilitating women's retreats. I read aloud into the night until my eyes would no longer stay open.

During retreats like these, I feel the richness of the tapestry of life. My senses and my imagination overflow as we share our stories with each other. I find comfort, value, and wisdom in their presence, luxuriating in the soul connection of women who are willing to affirm each other.

More women than ever are seeking adventure trips with other women. Katie, a lover of nature, began selecting women's adventure retreats when she retired at the age of sixty-four.

"I need time just for me," she said. "On these trips, there are only eight to twelve women, and nature. That's all. No one else. We bond as women, and experience nature together as a personal and spiritual event. It moves me deeply."

In addition to her trip up the Amazon River, Katie canoed the Florida Everglades for ten days, surveyed the canyons around the Utah Green River, explored the Missouri River in the footsteps of Sacajawea, Lewis, and Clark, and then discovered the northern mystery of the Alagash River in Maine.

"In Maine, one of the women played her flute to a loon. They actually communicated back and forth. And when I saw a moose, chills swept over me."

Sometimes, retreats for volunteers or professional women result in an unexpected closeness. When I trained Girl Scout leaders in Florida, a weekend experience changed my life forever. The Council sent me to the beautiful national training center in the New York mountains to join thirty other women from around the country. For two-and-a-half days, women explored the socialization of our belief systems. We examined the subtle messages in media that stir the frustrations with our physical imperfection to a buying frenzy. Stereotypes and prejudices that have prevented women, especially minority women, from realizing their potential as productive individuals were uncovered. Common messages from adults, who socialize girls to be passive and helpless, were defined. We looked with new eyes to heroines in our past, unique individuals who insisted that they deserved a better life and then worked hard to realize their beliefs. The group learned communication skills that empower girls and women to think for themselves. It was as if a shroud had been lifted from my eyes forever.

Returning to Florida, I enlisted Pearl, a dynamic dean from a black university, to join me in presenting this experience to our volunteer trainers. The power and electricity of that weekend charged all of us. Some of the women shared from their souls, some from their hearts, while all of us remembered moments of crushed dreams. We examined our hopes and ambitions as we acquainted ourselves with women achievers in various fields of endeavors. Our awareness grew by leaps and bounds as we practiced the new communication skills we had just acquired. Taking time to play, we celebrated our free-spirited uniqueness as women. The night passed quickly as personal stories continued to unfold. The next day, our closing ceremony ended with hugs, tears, and soaring spirits ready to spread the profound wonder of empowerment to our girls back home.

I sometimes forget the value of taking time for myself, of being in the company of women removed from the demands of families and routines. We have so much wisdom, compassion, and encouragement to share with each other. For centuries women have gathered together to share ideas and to find strength and sanity within the framework of our lives. Today's hectic lifestyles and demanding schedules prevent us from receiving the wonderful nurturing that can revitalize and uplift our spirits. When will we learn to take advantage of the opportunities to congregate as women? The time is now.

Dinner Questions

❏ Where do you like to go to renew your Spirit?
❏ Who do you enjoy being with?

How to Turn A Financial Alligator into a Priceless Purse
Give Treasured Gifts and Incredible Parties on Any Budget

Poverty on both a personal and worldwide level is supported by our collective belief in scarcity.

— SHAKTI GAWAIN, *REFLECTIONS IN THE LIGHT*

The simple mystic knows that we need very little, yet we choose to encumber ourselves with luxuries and unnecessary clutter—alligator bait for debt. We also find ourselves running a time deficit as well, since we spend huge amounts of time acquiring these luxuries and this clutter by shopping, searching, and organizing, rather than living life to its fullest. How many pairs of shoes, CD players, tubes of lipstick, purses, televisions, videos, and software do we really need to feel at peace? To some extent, our checkbooks and credit cards reveal our values.

Straightening out finances is never as easy as our accountants tell us. Feelings get tangled up with finances so easily. I have yet to encounter a marriage where money was not an issue. Gender expectations as to who should provide what, children's comparisons with their friends, family patterns of guilt, worry, or miserly thrift, and arguments over personal spending all fan the flames of anger and jealousy in most marriages. For some couples, there are even issues over the paying of taxes: procrastination, integrity, denial, and anger toward the government.

Analyze how you personally respond to your finances. How do you actually feel about money, bills, checking accounts, and taxes? Are you lacking self-control when it comes to spending? Do you track every penny, review monthly records, and make decisions as to where to cut back? Do you run your life like a business, or have you chosen to remain ignorant when it comes to financial decisions? Do you depend upon your husband/boyfriend/father to "handle" all things financial?

Managing financial matters used to be considered the strict domain of men, but we can't cling to that division of labor any longer. More and more women enter the financial arena every year. Women are CPA's, investors, bankers, controllers, and business owners. I cheer them on from the bleachers, squirming as I acknowledge my own dependence on gender stereotypes. My excuse? My husband enjoys math.

I plead guilty to leaving all financial decisions to my husband. Numbers terrorize me. My checkbook never balances. My temptation to spend overtakes me like an addicted gambler in Las Vegas when I enter stores. Recently widowed women have no inkling of their financial situation. Newly divorced wives find themselves without retirement after twenty years of staying home with the kids at their husbands' request. I would be in the same exact financial boat with these women, even though my husband assures me not to worry. "I've got insurance. If I die, you'll be good for a year."

We unconsciously acquire attitudes about money from our parents. I understood my own helplessness, financial incompetence, and fear of failure when I explored family patterns in my journal. My father aspired to become a doctor, like his grandfather. His own dad, an electrician, saw no need for a college education and refused to encourage or support a college dream. Studying chemistry challenged my father to the point of changing majors. Later in life, we would discover that he struggled with attention deficit disorder, a contributor to feelings of incompetence. Although Daddy successfully completed his master's degree in hospital administration, his feelings of worthlessness haunted him. Anne Wilson Schaef says that men feel either one up or one down. My dad felt one down all the time. In spite of his reputation as a creative businessman in a growing hospital, Daddy felt inferior to the other successful professional people that surrounded him. He wanted us to be prosperous in life, yet he unconsciously taught us children to feel inferior to doctors, lawyers, and other successful people.

My mother came from a family of devoted ministers and missionaries. She unwittingly communicated to us that having money was sinful. Money belonged in world missions, period. People with money, big houses, expensive cars, and fur coats personified greed. They should have given their money to world missions instead, Mother implied. She related stories about growing up during the depression. Her father accepted chickens or goats as payment for ministering to the small church. Mother would assure me that if I didn't find a husband in college, I could attend seminary and meet a fine, young minister. I made up my mind early. No way on earth would I ever marry a minister and live on chickens and goats as income.

My parents rarely discussed money when I was growing up. Daddy passed up raises since he felt he didn't deserve them and the hospital couldn't afford them. Mother sewed our clothes. She made sure that my paltry allowance went to church and savings for college. My parsimonious upbringing was not all negative, however. My parents' thriftiness taught me invaluable lessons that I could have never learned had I been handed everything I wanted. My creativity seems to be at its peak when my pocketbook is the emptiest. What an incredible legacy!

I still wrestle with the financial alligator but I have made the decision not to let that particular alligator better me any longer. I have hired a coach to teach me accounting with technical programs. To this day, I celebrate when my checkbook balances.

The acquisition of financial alligators begins at birth with our parents' perceptions, which are then passed down to us. The maintenance of these alligators is perpetuated by societal expectations as well as our relationships with others and our mental state at any given time. Although it is tempting to chase after happiness bought with plastic cards, the wealth in life lies in relationships that we heal, nurture, and value. Only in that context can we experience our personal growth, our true wealth, and abiding love.

In the pages that follow, I recount three of many memorable experiences that probably would not have happened if I had been privileged as a free spender. Financial alligators are only dangerous if you choose to allow them to dominate your life. I discovered that the alligator of financial challenge withers in the face of celebration. Celebrating friends and family concentrates one's focus on that which matters most in life, which are rarely things that money can buy, and denies this alligator any power over one's spirit. Using creative and sometimes free resources, success in accomplishing this equilibrium depends on imagination.

Dinner Questions

❑ How did your parents feel about money?
❑ What unconscious messages did they teach you about self worth, spending, and saving?

P.S. By the way, people change. My mother still gives generously to world missions, but she now drives a Cadillac!

The Flat-Broke Party

That was the best time of my life,
and only now that it has gone from me
forever— only now do I realize it.

— NATALIE GINZBURG, *THE LITTLE VIRTUES*

"I can never go anywhere, do anything, or have any fun. It's not fair!" I whined at fourteen.

"Throw a party!" was my clever mother's surprise suggestion.

"But Mom! I'm flat broke!" I reminded her.

"So, make that the theme!"

Mother knew how to hook my interest. My imagination raced with ideas as we concocted an event my friends and neighborhood would never forget. Invitations were scribbled on strips of torn newspaper with a black marker.

"Dress in rags," I instructed.

As baby boomers, we heard horror stories of the depression from our parents. At this time in my life, I had no such image of financial despair to compare to that. The era of homelessness had not yet infected our cities. Afternoon movies occasionally featured stories of hobos riding on trains but that was as close as I ever got to people who were truly without. This party idea captured my innocent imagination.

To decorate, I removed the furniture from the family living room. I stuck plastic wrap on the wall and drew a temporary crack with Magic

Marker. A single light bulb suspended from the ceiling declared the room a poverty zone. Scattered newspapers covered the floor. My confused but obliging guests arrived in torn shirts, ripped pants, and shoes held together with duct tape. One bedraggled guest even penciled in an unshaven beard, changing her gender with her appearance.

"I'm so glad y'all could come," I drawled humbly, "but since I'm flat broke, I hope you don't mind scroungin' around for some party food."

"You mean it's hidden?" a male guest asked, eagerly looking around, hoping to get a head start on a scavenger hunt.

"No, it's not hidden," I mischievously explained. "You have to *beg* for it from the neighbors. But don't worry, they're really nice and they have great food."

My guests stood glued to the floor, their eyes wide with disbelief.

"Beg!" cried Pam, "You're not serious!"

"Yes, I am," I hustled the kids toward the door. "Pam, you, Wilson, and Norma will take this street. Dorcas, you and Edith and Mike will take the houses around the corner, and Beth, you, Charles, and Susan will take the street beyond the corner. You only have thirty minutes so you better get started or we won't eat."

Flabbergasted, the three bands of young hobos took the paper grocery bags I handed them and stumbled out the door, headed in their respective directions. Jumping around the empty living room, exploding with laughter, I spied on my friends through the front window. I had forewarned the neighbors, but as part of the master plan, I had failed to divulge the fact to my friends. Little did I know that the neighbors themselves savored the idea of being approached by a bunch of shy kids timidly asking for handouts. They had prepared with gusto.

The raggedy revelers returned an hour later, excited about their loot, booty that exceeded my wildest expectations. Unloading their goods on the kitchen table, they laughingly interrupted each other in their haste to describe each adventure.

"This one lady made us sweep her porch first!" Edith grinned. "Then, she gave us left-over fried chicken bones!"

"But she gave us a can of green beans, too," added Mike.

"The lady we visited gave us chocolate chip cookies!" exclaimed Susan. "Right out of the oven, still warm!" She popped one into her mouth.

"We got a sack of candy from the lady across the street," chimed Beth, "and one chicken drumstick from the house on the end."

"Hey, you guys, that's nothing. Look at this!" Wilson hoisted his bag, heavy with beautiful produce, onto the table. "But you won't believe what we had to go through to get this!"

Wilson and his team of two girls had knocked on the door of Mr. and Mrs. Byler, an elderly couple living in a large, new home. Childless, the Bylers stayed to themselves, tending their garden that they composted, weeded, and pruned. I figured them to be people who didn't know how to relate to kids, polite, but having nothing in common with us. Or so I thought.

"Mr. Byler made us come in!" exclaimed Wilson. "Said we had to hear his bad luck story before he would give us anything." Strange, I thought to myself. They had never invited me inside! "We followed him into the kitchen where this old lady sat at the table crying. They were wearing old, dirty, ragged clothes." Their garden clothes, I figured.

Wilson continued his saga as I listened, amazed. "'We've just lost everything,'" Wilson imitated Mrs. Byler in a high, sniffling voice. "'You see, we only take *care* of this house. Mr. Byler is a gardener and a butler. I am a scullery maid.' Then she blew her nose, like this," Wilson imitated a loud honking noise.

Wilson switched to Mr. Byler's voice, "'My daddy left me filthy rich. Filthy rich,'" Wilson repeated for emphasis. "'Then the stock market crashed and I lost everything.'"

"And a burglar stole Mrs.Byler's jewels and kidnaped their children," Norma jumped in to continue the story as if it were juicy gossip. "They never found the diamonds or the babies."

"Then she turned my head and inspected my nose!" Pam's eyes flashed. A look of fake fear clouded her face. "She said I looked like one of her children! She had me worried, for a minute."

Wilson retrieved the story. "They work for a few dollars a week, just to live in the basement and eat table scraps. Mr. Byler actually cried when he told us that."

"Their masters are away on vacation, so they have some vegetables to spare. Then they thanked us for listening, and loaded us up with all of this," Norma finished. She dumped out the contents all over the kitchen table.

We stared in amazement at the fresh lettuce, carrots, peppers, and tomatoes that tumbled from the sack—the makings for a spectacular salad.

Proud of our hard-earned loot, we consumed it all. My guests even insisted on opening the cans of green beans. We washed it all down with Kool-Aid served from a new garbage can while rehashing our adventures, emphasizing new details and descriptions of our neighborly patrons.

This unique opportunity, born out of lack of money, turned into far more than either my mother or I could have predicted. I don't know who relished the party more, the hobo kids or the neighbors. The theme was based on being financially poor, but I realized that I was not just flat broke money-wise but also in my relationship with my elderly neighbors. As I think back, I regret not getting to know the Bylers better. In my own teenage shyness, I missed the opportunity to develop a relationship with imaginative, fun-loving people who became the hit of a teenage party.

Dinner Questions

❑ When have your neighbors surprised you with an adventure?

❑ Did you ever think growing up that your family didn't have enough money?

Seducing a Sailor

*A man falls in love through his eyes, a
woman through her imagination, and then they
both speak of it as an affair of "the heart."*

— HELEN ROWLAND, *A GUIDE TO MEN*

My first Christmas with Robert demanded resourcefulness. After combining our debts from the misfortunes of our former lives, we found ourselves struggling on a stringent budget. New love, however, brings a wealth of its own. We were determined to celebrate this special holiday in spite of our lack of extra resources.

We went searching for a Christmas tree, but were quickly discouraged by the expensive lots manned by enterprising vendors. We finally stumbled into a lot empty of its Canadian pines, save one small, scruffy tree languishing in the corner. In spite of the crooked trunk and branches on only one side, we forked out three dollars and loaded it into our car. Using bits of felt, sequins, and gold rickrack scrounged from my sewing box, I made ornaments for an effective transformation. We had achieved our first Christmas tree as a couple.

Affording gifts for each other presented another challenge. Robert had his own resourceful outlet for generating spending money. He mysteriously disappeared to a weekend poker game with his Army friends. He didn't play often, but when he did, he rarely lost. I knew from his cocky manner that he had been successful. I had to create my gifts solely from imagination. I searched old magazines for ideas. Aha! A travel magazine featured a picture of a geisha enticing visitors to Japan. I grabbed my scissors.

On Christmas Day, Robert's eyes danced with glee as he presented me with a pile of gifts. "For my sweetheart," he said with a satisfied kiss.

Overwhelmed, I gingerly removed the wrappings, revealing a set of new cookware and a tiny, red satin bikini nightie trimmed in marabou feathers. Function and fantasy, I thought to myself.

"I love the cookware," I kissed my husband. We both knew the nightie was purchased mainly for Robert's pleasure.

"Here," I handed Robert a rolled up parchment, tied with a red ribbon.

He slipped off the ribbon, and unrolled the handmade document.

"Ohhh!" He exclaimed enthusiastically as he began to read aloud. "You are invited to spend an evening with Madame Dragonfly, the famous Geisha. You must give notice one week in advance."

Two weeks later, Robert gave notice.

At a local consignment store, I discovered a turquoise satin robe with a colorful dragon on the back and decorative scrolling designs on the front. Oriental, yes; Japanese, not exactly. I sewed glass beads and rhinestones on the dragon. A big sash around the waist with a fan stuck in it, and I was all set. Throughout my career as an entertainer, I had accumulated several wigs. I selected a black, Gibson Girl upswept 'do and searched for silk flowers to adorn it.

The day of our soirée, I busied myself with details. Our apartment easily converted to a Japanese house of entertainment after I plopped the sofa cushions onto the floor around the coffee table. A treasured tape of Japanese nightclub music played softly in the background. Candles lent a flickering glow. Ramen noodles in a tasty broth waited on the stove. I stuck a Chinese fan from my grandmother in the front of my sash and added a chopstick to the silk iris in my hair. I applied pale makeup and outlined a tiny red heart-shaped mouth.

An urgent knock on the door announced Robert's arrival. His eyes grew wide with anticipation when I cracked the door. Robert, a recruiter for the Army, wore his khaki fatigues.

"Are you American sailor?" I inquired in a high soft voice, affecting a lilting Asian accent.

"No, ma'am, I'm in the Army," he replied.

"So, sorry…I only take sailors." I began to shut the door.

"I'm a sailor, I'm a sailor!" He quickly changed sides. I let him in, a kid in a candy store. He reached up to touch my sash.

"Oh, NO!" I slapped him with my fan. "We go slow!"

He jumped to attention. Putty in my hands from here on.

Our evening began with Robert soaking in a hot bath while I faked a fan dance.

"First I dance with robe ON!" I teased. The bathroom steamed up quickly as I coquettishly fluttered the fan.

Usually a steak and potatoes man, Robert never complained about the bowls of noodles in broth that sufficed for supper.

"I feed you," I directed. "Sit down."

The noodles dangled from my chopsticks as I attempted to put them in his open mouth. We giggled uncontrollably throughout dinner as noodles slid all over his chest. Without going into further details, suffice it to say that, to Robert, this was one gift worth far more than money could buy.

When the money alligator comes knocking at our door, we often let him in and watch him devour our most precious celebrations of the heart simply because we cannot conceive of celebrating without money. We fail to look into our inner resources and recognize what true gifts we really have to offer to each other; gifts that no amount of money can buy. For me, my gift to Robert was my love for him, all young and fresh and new. Young romance is itself one of life's richest gifts. We can play with abandon, and give freely without holding back. Money and maturity can't replace those early moments of pure emotional prosperity.

Dinner Questions

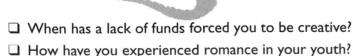

- ❑ When has a lack of funds forced you to be creative?
- ❑ How have you experienced romance in your youth?

Sara's Pleasure Lunch

*It isn't the great big pleasures that count the most,
it's making a great deal out of the little ones.*

— JEAN WEBSTER, *DADDY LONGLEGS*

My friend, Sara, deserved a wonderful birthday. Sara is one of those people who relish her birthday, anticipating hers weeks in advance. She alerted her family with a birthday list on the refrigerator suggesting numerous ways to appease her heart's desire. This list went from the sublime to the ridiculous, with suggestions ranging from a compact CD player or a homemade birthday card to an elephant ride in New Delhi or breakfast with Robert Redford.

Confined with two young children at home and limited to a shoe-string budget, I pondered my challenge. How could my gift be one of a kind, a priceless present worthy of my friend? To provide Sara with fodder for her favorite pastime, storytelling, I decided to serve her lunch with an unforgettable twist. I knew *I* would love it as well since Sara's generous way and easy laugh made her fun to entertain. Always bringing treats and little gifts for others, she definitely savored the art of surprise.

I assessed my available resources like a card player studies her hand. A close neighbor had suspended a giant new hammock between two shade trees in her backyard, a setting as lush as Tahiti with rich green foliage, exotic plants, and a swimming pool. The red geraniums, cheerful daisies, and vibrant clusters of hot pink impatiens seduced the senses with luxurious color. Perfect weather with an ideal temperature enhanced by a slight breeze coupled with the children's afternoon naptime added to my advantage.

My trump card consisted of a raunchy fantasy book for women, a bizarre collection of erotica written by a group of older women in California. The authors, who were all mothers and grandmothers, gathered monthly bringing sensuous food for feasting while sharing their written fantasies about real women in normal life settings. They composed their stories while waiting at soccer practice, piano lessons, and school functions. They imagined scenarios charged with sexual chemistry between their everyday heroines and the gardener, the soccer coach, or the lifeguard. Their stories of succulent passion and ripe desire, peppered with raucous humor and sweet surprises, enticed the reader to enjoy sexual salads of titillating imagery. I knew I possessed a full house, a winning combination for her birthday. I fine-tuned the details, energized with excitement and satisfaction as I imagined Sara's delight on her big day.

Sara arrived on time, her eyes shining as she suspected an adventure about to unfold. She accepted a blindfold without resistance, and followed me cautiously. I led her next door, through the big wooden gate, around the pool and between the fragrant, flowering shrubs. Sara sunk into the hammock as I adjusted headphones and turned on a cassette tape of Handel's "Water Music." Removing her blindfold, I left her rocking like a baby in the cradle of paradise. Phase 1 completed.

My five-year-old daughter retrieved Sara when lunch was ready. An animated, talkative child, Simone adored Sara. The child provided most of the conversation as I served marinated chicken, stir-fried vegetables, and sesame spinach salad on our finest china. I knew that business people, like Sara, who are frantically on the run meeting deadlines, appreciate any home cooked meal prepared just for them. Phase 2 completed.

Phase 3 was my pièce de resistance, but required that I initiate naptime for my children. After serving Sara dessert, a rich, chocolate mousse with whipped topping, I retrieved "The Book." I read aloud to Sara, stressing physical descriptions with exaggerated inflection and increasing my pace as the pursuit of lustful love grew hotter.

In fits of laughter, we related our own histories of unrequited lust and deep secrets of female yearning. We professed private admiration for the melting eyes of a local librarian, the sexy yet gentle hands of

Sara's veterinarian, and the seductively smooth manners of the grocery store butcher who always aimed to please. We created our own scenarios of risqué possibilities amidst library archives, canine kennels, and the supermarket meat cooler, reliving the unabashed delight of two schoolgirls telling naughty secrets. But alas, our two-hour escapade came to an end. Sara rushed off to her next appointment and I responded to whimpering children waking up from afternoon naps.

Women cherish nurturing. They appreciate peaceful, relaxed moments as offered by the sensual hammock. They savor simple yet beautiful meals served with elegance. For some women, the idea of sharing sexual thoughts would violate deeply personal secrets, hidden from the universe in a carefully guarded part of the psyche. For others, it is just fun, silly girltalk, spiced with taboos imposed by our mothers. In some cultures women openly share with each other stories of their marriage beds, explaining and demonstrating sexual positions so as to teach their daughters. Most women raised in my white, middle-class culture are lucky if their mothers inform them where babies come from, and wouldn't be caught dead talking about sexual pleasure. Regardless, to laugh about our own humanness together in a moment of female bonding results in a special validation while energizing our own sensuality. This was my gift to Sara —the same as the gift experienced by the mothers in Berkley who had the nerve to write those stories.

Dinner Questions

- ❑ When do you treat yourself with time for girl talk?
- ❑ How have you created an unforgettable birthday for a girlfriend?

Alligators in the Workplace:
Learning to Wrestle in a Different Swamp

*The question was not how to get a job, but
how to live by such jobs as I could get.*

— DOROTHY M. RICHARDSON, *THE LONG DAY*

At least twenty different kinds of alligators and crocodiles exist in the world, each distinctive according to their varied environments around the globe. Some jump high in the air, others run fast chasing their prey, still others swim in the ocean. The most deadly of all these reptiles is the saltwater crocodile. That is, of course, in the animal kingdom. For me, the most fearsome kind of alligators lurks in the workplace. These alligators are disguised as bosses with hidden agendas, destructive co-workers, and employers with uncontrolled sexual energy.

Since my mother's work experience consisted of a few years in a conservative church before she committed to working full-time as a mother, she was unable to give me a list of do's and don'ts in the workplace. I, like most women my age, had few examples of career women to base my opinions on, since most women who had a financial choice did not work and those that didn't have a choice worked in low-paying, low-status jobs. Television, though mostly representing adult women as young, non-working wives or stay-at-home moms, did supply my early impressions of professional women in shows like *My Little Margie* and *Our Miss Brooks*. Lucille Ball joined their ranks much later, after she was no longer married to Ricky, who would have never let her have a career. These actresses represented warm-hearted women who solved problems by conniving against older male decision-making superiors while enjoying the attention of handsome men passing through their particular series. Lucille Ball could have hardly been considered a role model for a young girl with aspirations for a real career.

Since my father subconsciously taught me to fear professionals, and my mother unwittingly taught me to fear men, I began my career afraid to speak up for myself, too intimidated to confront a co-worker or a boss, and uneasy about correcting support staff. Authority figures reminded me of my father and my grade school teachers, prohibiting me from establishing an adult relationship with them. I continued to feel as if I should follow my childhood authority figures' advice. "Do as you're told and don't talk back."

One of my first bosses, a strong, dynamic woman, elicited the fear of God in me. I hid in the bathroom, turned down a hallway, or remembered an urgent phone call to return whenever I saw her coming. I still remember the heat from my reddening face when she confronted me about my allusiveness.

With time, I gained experience, developed great relationships with many of my bosses and co-workers, and loved the challenges of meeting goals in my jobs. But I have never learned how to handle hidden agendas and destructive, dysfunctional people. The aging process has relieved me of encounters flavored with the dangerous sexual energy that permeated my younger workdays. Although no longer a problem for me, I worry about the inevitable potholes that await my daughter. I think back to the years of stumbling around, making mistakes, stepping into hidden traps, and getting my feelings hurt while withdrawing to the safety of my office or worse, the bathroom. I marvel how my young daughter-in-law manages her role as an army captain with such apparent ease. I envy the young women emerging from school armed with MBA's and a clear understanding of their own career path, corporate cultures, and human dynamics. I had no guidance, no role models, and no support systems when I embarked on my career thirty-some years ago. That's all different now, as women are breaking into previously forbidden careers in record numbers. They are forming network systems of support and mentoring, both in formal and informal venues. However, all the education and support in the world cannot fully prepare one for the existence of hidden agendas, the presence of dysfunctional people, and the danger of uncontrolled sexual energy.

One thing I have noticed about many other working women, myself included: we tend to wear our feelings on our sleeves in the workplace. In order to attain any level of comfort, we try to recreate a semblance of "family" among co-workers. We seek a friend and confidante in our fellow employees; we long for a close, trusting relationship with the boss. We expect to find an active support system that acknowledges and rewards us for our hard work. But these are all unreal expectations of the real workplace. I think back to the times when I quit a job because I felt disgusted, depressed, or just fed up, emotions having little to do with whether or not I was good at the job or I liked what I was doing professionally. In every case I was driven from a job I enjoyed by a fellow co-worker or a boss. I would tell myself that I didn't deserve being treated that way, and that I could do better.

Repeatedly, I walked away from big salaries, trappings of prestige, and opportunities I was emotionally incapable of pursuing. Each time I left, I felt relieved. I celebrated as if a weight had been lifted, though when the dust settled and I was once again jobless, I felt as though I had failed to succeed. I am just now learning that, as women, we must learn to work differently and have different expectations of our work.

I have interviewed many powerful women in business who were all too willing to share their secrets of success with other women. Women who succeed in business learn to utilize excellent communication skills. They know they must state the facts and have clear expectations before asking for compliance from their employees. They draw firm boundaries with both subordinates and employers, and maintain strong personal policies that prevent awkward or compromising situations. Successful women use specific proactive strategies for getting along with people instead of taking everything personally and avoiding situations of conflict. They position themselves for opportunity and advancement, tooting their own horns when necessary, and cultivating advocates who will do the same for them. This new breed of females negotiates their own raises with the same calculated precision as their business deals. They delegate whenever possible and seek out specialists to help them make decisions.

Women must also come to grips with the price of success. They must understand that for every gain in business there may be a loss in family time. These productive working moms know they will miss ball games, school parties, and bedtime stories. They pass up the opportunity to lead the Scout troop, teach Sunday School, or make class cupcakes, opportunities which make them active participants in their children's lives, in favor of pursuing their career goals. This is not an easy decision to make; it is never an easy sacrifice.

Alligators in the workplace will never go away. If anything, the age of technology has increased the speed and subtleness of attacks. The drive for power remains; destructive, dysfunctional people make lives miserable; and women continue to struggle with sexual energy. Mentors, training that empowers, and the increase of successful women role models brings new wrestling skills for dealing with these workplace alligators. In the meantime, I see a terrific therapist.

Dinner Questions

❑ How do you let the workplace affect your mental well-being?

❑ Where do you learn strategies for dealing with difficult people and the politics of business?

Hidden Agendas

The more hidden the venom,
the more dangerous it is.

— MARGUERITE DE VALOIS, *IN "FRENCH*
WIT AND WISDOM"

Sometimes, even when we do our jobs well, we are unable to blow the whistle on unethical business practices. How can we work with a sense of pride and accomplishment when circumstances are laced with dishonest politics?

"Frustration, continual frustration!" my government clients exclaim with exasperation. "Our hands are tied. We can't assure our customers of a quality service when we are required to work with a dishonest vendor who gouges them for expenses, uses shoddy materials, and hires workers who take advantage of them without hesitation. We have no power to determine how the vendor is chosen. There are political kickbacks. Our clients suffer and we can do nothing about it."

Hearing their anger, I had no idea how to help. This is not an unfamiliar scenario in the workplace. Another friend, Mary, who works for a large business, discovered how her company mishandles thousands of dollars of expenses for a client company. Thinking she was doing the client a service, she mentioned her discovery to a supervisor.

"Forget what you know!" the threat from above came loud and clear.

During a sales call to another company in Florida, an enthusiastic meeting planner impressed me with her determination to achieve a high attendance goal for an upcoming meeting.

"I organize conferences for our salespeople," she explained. "If I reach my goal, the president promised to buy me a fur coat!"

Admiring the coat featured in a picture taped on the wall, I envied her incentive.

"I'm going to reach that goal, too," she announced confidently, "in fact I'm almost there."

And reach that goal she did. Instead of receiving the coat, however, she received walking papers, with a promise of severance pay only if she kept her mouth shut—the company's way of keeping new blood in a burnout job. Hidden agendas can come in the form of threats communicated by subtle or not so subtle means, enforcing the upper echelon politics of power and greed.

Not necessarily a gender issue, the hidden agenda is a workplace issue that many of us simply can't handle. Even the manipulative prowess of television's *My Little Margie* doesn't come close to the cutthroat deals and personal threats made regularly in today's workplace.

For a short period of time, I trained laid-off employees as they prepared to re-enter the marketplace. It broke my heart to hear the stories of faithful employees just months from retirement, some still celebrating from a recent raise, only to be escorted to their cars the following week, the company doors locked behind them.

Occasionally employees themselves foster hidden agendas. One disgruntled employee plotted secretly with former employees to develop a lawsuit against her boss. Twisting information, fanning fires of racial unrest, misinterpreting fragments of conversations, she triumphantly "got even" for being reprimanded. A competent non-profit executive dedicated to building community race relations paid dearly for crossing the path of this vengeful woman.

What is the answer? Or is there one? People are always going to be afraid of losing their jobs. Layoffs seem to be increasing by the day. As an entrepreneur, I never miss that aspect of the workplace. I am encouraged to hear of companies who are committed to honest, open communications with their employees. Recently I attended a program at Wake Forest University where Mary Ellen Sheets and her daughter told their own story of building a successful business, Two Men and a Truck, International.

"We treat everyone the same," exuded Melanie Bergeron, the daughter-turned-president. "We set rules and have high standards, and terminate agreements that aren't kept. We know that all of us together are smarter than one of us alone. We believe in empowerment. When Mother hired me, she gave me complete empowerment."

Mary Ellen and Melanie's presentation left me dreaming of possibilities for women to run businesses with integrity, empowerment, and high standards. We are all challenged to dream of women who might possibly change the face of the workplace by importing new standards and new practices that don't tolerate hidden agendas and don't reward people who employ them.

Dinner Questions

❑ When have you been aware of shady dealings in the workplace?

❑ Who were the victims?

❑ What women business owners have inspired you with their commitment to ethics?

Destructive, Dysfunctional People

*Cruelty, like every other vice, requires no motive
outside itself; it only requires opportunity.*

— GEORGE ELIOT, *SCENES OF
CLERICAL LIFE*

Avoiding alligators in the workplace takes great skill and concentration, and being familiar with the territory is necessary in order to avoid bumping into one. A new employee does not have that advantage because it takes a while to feel comfortable in the unfamiliar work environment. In addition to the job description, there are new procedures, new terms, new equipment to master, and always, whose toes NOT to step on. The number one reason that people leave a job is because they can't get along with someone else in the company. Every workplace contains a mix of personalities with different ideas of how to get things done. Conflicts and disagreements are inevitable. Fortunately, good employee training can teach us how to wrestle with alligators that inevitably arise in nearly every work situation.

Alligators have been around since the age of the dinosaurs—huge, mega creatures that were even more voracious than they are now. These dinosaur-aged alligators hunted their prey, hapless gentle plant eaters, in much the same way as they do today, only they were much bigger, much faster, and much more destructive in the Jurassic age.

The dinosaur alligator, the dysfunctional person who thrives on destroying the self-esteem, productivity, and sometimes even the reputation of others in the organization, is often the deadliest alligator in the workplace. This person secretly plots ways to sabotage projects or individual successes, maintaining a veneer of innocent compliance that can fool even the most experienced boss, at least for a while. For women who value a safe environment where friendships can abound, dinosaur alligators in the workplace can be lethal. These people infect the whole territory with their neurotic negativity. There are emotionally dysfunctional people in every walk of life, on every street corner, and in every crowd.

The Dinosaur Alligator that I worked with, I'll call her "Dina," targeted enthusiastic, eager professional women who loved their jobs. While Dina knew ways to make all of us miserable, she typically stalked her victims individually, framing them to appear as if they were dishonest thieves, incompetent managers, or sloppy workers with poor judgment. Dealing with Dina was practically impossible because all standard techniques for working with difficult people systematically failed. Behavioral strategies didn't work with Dina; being nice didn't work with Dina; avoidance didn't work with Dina; and honest conversation didn't work with Dina.

One by one, my aspiring professional co-workers disappeared. The reasons for their dismissals always astounded me.

"But she couldn't have stolen the money!" I cried in disbelief.

"You may not believe it, but we have proof," came the suspicious but indisputable reply.

Dina never spoke to me personally. She refused to return my wave in the parking lot, nor did she enter into conversation at office parties. She left accusatory notes scribbled in red ink in my mailbox, scolding me for leaving someone else's mess in the conference room, for not cleaning up someone else's trash in the kitchen, or for parking in someone else's parking place. She left threatening notes on the fragile, frequently non-functioning copier. She scowled in irritation whenever the paper jammed, forcing me to wait helplessly for her to come rescue me since she deemed herself the only one capable of removing the offending paper. She delayed paychecks and held back my use of support staff without explanation. I became paranoid at work.

Unexplained mysteries incriminating fellow office mates continued to unfold as another outgoing professional woman was fired. Important computer files were enigmatically destroyed. A deep scratch, obviously gouged by a set of keys, the entire length of the vehicle, marred a new car of yet another co-worker. Dark, heavy clouds seemed to settle over our office space. I dreaded going to work.

Should I leave a job that I loved and customers that I enjoyed serving just because this woman was determined to make my life miserable? I weighed my situation seriously; there did not seem to be an easy solution that did not involve unemployment or death, either hers or mine.

Fortunately, fate smiled upon me, and saved me from experiencing either catastrophic outcome. Dina finally did herself in after directing her caustic criticism to the wrong person. The executive director herself had become Dina's target. The day our Dinosaur Alligator lost her job, the dark clouds magically lifted. I will never forget the relief and the instant surge in productivity in our office, as our enthusiasm for our mission once more became the driving force in the organization. Looking back, I am so grateful that I stuck it out. The opportunities and job success that I would have sacrificed by leaving weren't worth it, though in the short run, it seemed to be an even trade-off.

Sometimes the Dinosaur Alligator in my life wins. Each time I have to ask myself the same questions: Can I use strategies to survive in this environment? Can a professional friend in another organization advise me as to how to deal with this? Can I build up support systems in other areas to keep my self-esteem high? If all the answers to these questions come up "No," then I ask myself a different question: Can I arrange to be moved to another department? Do I need to look for another job?

I don't always know when to ask these questions of myself. One time I needed an outside friend to confront me as I stubbornly held on to another negative work situation. Working longer and longer hours as the situation deteriorated, I had started to let the destructive Dinosaur Alligator affect my well-being at home. As my family reacted to my stress, arguments and tears increased. Often, I threw up after breakfast, unable to calm my nervous stomach before facing work each morning. The intimidation I experienced at work was definitely beginning to affect my personality.

"Ana, what is happening to you?" demanded Shary, "I've never seen you like this!"

Her observation was totally correct. I knew no one had the right to rob me of my own personality and chip away at my spirit, much less destroy my relationships with my family. I left the job. Sometimes we need to be reminded when to let go of a job, a husband, a nagging parent, or even a friend. We must value ourselves and take whatever steps are necessary to preserve that which we value.

That painful situation became a launching point in my life. After taking three months off to heal myself with meditation, exercise, and a healthy diet, the ideas began to flow.

"*It's time to speak*," my inner voice encouraged me.

Me? Speak? To whom? About what? I asked myself incredulously.

"*Trust me*," the inner voice responded.

Two days later, the phone rang.

"Ana, it's us! Your church in Florida! We have a plane ticket and a check for you if you could come and speak to us!"

My new career began. Maybe the Dinosaur Alligator didn't win, after all.

Dinner Questions

❑ How have you wrestled with Dinosaur Alligators?
❑ How do you create support systems in the workplace?

Uncontrolled Sexual Energy

The only women who don't believe that sexual harassment is a real problem in this country are women who have never been in the workplace.

— CYNTHIA HEIMEL, *GET YOUR TONGUE OUT OF MY MOUTH, I'M KISSING YOU GOODBYE!*

Alligators travel long distances to fulfill the mating urge. Unfortunately, so do humans. The workplace offers lustful alligators at every turn for the unsuspecting career woman, particularly one who happens to be young and attractive. Far from helpless, a woman can train herself to recognize these alligators in men's clothing and learn techniques to wrestle them to the ground and render them harmless. This type of wrestling could use a course not taught at most high schools or universities. Imagine the outline for an effective course on dealing with uncontrolled sexual energy in the workplace:

Sexual Politics 101: How to Stay out of Trouble on the Career Path

- How to handle men who stand in your office door and stare at your breasts
- What to say to the married business owner who insists on walking you to your car

- The peril of wine or mixed drinks at lunch (or other business engagements)
- What to do when a big opportunity depends on a sexual favor
- The danger of business mixed with flirtation
- Hazards of jealous co-workers, ex-girlfriends, and spouses
- How to handle your own burning desire in an appropriate way

How do young career women acquire these workplace survival skills without having to learn the hard way—through experience? There may not be a formal course such as the one outlined above, but every woman should arm herself with knowledge of the laws protecting her as an employee and her company's written policies regarding employee relationships and harassment. She should read some of the numerous articles published on the subject, and seek further help through books specifically written to advise women in the workplace. Dealing with sexual situations is almost always included as an important topic. Finally, a woman entering the workplace should talk with other women about how they have managed to fend off uninvited advances and to avoid a full-blown harassment situation.

Even if you enter your job fully equipped to do battle with the opposite sex at work, sexual politics, power, loneliness, and flattering attention often muddies a woman's judgment, as does alcohol. We expect a certain amount of sexual aggression from male bosses; the entertainment industry suggests this is a natural part of how things should be. When we are twenty-something, we think we know it all, and we believe office sex will never hurt us. I still didn't know it all at thirty-something! Looking back, I can't believe how naïve I was!

One of my first jobs after leaving the education profession was as a sales representative for a big hotel. I really wanted to fit in to this glamorous job, and appreciated it when the sales director coached me for my interview with the hotel owner.

"He'll want to know what you drink. Tell him whiskey sours," she replied knowledgeably. I sat before her, young and eager, admiring the way she talked, the way she moved, the way she looked. The hand she smoked her cigarette with sported an enormous diamond ring, and I thought, sitting there, that she was definitely one of the most glamorous women I had ever seen. "Smile a lot," she continued, "tell him you like to entertain."

The sales director certainly knew her boss. Although my drinking experience was limited to wine consumed while touring Europe and a little beer, I lied as instructed, smiled like a beauty queen, and found myself employed.

The hotel sales department consisted of the married director and her single assistant. Together, they booked rooms and meetings for area businesses and entertained during "happy hour" on Friday nights. A willing student, I attentively watched and listened so that I could become part of this "glamorous" business. Apparently, it consisted mainly of flirting. While the sales director ran the show, the assistant managed the meeting functions, and dated men she met through the job. Lunches could be scheduled at the property or as the guest of a client. I had been hired to conduct sales calls off property. It didn't take me long to find myself in over my head.

As I flirted my way through business calls, I found it harder and harder to know when to draw the line. Offers for dates poured in. I quickly learned that the absence of a wedding ring didn't mean a thing in the business world. I grew confused as to whom I could date and whom I should not date. If my lunch with a client included drinking, wouldn't it be okay to drink a glass of wine with him? I couldn't understand why a client would take me to a restaurant that featured a fashion show that only modeled revealing lingerie.

I became very successful, even in my daily dilemmas regarding possible sexual situations. But when I would return to the hotel, I began to detect a cool attitude in the office towards me, one easily detectable as jealousy.

That just doesn't make sense, I thought to myself. I am doing exactly what she taught me to do! I decided that this, too, was part of the job.

Surprises occurred constantly. One of the clients I enjoyed the most, Ray, had impressed me as a funny yet respectable man. His genteel manners and professional countenance assured me that we had a nice, safe, business relationship, or so I thought. It flattered me when Ray invited me to have dinner with him and his boss from out of town. Little did I know that their plan included for the boss to sleep with me at my place! Fortunately for me, Ray's boss passed out, giving me an escape from an unwanted predicament.

One afternoon, during a pouring rain that caused hotel traffic to slow to a standstill, I had the privilege of joining in some "girl fun." I returned from lunch to find the hotel sales director and her assistant scheming together like schoolgirls planning a prank. To my surprise, they decided to let me in on their secret, encouraging me to innocently participate in another form of sexual harassment, only this time the tables were turned. It would be women harassing men.

"Wanna have some fun?" the director invited me to join them with a naughty look.

"Sure," I replied, eager to join in an activity that might promote office camaraderie.

The assistant explained the plot. "*Playgirl* has printed a list of men all over the country who will accept a long distance call from sexy women," she giggled. "We're going to call some of them."

The assistant and I stuffed hotel washcloths in our mouths to smother our giggles while the sales director began calling numbers on another extension. Asking for the men listed in the magazine, she found them eager to accept the calls. Each time, we reached a business, contacted the party, and patiently waited while he shut his door.

"John," cooed my associate in crime, "this is Janet, one of your *Playgirl* callers," she began. "Tell me about yourself."

"Just a minute, I'll be right back," a man's anxious voice replied.

We could hear him close his office door.

"Okay, Janet," the man's voice recommenced in an excited tone. "Tell me what you look like."

Of course, our hotel sales director painted a vivid picture of her imaginary persona, nothing like her actual physical description. We could hear John breathing heavily. After a little teasing, "Janet" ended the conversation.

"Now, I'll call you tomorrow, at one o'clock, you hear? Don't schedule any appointments. You'd better be sitting there right by the phone!" She hung up to our peals of laughter.

I couldn't believe my ears! My boss, on company time, titillating a CPA she didn't know on his company's phone bill, just to pass the time!

In most of the instances, however, I found myself to be the victim of misleading come-ons. I try to forget those encounters, but a few still make me laugh. A year later, after one rather strange business lunch, my host requested permission to show me a package in his car. Asking for my strictest confidence, he pulled out a paper bag from the back seat.

"Look in there," he ordered.

A dress, stockings, and large high heels. His high heels. While I struggled for my composure and concentrated on maintaining a poker face, my luncheon host pulled out another item. His album of photographs!

"I think I need to get back to the office," I added, hurriedly.

To this day I have no clue what his purpose was in showing me his bizarre personal effects.

To top that occasion, my boss from a large company ended our first official day with a meeting, and an offer to drive me to my car parked in the parking lot on the other side of the company. By all accounts, he was a nice man, talented, and prestigious within the company, so I was completely surprised when he asked for my personal opinion as he pulled to stop next to my car.

"Regarding what?" I asked naively, feeling flattered about the importance of my new job.

"This," he replied, pulling out his male organ. "Is it too small?" he asked meekly.

I tried not to act shocked.

"It's just fine," I replied, as if I were an expert on the subject. "Well, good night!" I mumbled in one breath before jumping out of his car.

We never referred to that incident again, but I began to question why he hired me in the first place. I felt betrayed and duped. All this time I thought he had hired me for my creative talent, not to render him an opinion on his penis size! I do not know if that was an insensitive yet honest attempt at confirming the worth of his manhood, or an attempt to entice me to jump in bed with him by letting me have a glimpse of his private parts. It took me years to get over the disappointment that he had disrespected me so much that he felt free to embarrass and humiliate me. I didn't stay long with that company, feeling ashamed, incompetent, and, once again, a failure for something I did not do.

When I think back to that time and to my short employment as a hotel sales rep, I realize how sad it was that I never received any kind of orientation about the company mission or vision. There was no formal training for achieving goals, no teambuilding with company employees, no mention of a possible career path I might hope to follow. I merely worked a job. In later years, I proved to be an exemplary employee. A nonprofit agency inspired, trained, and motivated me to be a high producer. Those early companies received only a small bit of what I was capable of giving them. It was, of course, their loss as much as mine.

Other instances of uncontrolled sexual energy have affected me inadvertently. I have endured the awkward dynamics of other office relationships: overt or covert affairs and flirtations between boss and secretary, boss and subordinate, boss and client, or boss and another department head. One boss made a total fool of himself over a secretary who had absolutely no interest in him. I felt angry and devalued as he dismissed me from the office, laden with unrealistic sales goals, while he showered bouquets of roses and wrote little love notes to "Diane."

In my forties, temptation and sexual chemistry in the workplace evaporated, an era gone by. I guess I had outgrown it, but as a married woman I also worked hard to avoid it. I looked for employers who fostered family friendly workplaces. I even worked in places where sexual misconduct would be virtually impossible, like the Girl Scouts.

Human sexuality is an integral part of us, and I suppose will always be a potential problem in anyplace where men and women work together. The question is, how can we better prepare our younger co-workers and, more importantly, our daughters to avoid the deceitful alligators in business suits? We need to give them the confidence and the tools they need for fending off a boss or fellow colleague if he or she makes an advance. And we need to help them accept their own sexual feelings without guilt and learn to manage being in sexually-charged situations without acting on them

Maybe if we talk about it more among ourselves, we can collect ideas for powerful woman-to-woman, mother-to-daughter discussions. Then we need to develop that course.

Dinner Questions

- How do you talk to your daughter about the gains and losses involved with sex in the workplace?
- If you don't have a daughter, what do you think every young woman should know?

Baby Steps for Supermoms

Lost time was like a run in a stocking.
It always got worse.

— ANNE MORROW LINDBURGH,
THE STEEP ASCENT

"I didn't do all the things on my list. I've been bad."

Barbara's face clouded over with disappointment. One of the more popular trainers at the women's gym, she also sells cosmetics as a home business and dreams of becoming rich as a business owner. Thus far, however, her dreams seemed to be a long way away. Recognizing a fellow dreamer in need of a boost, I had suggested to her that she write down specific, achievable goals for her business. Her list included six goals for building her business; each goal involving repeated efforts on a daily basis. Though naturally a warm and friendly person, Barbara froze in the face of personal sales calls, which was a critical part of her business. I certainly could relate to this resistance. Now, on top of her fear, she had just added a truckload of guilt by trying to achieve goals that may not be realistic for her. I wanted to help her release some of the guilt that seemed to challenge her more than building her business. I needed to help her find validation for being the wonderful person she was right then, rather than after she had accomplished business success. How could I help her, when I myself was in the same boat?

How many of us women decide to shoot for the stars, then beat ourselves up when we find that the process of building the necessary equipment to reach that high is not easy? Or we discover that we don't have the skills yet to reach those lofty heights? Or we feel overwhelmed by the effort required and the sacrifices demanded of us? We cry in frustration and deem ourselves failures for not reaching our business goals. Meanwhile, we are raising children, nurturing an active marriage, supporting aging parents, volunteering in church, PTA and Scouts, working hard to enhance our own health, and maintaining a full workload. Many of us do all these things as single parents. We share a need to be considered somebody of worth, to feel validated in what we do, and to achieve financial freedom. We often feel that there just isn't time to do much beyond getting food on the table and the kids tucked in bed. The bottom line is that we are emotionally drained from our everyday lives, and don't need another pound of guilt added to our shoulders, self-imposed or otherwise.

Recently, I have encountered three different friends with work-related crises. One woman, Jan, an executive director for an Alzheimer's facility, found herself challenged by low-paid workers who did not show up for work. In our area, there is such a small worker pool that hotels and nursing homes are scrambling for qualified employees. My friend received calls from her facility at all hours of the day or night, notifying her of employees who refused to come to work. She found herself cooking the patients' breakfast, helping patients get dressed, and soothing upset families. Meanwhile, she drove three children to three different schools, and carrying one with learning disabilities to special tutoring. Her own mother was a recent widow suspected of having Alzheimer's herself. Jan received crisis calls during her family dinner on Thanksgiving, as well as on most weekends, and on the day of her husband's fiftieth birthday party. Whenever I saw Jan at church, the tears of frustration filled her eyes, threatening to spill over at any instant. She was being beaten down by all her commitments, both at work and at home, and I wondered how much longer she could bear the multiple burdens weighing down her shoulders.

The other two women were in similar sandwich generation situations, each with a teenage daughter and an elderly mother. While Nancy struggled to help her mother adapt to the assisted-living home, a business crisis with her unsavory partner required immediate evacuation from her building. After a day negotiating with a difficult landlord, loading massage tables into a truck, and signing legal papers, Nancy dropped into bed exhausted. Within minutes, a knock on her bedroom door announced her teenaged daughter who needed to unload her own anxiety about school. And then the phone rang, imploring Nancy to please coax her mother to ride in the ambulance. The assisted-living facility suspected a stroke.

The other woman, an art teacher for middle school children, exerted her emotional energy on a daily basis, maintaining discipline with unruly preteens, all the while determined to help her students produce quality art. A soft-spoken woman who felt empathetic to teenage angst, she participated in a teaching team with strong, intimidating personalities. By the end of the year, the job totally deflated her stamina and motivation. She, too, craved validation for all that she was doing for her students. How sad that our system is such that a teacher feels that no one cares whether or not she is doing a good job!

All three of these women work in the demanding fields of human services. All three nurtured husbands, children, and elderly parents, and all three desperately need support themselves. My heart cries for them when I saw them fighting exhaustion and tears, feeling so defeated and overwhelmed. I have felt that way, too.

Many of you reading this book may live the supermom lifestyle that others around us take for granted. It is incredible what we achieve before eight in the morning. One Friday, I had purchased groceries for the weekend, washed and dried three loads of clothes and hot-glued a brachiosaurus eating tree leaves in a shadowbox, all by eight in the morning. Today, I vacuumed the house before seven. Most days I complete my aerobic workout, make three lunches and wash clothes by seven-thirty. Many of us make a major purchase of groceries at midnight!

I will never forget the day that I delivered a proposal and met with two separate clients on different sides of town while picking up printing for a major presentation the next day. I had a window of fifteen minutes to accomplish the most important errand of all: convert a pair of girl's rollerblade skates purchased at a yard sale into a "looks new" pair of boy's skates. I worked like a madwoman, ripping out the pink laces and the pink shin guards, spray painting them gold and re-lacing the skates with new black laces. No one will know the tremendous triumph I experienced at pulling off this major transformation while in my business suit, the clock ticking as if for a television game show with a million-dollar ante. I raced off to the next appointment with gold paint on my fingernails and the smile of a winner on my face.

As a small businessperson working out of my home, the accumulation of small alligators gets me the most. The computer, sick with a virus, threatens to stall out completely the week of my deadline. The toilet overflows the same day and the dog pees on the carpet. The fax quits working, we're out of milk, and Simone can't get her math done in time for Girl Scouts. The family is tired of eating Beef-a-Roni three days in a row and there are no beans to go with the hot dogs. Meanwhile, an old friend writes to update me on her global business, her global romance, and her new CD out this month.

It is so easy to feel envious of another's success. My brother is a successful management consultant. He is in demand by the business world, accruing frequent flyer points, the latest personal organizer, hi-tech presentation skills, and a list of notable clients. However, he pays a price for his success. His children only see him on weekends, when he is worn out. He fights a weight problem, and his wife gets little attention from him. For every gain there is a loss, and his losses are too great for me.

I try sometimes to make myself more competitive in my field by putting in the extra effort required to put me on the cutting edge. Last year, I decided to upgrade my presentations with references to current affairs in the business world. I subscribed to the Wall Street Journal and read my stack of newspapers throughout our family camping trip. I totally defeated the purpose of getting away with my family by blocking them out all weekend. What a loss for both of us!

I remember other destructive habits I have fostered in my past. In addition to comparing myself to my peers, setting unrealistic goals, and eating to smother my feelings, I used to brag about my accomplishments. One school chum had the nerve to tell me that my Christmas letter made him sick to his stomach. I usually brag when my self-esteem is low, or when I am not feeling good enough about myself. I am sure that people are barely able to tolerate me when I do that.

Practicing positive habits makes life richer and more enjoyable. Every night, list the accomplishments and blessings that you have experienced that day. We all have unproductive days when it feels that we have gone backwards instead of forwards. By acknowledging the small signs of progress each day, you confirm the baby steps you are taking toward your goal. No success is too small to count. Then, when you look over the pages of past achievements, you will clearly see the overall progress you are making. Here are some other daily practices that have made a difference for me:

Keep a gratitude list. This helps me to let go of the "Not Enough Syndrome." Whenever you catch yourself feeling negative about your body, your closet, or your checkbook, work on your gratitude list. For example, I tend to feel fat when I focus on my stomach in the mirror. So I add to my gratitude list, "My abdomen has carried two wonderful babies," "My husband loves its feminine softness," "True women never have flat bellies," and, a constant source of gratitude, "My body is cancer free."

Set small goals that lead to larger goals. Remember my friend Barbara with the cosmetic business at the beginning of this story? After writing her smaller, more attainable goals down for two weeks, she added four clients and doubled her income!

Set boundaries. This is a really hard one. A therapist can help a lot with the process. My therapist reminds me to assess gains and losses. Writing this book, for example, has resulted in losing income because I am not working. My family agreed to give up some of their creature comforts in order to support me. The gain is that I have been much more accessible to them and I am having more fun as a wife and mother, while still contributing to my career. The process of writing has deeply affected my future business mission to one of supporting women. I am beginning to understand my boundaries, and know now that I can accomplish what I need to within the confines of my boundaries.

Spend time in solitude. I know what you are going to say—when can mothers do this? Yet, it is when we meditate that we are able to feel waves of gratitude and inspiration that can fill our hearts with enough positive energy to last us all day. Walking my dog at five-thirty in the morning is part of my solitude time.

Exercise with other women. I can finally say that I actually enjoy going to the gym as much as to a restaurant. Find a women's fitness center that fosters a positive body image. Remember that you are there not to morph into the anorexic models in the fashion magazines, but to become strong, healthy, and content with your own unique body. Focus on fitness as a personal journey. The camaraderie, energy, and stress release you can experience with other women who are equally committed to becoming fit and healthy are invaluable. Or find a walking buddy. She can make an hour walk seem like five minutes.

Read books by other women. Ann Morrow Lindburg writes beautifully about balance and a woman's need for solitude. Maya Angelou writes about sexuality and pride in an inspiring way that could change the way you feel about yourself. For other good reads, find Oprah's reading list on the Internet. Read Julie Cameron's *The Artist's Way*, and follow her suggestion that you write morning papers—an awesome experience, even if you can only do it on weekends. Indulge in a great women's novel, such as *The Red Tent* by Anita Diamant, or ask your local librarian or bookstore clerk (find a woman for the best suggestions). I have included a list of some of my favorites in the back of the book.

Write down your frustrations and your prayers. On days when the alligators of frustration seem to consume you, list them. It is much easier to conquer a known enemy than one that has no name. Then, write a prayer asking for the inner quality you need to do battle with those alligators, whether it is strength, courage, patience, perseverance, or humor. Ask for reassurance, a sign that you're on the right track, or a signal that all will be well in due time. Be sure to date the prayer and keep it in a safe place. Never forget to pray for a sense of humor.

Have parties where women tell their stories. Celebrate your birthday, a new job, a promotion, a new baby, or a new lifestyle by inviting women to gather together to share their stories with each other. To get them started, write topics on slips of paper and put them in a basket. After each story, ask if another woman has a story about the same topic. This is inspiring, entertaining, and insightful to everyone. Ideas could include:

The silliest thing I ever did to look good.
The time my wits got me out of a tight spot.
The most outrageous thing I ever did…
A woman who inspires me is…
The most afraid I've ever been…

Look for opportunities to acknowledge other women. Acknowledge other women in your life specifically and sincerely. Be sure to acknowledge the women in your past by remembering their stories, passing them down to your daughters. The more you do this, the more you validate yourself. Every woman deserves a medal for her courage in some way. Every woman has the instinct of a lioness. Discover how women are the music of life! Observe how they bring drama, lightness, and flair to your surroundings. Ascertain that which is special in every woman you know, and then tell her about her own uniqueness.

Leave situations or people who hurt your Spirit. You don't need those people, but it is sometimes hard to imagine life without them. I have never regretted leaving a husband, boss, partner, or client if he or she were abusive to my spirit or my body. Instead, surround yourself with positive people whose infectious energy will uplift your Spirit. Learn skills and strategies for dealing with difficult people who are impossible to leave, such as in the workplace. Participate in workshops where you practice communication skills that will empower you to deal with unpleasant, negative people.

Remember the Stages of Birthing. I have had two babies by natural childbirth, which means, for those of you unfamiliar with the concept, I did not use drugs or artificial contrivances to bring my babies into the world. Whether you have or not, there is an important lesson to be learned about the birthing experience. A birth is broken down into stages of labor. During one particular stage, called transition, sometimes after hours of pushing, the mother wants to give up. I remember distinctly telling my husband, "It is no use, I just can't do it." At that very moment the baby's head crowned, then popped out. In life, whenever I am giving birth to a major project or trying to achieve a goal, I remind myself that just when I feel like quitting, the baby's head is crowning, and the birth is around the corner.

Foster your pride in others. Pride is a much more positive way to feel about yourself than feeling frustrated all the time, yet we have particular trouble admitting that we feel proud of ourselves. Vanity, and the pride that is implied, is, after all, considered a sin. Yet we readily swell with pride when our child does something remarkable, or our spouses accomplish some goal. If you can't feel proud of yourself, think of women you are proud of. When I meet successful businesswomen, young and old alike, I know the courage and tenacity it took them to achieve success in a male-dominated world.

Included in this book are stories about the difficult times I have endured as a step-parent. I have never felt more unprepared or incompetent than I have as a step-mom for Robert's three sons. Looking back, I can think of many things I would do differently. However, I need to share one success story regarding Robert's middle son, Roger.

Sixteen-year-old Roger had mixed feelings about entering our household, I'm sure, but he recognized the opportunities that the newly-formed relationship offered him. Roger became active in our church's youth group, and represented our church at the international youth conference that first year. He found a job at the hospital nearby, thanks to the help of a neighbor. Although Roger had high grades, he became involved in an unhealthy relationship at an early age and, consequently, showed no interest in going to college. He seemed doomed for early marriage, children, and a dead-end career. Suddenly, Roger enlisted in the Army and was shipped off to Germany. We lost touch for several years after that, but one day we received a phone call that he had fallen in love with an officer in his unit.

Two years ago, Roger contacted us again. Anticipating his return to the States, he wanted us to meet his wife and son. After all those years, Roger wanted to be a part of our family again. Roger and his lovely wife, Lynn, brought three-year-old Tristen last summer to meet his grandparents. The couple has set high goals, working hard on their marriage, and plan to continue their education. We were delighted to discover that he had adopted many of our values, and was now requesting our emotional support. Roger is considering a teaching profession, building on his love for children. After taking a Marriage and Family class, he proposed ground rules to his wife for their marriage. Roger even sited our marriage as an inspiration for him.

No grandmother has felt more love than I while packing Tristen's Easter presents. He calls me "Granna" and sings to me on the phone. As Roger and Lynn await the adoption of a baby girl, I am scheduling a plane trip to go and help them when she arrives. This will slow down my work, but I will simply adjust my goals. I never thought I would feel this close to my teenage stepson, but now I am so very proud of him. It is a privilege to have Lynn for a daughter. This young family is such a wonderful addition to my life that I thank God for making this happen.

It's all about baby steps—just take baby steps and you will eventually reach your goal in life.

Dinner Questions

❑ How do you handle situations that feel overwhelming?

❑ What tasks do you delegate to family or assistants to relieve your workload?

Wrestling As We Age:
Warrior Queens of Greater Gaters

Age puzzles me. I thought it was a quiet
time. My seventies were interesting, and fairly
serene, but my eighties are passionate.
I grow more intense as I age.

— FLORIDA SCOTT-MAXWELL, *THE MEASURE*
OF MY DAYS

Some alligators stay with us throughout our lives, lurking in the bushes, ready to growl, nip, or even bite if we ever let our guard down. These alligators are hatched from character weaknesses, personality flaws, physical limitations, or unfortunate relationships. They have become regular features of our backyards, like kudzu that won't go away, threatening to overgrow the good things about us.

All my life I have wrestled with my need to be perfect. As a performance artist, I even created a character of perfection with a heavenly costume and an endearing personality that evolved as I matured. As a young woman, I wrestled with the lack of perfection in my looks. I wrestled with my inability to be the perfect daughter, wife, and mother to my family.

Today, I wrestle with the perfectionist within me as I try not to impose my unattainable standards on my children. I still haven't figured out how to respect the thin line between encouraging them to do their best and insisting that they excel. In business, I strive to be a successful professional, I find myself teetering on another thin line between delivering excellent service while growing a business and maintaining a balance between work and family.

Other women wrestle alligators of poor health and disease. Still others wrestle the alligators of divorce, children in trouble, or grandchildren too far away to cuddle and hold.

I recognize that I am not alone in my fight. I am, in fact, surrounded by women who are fighting noble battles with greater gators. Many of these women wrestle with multiple alligators as they nurse a spouse with cancer, care for an aging parent, support a son or daughter's blossoming career, or overcome their own physical challenges. In spite of all of these personal difficulties, they continue to focus on a bigger life mission. Global warriors they are, warrior queens who develop and maintain networks and contacts to help others and attend and support conferences and rallies as they fight relentlessly for change.

Dinner Questions

- ❑ In what area of your life does your drive to be perfect rob you of happiness?
- ❑ Who do you recognize and admire as a "global warrior queen," someone who wrestles multiple alligators while contributing to society?

Learning from Experienced Alligators

*If we all tried to make other people's
paths easy, our own feet would have a
smooth even place to walk on.*

— MYRTLE REED, *A WEAVER OF DREAMS*

In a society obsessed with youth, we aging women often struggle with our own sense of worth. Foods, drugs, and plastic surgery promise to be the proverbial fountain of youth. We are constantly reminded that we must do everything within our power and pocketbooks to prevent the ravages of this horrible, albeit inevitable, process of growing old. We fight the alligator of aging as if it were truly the devil incarnate, ready to condemn us to a life of failing health, fading beauty, and faltering mental capabilities. No longer considered attractive physically or viable intellectually, we fear being relegated to watch from the sidelines as a younger population begins to call the shots.

But this doesn't make sense. We, as a cohort, compose the majority of the population, owing to the fact that we are members of the baby boomer generation. While some of us still hover on the border, many of us have already gone over the hill, taking with us our powerful voices. Our boomer members have dictated fashions and trends for over three decades and have made our age group the top priority for public policies regarding health care and education. This group has also determined what issues and concerns will gain the most attention in our society. As women in the majority, we have seen significant changes in our status in the home and in the workplace. We, as women, have been able to influence massive changes in the social fabric of our country, including race relations, treatment of children, and, ironically, care of our elderly. Are we going to surrender this position of power just because we find ourselves aging?

Thousands of vital women bloom in their greatness during the second half of their lives. Older women not only possess a sexual maturity that exudes confidence and compassion, but their wisdom and accomplishments strengthen the framework upon which our society was built. While the media often ignores dynamic older women, touting instead pretty young superstars, let us respect and honor them, and be inspired to follow their paths.

We need to reconsider who our role models should be, particularly as we face increasingly complicated life decisions. Instead of ignoring our elderly women we should sit at the feet of these wise matrons, reveling in their stories of courage. Look around you and assess your opportunities to learn from the voice of experience. Do you work alongside an older committee member, yet fail to listen to her knowledgeable past? Have you incorporated grandmothers into the lives of your children, blessing them for the unconditional love they bestow? These women of age surround us, offering their wealth of experience for our use, if we will just look for them instead of treating them as if they are invisible. For the most part, these women ask for little in return, delightfully grateful when we accept the legacy they offer. I would like to introduce to you a few of my favorite women who have graced my life.

Margaret Scruggs

Chocolates, poetry, and church bulletins—these are my mother's tools for sanity. Margaret Scruggs is a remarkable woman in her early seventies, who believes in pleasure, faith, and service. I brag about her all the time to people, and add that I am thrilled by the fact that I have her genes. I could go on and on about my mother's talents, strengths, and legacy she has left her children, her grandchildren, and now her great grandchild. Even as an older woman she continues to make an impact on the people who love and depend upon her. After digging enormous rocks from the sloping terrain of her property, she transformed her entire backyard into a terraced garden that feeds two families, with plenty of vegetables left over for neighbors. This act is symbolic of how my mother has managed her life—by working hard, conquering obstacles, combining functionality with beauty, and reaching out to others.

After raising four children, Mom returned to school for a teaching certificate. She tackled literacy with persistence and creativity, developing an approach to reading that brought new hope to children with learning difficulties, and helping teenagers previously labeled as slow readers. As her successes in the classroom grew, she wrote a book for parents so that they, too, might understand and follow her triumphant methods. She also pursued a personal dream, to spend time in the mission field. Mom flew to the Philippines, at the age of sixty-six, to donate several months of her time to a school for young girls.

Today, Mom considers her role as Daddy's caregiver her foremost function. She carefully regulates his many daily medications for diabetes and manages his Alzheimer's type of dementia. In spite of the restrictive life she now must lead because of my father, she still maintains her ample garden, stays healthy and fit for her seventy-six years, and contributes to her family and her community. She tutors children at a nearby school and has adapted her reading system for Hispanic women eager to learn English. She sells her personally illustrated instruction books to parents, sending the profits to a global medical mission. Since her life revolves around the church, she grows flowers to glorify God on Sundays.

Martha Jones

Crates stuffed with files fill Martha's car. An officer in a myriad of service organizations, Martha donates her expertise to community projects, church committees, and personal celebrations. Because of her, life runs smoothly for thousands of others. Smartly dressed, her refined flair for fashion attracts advice seekers, including brides and celebrities. I am proud to be her friend.

Martha knew prejudice as a child. When her stoic Native American father married her African American mother and gave birth to multiracial offspring, they learned a hard lesson about the repercussions of being culturally different. Putting the kids in the back of the family pick-up truck, the family set off to visit relatives. Ashamed of her black daughter-in-law, the Native American grandmother offered no warmth or affection to her grandchildren. Visiting the maternal grandparents, however, the family discovered a completely different experience. Running throughout the farm, the children enjoyed the freedom and adventures of country living before ending the day in grandmother's arms. Martha experienced family closeness, the joy of family storytelling, and the pleasure of family holidays from her black grandparents.

Obtaining a teaching certificate, Martha dedicated herself to raising nutritional standards for young mothers with limited resources. For twenty-five years she taught nutrition for the cooperative extension service, teaching young mothers as well as 4-H children. She stays in touch with many of these children, now grown with children of their own.

Martha refused to let prejudice prevent her own children from obtaining opportunities in life. Although she has sadly buried two husbands, she has raised five children who set and achieve goals, resulting in prestigious careers for each of them. Today, Martha still speaks up for the disadvantaged, this time for the transportation-challenged poor. As the vice-chair for the Transit Authority Board, she speaks boldly at televised Alderman board meetings, insisting that bus routes offer transportation for working people without cars.

There is a creative, fun-loving side to Martha. Responding to frequent requests from families overwhelmed with details of special events, Martha willingly takes charge, fitting in one more wedding amongst funerals, a family reunion, and a community conference for women. Nothing, however, takes precedence over her own family get-togethers. With seventeen grandchildren and twenty-seven great grandchildren of her own, Martha is the family matriarch in every sense of the word, providing for her extended brood the love and affection she had sensed long ago cuddled in her grandmother's arms long ago. Even now Martha influences and nurtures many young women, related or not, as she continues to encourage them to overcome their obstacles and to strive for a better life.

Ann Barefield

You would think Ann would welcome retirement. For forty years she had dedicated herself to her career as a teacher, principal, curriculum director, administrator, and research center director. Her current life as a university professor continues to demand a rigorous schedule of teaching, exams, and student consultations. A devoted mother, Ann fits plane schedules into her weekends, taking in her son's organ concert in Texas one weekend, then flying to New York to visit the other son another weekend. Grandchildren come for the holidays and the summers, staying in the upstairs bedrooms or at her condo at the beach.

Still young in her sixties, Ann fights and nurtures simultaneously, leaving retirement to teach education at a local black university. Ann's students adore her. My own children love her. My daughter has fed her kitties when she traveled and my son plays Nintendo with her husband, Bob. Ann and her husband fill their schedules with events, meetings, and dinners, all devoted to fighting racism. Ann inspires me with her passion that fuels her energy for work in race relations. As the editor of an expansive community online newsletter, Ann motivates community leaders to participate in supper clubs, sponsor poster and essay contests, and to attend a myriad of conferences and discussion groups. Ann co-chaired a conference for women of different ethnic backgrounds to explore issues and devise solutions that might heal conflict. With all of her responsibilities and projects, Ann finds time to feed and care for her elderly mother in a nursing home while dealing with her own physical limitations.

Katie Sollohub

Katie loves children and nature. When her husband retired as a colonel from the Army, Katie launched her own rocket, so to speak. At the age of sixty-four, Katie developed wildlife programs for children at St. Mark's Wildlife Refuge outside of Tallahassee, Florida. Because of Katie, thousands of Florida schoolchildren respect water moccasins, recognize animal tracks, and appreciate the beauty of Florida's waterfowl. In addition to the Wildlife Refuge, Katie, much over the hill in age, trained Girl Scout leaders in camping skills, read to the blind, and tutored children with learning disabilities.

"The key to staying young is to take advantage of opportunity," Katie advised me. "If the door's there, open it!" Katie has opened many doors. After raising four children and moving fifteen times during her husband's army career, she took advantage of his tour in Thailand and

completed her education degree at the age of fifty. Katie taught reme-
dial reading while seeking even more opportunities for her own learning.
Putting her name on a waiting list for Kent State University teacher's
tour, she rallied to a phone call at the last minute.

"We just received a cancellation on the tour," the guide told her.
"You can join us for a trip to China if you let us know by tomorrow
night."

Katie knew how to pack in a hurry.

Today, Katie takes religion courses to keep her mind active and com-
mits to her daily swim to keep her body active. She celebrated her
eighty-fourth birthday the same year that the State of Florida honored
her with the Points of Light Award for four thousand hours of volunteer service.

Maxwell Grier

Dressed in a saucy hat with a sparkling blouse, Maxwell Grier beamed
at the ladies luncheon I attended in a community center. A retired schoolteacher, Maxwell generated energy and wit as she recognized her friends
from the podium.

"She's quite a speaker," the lady next to me commented. "You should
hear her speak at a function. She keeps everyone laughing!"

Admiring the decorations, I inquired about the meticulous handiwork that adorned each of the sixty placemats.

"Maxwell did them," the lady replied. "She provides a surprise for
us every single month."

Did I mention that Maxwell is 101? Spry, happy, and smiling with
all of her own perfect white teeth shining from her dark face, Maxwell
is an inspiration to everyone who knows her.

"Maxwell raised one daughter," my new friend continued, "and one
of her grandsons. All five of her grandsons are ministers. "With
churches," she had added emphatically.

These older acquaintances of mine have many qualities in common. They all radiate a serene happiness in their later years. They exude
vitality, love adventure, enjoy the spirit of youth, and embrace the challenge of aging. They have seen birth and death, personal gains and losses,
and devotion and betrayal. They experience the inevitable signs of ag-

ing, physical pain from arthritis, and other personal irritations that frustrate their busy schedules. They grieve over children's marital problems and celebrate grandchildren's triumphs. They are mothers of women who pursue career goals and men who can cook.

We mustn't forget to bask in the radiant wisdom of these women. They are like rays of divine energy. A psychologist friend of mine, Smeeta, recently shared with me her special love for her work counseling older clients.

"I feel like I am absorbing their wisdom and insights," she acknowledged gratefully. "They are profoundly spiritual and reflective."

Just as Janet Reno recalls the strength and determination of her mother as the foundation for her own leadership ability, we, too, can draw from the passions of our own mothers. We reap great wealth from the wisdom and insight they embody. Their stories can inspire our own stories. Their mentors can provide valuable lessons for us, too, generations later. As we pass down family recipes, quilts, and photographs to our daughters, let us also pass down our mother's and grandmother's triumphs over their own alligators, and the tools they used when they wrestled the beasts and won.

Delores Smith, Ed.D., the president/CEO of our local Urban League, closes functions by leading a community chant that includes the line, "If you lose your history, you lose your power." We women must find our history before we can find our power. We must hear the stories of our great-grandmothers who fought in wars, progressed in every field of knowledge, and succeeded in nurturing husbands, children, and communities. We must learn the names of the women who swam the English Channel, who painted with Michelangelo, and who led tribes of Native Americans. These women are reminders of our own greatness, our heritage of feminine wit and courage. We have a lot of studying to do, stories to share, and sisters to cheer for as we go along our way through life. We need to explore our own pasts and discover our authenticity. Only by doing this will we are able to discover that they have the ability to wrestle our present-day alligators, no matter the size or the source.

The women I have known who have reached the second half of their lives with their wisdom and wit in tact are, without a doubt, shining examples of how one's commitment to living life to its fullest can have universal ramifications. Alligator wrestling on a global scale requires a burning sense of purpose, faith in a higher being as an anchor, and commitment to personal balance. In their often meager, unassuming ways, women who wrestle alligators, and live to tell about it, touch thousands and thousands of lives. They demonstrate loving courage, flexibility in the face of change, an unwavering work ethic, and a solid commitment to their missions. Their visions for quality life inspire others to raise the bar for their own personal goals. They are concrete examples of how women supply humankind with the music of life.

Dinner Questions

☐ How did older women impact your life as a child?
☐ Can you describe a lifestyle you would like to grow into?

Dancing with Death

Life is not separate from death.
It only looks that way.

— BLACKFOOT PROVERB

The group of women huddled together in the small gazebo, pouring sangria for each other and passing plates of salmon and crackers. We had settled in for storytelling, trusting each other with experiences that came from deep in our hearts.

"I helped a woman die," Pam offered. "I mean, I took care of a woman as she was dying." Quiet and pretty with medium-length blonde hair framing her face, Pam surprised us by volunteering to share what must have been an intensely personal and intimate episode for her. We sensed a certain urgency in her voice as if the story needed to be told, so we settled back to listen.

"She wasn't a relative…. I didn't even know her that well. But she had cared for my husband as a child. She didn't have any family or even insurance," Pam continued. "I called my mother and asked for advice. Should I get involved? This woman is dying of cancer and has nobody. My mother simply said, 'Pam, it's your decision. Just be sure that you make a decision you can accept without later regrets.'

"So, I did. I monitored her medicine, gave her baths, changed her sheets, and cleaned up bodily functions. I didn't know I could do this, but I found out that I had a deep reservoir of strength. I could do what I needed to do for her until hospice stepped in at the end."

We all sat silently, each of us wondering what we would do in that situation, contemplating the capacity of our own reservoirs. How fortunate that poor, dying woman was to have Pam's selfless, loving care, I thought to myself.

Pam's story would reassure me five months later, when I, too, volunteered to help care for a woman as she prepared to exit this life. Although I didn't take care of her physical needs, I felt closely connected to her in the end. Helping this woman reach some sort of closure, providing her with some warmth and comfort, and being present at the completion of a life became a special spiritual and physical process for me.

Susan was neither a stranger nor a friend. As my sister-in-law's mother, our encounters had been limited to only a few family dinners since we moved to North Carolina. One would not describe Susan as warm and friendly. Although she participated in the dinners as a family member, she remained silent until the opportunity presented itself to converse with one person. Then, she would talk endlessly about herself.

Still, Susan piqued my curiosity. With her long red hair curling down her back, and black eyeliner tattooed in permanent upward slants at the outside of her lids, she maintained an aura of mystery for a woman in her mid-sixties. Susan had swirled through life as a professional belly dancer. My sister-in-law, Allison, had struggled for years with her mother's dysfunctional lifestyle. Multiple marriages, torrid affairs, addictions to drugs, alcohol, and other emotional clutter interfered with Susan's attempts to mother Allison. Even before her illness, the daughter had become the parent for the mother.

"Susan has pancreatic cancer. Allison has left for Florida to bring her here for surgery. She might not live much longer." My brother David's voice conveyed the seriousness of the situation. Allison needed to hastily organize the many details for a smooth family transition in her absence, all before her sudden departure. Carpools, Girl Scouts, homework support, and childcare during my brother's business appointments needed to be put in place immediately.

"I'll help," I jumped in instinctively. I had no idea to what extent I was actually volunteering for, I just heard in my brother's voice a sincere plea for help and I did the natural sisterly thing by volunteering.

My past experience with death has been removed, to say the least. My grandparents died in hospitals, three of them miles away from where I lived. I had not even been encouraged to attend the funerals. My parents and three brothers were all living. But I maintain my conviction that death is a family process, one to be experienced and revered together. I thought of the testimonials shared by friends who sat with parents, co-workers, and grandparents, either to be with the dying family member during their last days on earth or to comfort and support the people remaining. I contemplated the family whose daughter drowned in the swimming pool. Their loving ceremony of goodbye in the hospital room for the child who had graced their lives for three short years had brought a profound spiritual peace to everyone. And I remembered Pam's words, "I found out I had a deep reservoir of strength."

It was not difficult to find things to do to assist David and Allison's family. They had situated her mother in their guest bedroom, and their busy family life strained to accommodate the demands of their patient. Allison dropped her part-time job, rearranged her schedule and filled her calendar as she managed details for five lives instead of four. Susan needed transportation to a myriad of appointments, she had no clothes with her, and she desperately needed to talk through the shock of her predicament. I didn't know exactly what I needed to be doing to help her through this time, but I did know she was in dire need of human comfort, and that I could give her. I drove her to a massage appointment, shopped at Goodwill for clothes in her favorite colors, and led her through visualizations and peaceful meditations.

We only made vague references to Susan's "healing," her actual needs were for transition and closure. There were many little details to take care of, things that would bother her until she could satisfactorily resolve them. "You've got to help me find homes for my cats, Ana," she pleaded. I called a friend who agreed to take two of her six cats. Susan arranged for their air transportation.

I decided I would distract her from her morbid thoughts by getting her to talk about herself, something I knew she had enjoyed doing in the past. "Will you show me your belly dancing scrapbook?" I asked. Susan responded eagerly, lugging out her heavy book filled with pictures and mementoes. There were pictures of Susan with her troupe of dancers, Susan with a candelabra on her head, Susan in veils, bells, and feathers. From the pictures came the stories, tumbling forth in rapid succession. I could feel her excitement as she talked. For the moment, she was not thinking of her pending death.

"Would you brush my hair?" Susan requested her favorite ritual, giving me directions for just the right touch.

As an "inside outsider," or one related only by marriage, I could offer Susan family assistance unimpeded by a history of emotional entanglements. I found that I could be beneficial to Allison by giving her an ear and permission to unload her own frustration. If anybody needed a deep reservoir of strength, it was Allison.

"She watches junky TV shows and reads trashy magazines," Allison vented. "She doesn't seem very interested in seeking a spiritual path. And we think she's drinking again."

As time went by, David and Allison retrieved Susan's car and belongings from Florida, helping Susan to find a small apartment for her own privacy and theirs. Her condition seemed to have stabilized after her radiation and chemotherapy. The cancer support group provided a cocoon of unconditional friendship for them all. Life flowed smoothly, at least for a while. Then it came. The phone call we all dreaded.

"Susan's tumor is worse. She needs surgery again and might not come home. Allison is spending nights at the hospital, and we're taking the girls to see her. "

Again, I responded instinctively. "What can I do?" I knew, however, that David was not the one to ask. Allison was the commander-in-charge of the home operation.

"Food would be nice," Allison said wearily after our brief visit, "We don't have time to shop or cook."

I dashed to the store. I filled my basket with the makings for comfort food, mashed potatoes, turkey and dressing, gravy, and chocolate pie. My mom agreed to fix several other casseroles for the family.

The hospital visit to see Susan required courage. This could be goodbye, I told myself. What do I say to a dying woman? I had coached Allison earlier, remembering a public radio interview about supportive moments before death.

"There are four sentences to remember," I had wisely quoted. "I forgive you. Please forgive me. I love you. Thank you." I had burned these words into my memory, my first aid kit for emergency deaths. But these sentences were for Allison to say, leaving me unprepared with my own last words to the dying woman.

Allison and her sister left me alone with Susan in the tiny hospital room. Susan looked white and weak. She spoke in faint gasps. "Help me...turn over," she implored.

Her strength depleted, moving an arm or leg seemed to exhaust her.

"Susan, are you scared?" I ventured to ask a direct question, one that was worrying me as I contemplated my own death years from now.

"No, just angry," she replied. " I promised my cat I'd take care of her."

"What can I do?" I asked, hoping she wouldn't ask me to commit to taking the cat.

"Just rub my back," she whispered feebly. Gently I rubbed, lightly scratched, and soothingly stroked her back. The wasted body had lost all of its firmness, even her white skin seemed old and tired. The dancer's muscle tone had abandoned her. "Feels good," she murmured, encouraging me to continue. In an inspired moment I knew exactly what she needed—affirmation. I began to list all the ways that she had contributed joy, pleasure, and beauty to her family, her audiences, and even to her cats.

Allison and her sister shortly returned, my cue for departure.

"I need to go and let you rest, Susan."

"Give me a hug," Susan held out her arms. As I bent over her, I felt her hold me close, mustering all the strength she could for our embrace. A long hug. A goodbye that words couldn't express.

We were all surprised when Susan was dismissed from the hospital the next day.

"She seems to be holding her own," Allison said. "The doctor said it could be much longer. But now she needs round-the-clock attention. She is in pain. My sister, Erin, is staying with her while I go away for the weekend."

"I'll give your sister a break," I offered. Pleased that Allison was going with the family on a weekend trip, I knew the sister could also use a little reprieve. The two daughters had been with their mother non-stop; taking turns at night, giving her baths and medication. Everyone felt stretched to their mental and physical limits. I remembered a complimentary ticket to the movies I had tucked away in a drawer and took it to the sister.

Susan made little effort to greet me this time. It hurt to move. She kept a VCR playing continuous Disney movies as distraction for her pain. Her one last cat curled up at her side.

"What can I do, Susan?" I asked my customary question.

"You can pat my head," she whispered.

Gently, I stroked her head, pulling her hair behind her ear, imagining that I was a mother comforting my daughter. I gazed around the room, noting the bottles of painkiller with a list of instructions, the clipboard on which I was to note any food eaten or bodily functions, the bottle of Lysol left for me to clean up any accidents. Again, I thought of Pam calling upon her reservoir of strength.

Allison returned from her weekend trip, and Susan died in the night soon after. We were all aware she was dying, but we still felt stunned when the actual news came. Even though she was gone, there was more for me to do to help out. Allison would need help in going through her things.

Susan's apartment exceeded my wildest imaginings. Framed pictures of Arabian princesses, idealized Art Nouveau women, and Buddhist temple rubbings graced the walls. Stacks of pillows on a futon, a mamasan wicker chair, and exotic candle holders kept secrets of past nights when Susan held court, lounging amidst her cats and entertaining her fantasies. Woven baskets of different shapes contained snake skins and talismans; rubber snakes coiled on bookshelves reminded one of the real serpents that once curled around Susan's dancing body.

I felt like a voyeur as I explored Susan's closets. Embroidered caftans, flimsy chiffon skirts bedecked with mirrors and bells, matched with veils, and glittering gauze trimmed in sequined fringe. Another closet contained spears, seven to be exact—plastic party props. Headdresses hung from a hat rack—turbans, crowns, plumed tiaras. A frame of scarf hooks held layer upon layer of fringed shawls in every color imaginable. Jeweled bras and wide sashes bedecked with ropes of pearls, coins, and golden tassels meant to sway seductively from a dancer's hips rested in a treasure chest of drawers. All the tributes to Susan's fantasies, her art, her passion, and her seductive skills lay open to our inspection. Allison invited me to pick out some keepsakes to remember her by.

Susan was a wild woman, a free spirit. As I have been. She was a performer, a costume designer, and a woman of dreams. As I have been. In spite of her denial and dependence, her neediness and addictions, she left a legacy to those who knew her, especially to her daughters and granddaughters. She danced through life, loving its drama, and listening to the beat of a decidedly different drum. I am thankful to Susan, for giving birth to Allison and her sister, incredible women who also listen to the beat of their own drums. And I am grateful that I was given the chance to participate as she made her exit from life, a Sister helping another Sister to take her final bow.

We all want to avoid death—thinking about it, talking about it, witnessing it. But death, like life, is unavoidable. Instead of shunning the inevitable moments of death, embrace them by reaching out to someone who is in need of your comfort, your help with closure, and your participation in the completion of their life. Though it is always sad, it is also always powerful. Like birth, death is a time of great transition, and being in the presence of someone whose life force is leaving his or her mortal body to go on to the afterlife is an amazing phenomenon.

Dinner Questions

❑ When has a death touched your life?
❑ When have you experienced your deep reservoirs of strength?

The Bell Curve

When you stop looking for something,
you see it right in front of you.

— ELEANOR COPPOLA, *NOTES*

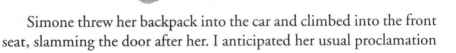

Simone threw her backpack into the car and climbed into the front seat, slamming the door after her. I anticipated her usual proclamation of the day.

"Today sucked."

At thirteen, my daughter finds misery a part of her daily routine. Everyday she comes home from school and recapitulates the day's catastrophes. She scored poorly on a test, forgot to get a parent signature, burned her microwave lunch, and lost the student council election for the third year in a row. Bummer. It's all terrible to my teenaged daughter. Life seems to be on a negative roll for her, during this awkward time when hormones are going wild and nothing seems to make sense for her anymore. One bad piece of luck has the power to taint her whole day.

At first, I found this constant negative outpouring distasteful. It grated on my generally upbeat, optimistic nerves and threatened to bring my own mood down every time I was around her.

"Simone, you did great on your test yesterday!" I would argue. "And you have photography class tonight! Isn't that something to look forward to?"

"You don't understand," Simone would glower at me, rolling her eyes and sighing in teen angst.

Oh, but I do.

I remember being thirteen; I remember it all too well. My life as a teen was an ongoing series of one hurt after another, all rolling into one enormous sucking life. I remember the total embarrassment I felt when my mother had the audacity to wear socks with pedal pushers in front of my friends. Everyone knew the written-in-stone rule regarding pedal pushers. Loafers without socks. Period. I remember the disdain I felt for my younger brother who acted differently from the other boys. I remember the stinging hurt of rejection when girls from my Girl Scout troop were voted into a high school sorority but I was not. I remember with pain the plain white Sunday dress my mother made for my piano recital when all the other girls performing wore formals with ruffles and lipstick. And I remember lying on my bed in my room, wondering how my family could possibly love someone as despicable as me.

Life definitely hurts at thirteen.

Today I wait for my parents to return from a riverboat cruise. Whereas I live with a thirteen-year-old who suffers life's trauma on a regular basis, my father lives with a seventy-five-year-old incurable optimist. While Simone is determined that life is out to get her, and lets anything and everything stop her in her tracks, no matter what, her grandmother is determined to enjoy life, letting nothing stop her, no matter what.

As Daddy's caregiver, she travels with his portable urinal, a complete pharmacy of medications, and extra clothes "just in case." Mother cuts Daddy's meat, watches his diabetic diet, and finishes his sentence when he can't, which is most of the time. When Daddy has nightmares, Mother sleeps on the floor next to his bed.

"It could be worse," she assures me.

My mother has mastered the art of coping with her losses. I wish, for her own sake, that my daughter would at least attempt to learn this same lesson. Simone grieves stridently, seeming to focus only on the things that are wrong with her life. But I know from experience that grieving is the beginning of letting go. I listen empathetically, and pretty soon she has forgotten what caused her such pain in the first place. Better to grieve and let go than to hold on and silently fume forever. For this I am proud of her. Champion alligator wrestlers let go with adept speed.

When I first learned to train adult learners, I discovered that evaluations from a class or an audience represented what statisticians called a bell curve. It is statistically true that some people will adore the training, while some people will hate the training. A trainer learns to focus on the majority in between the two extremes. It seems to me that life itself is a bell curve. We have gains and we have losses. We suffer trials and disasters but we also celebrate loving relationships and moments of triumphant success. We harbor defects and lack abilities but we also possess incredible talents and innate gifts. Our battles with life's alligators mimic this bell curve; we blast away a few, a few blast us away, but mostly we experience moderate successes and moderate failures—somewhere in the middle. We lose to the alligator when we compare our losses to the gains of others, or when we refuse to recognize our Spiritual connection. We beat the alligator when we acknowledge our past, embrace our present, and dream about our future.

In the end, the alligators really just represent life's gifts. The tragedies we survived, the problems we solved, and the obstacles we overcame bring us skills, insight, and wisdom. Some of the most gracious, successful women in this lifetime have been women with overwhelming losses. All of these women, having suffered the ravages of their own personal alligator battles, reached out to other women, sharing themselves, their talents, and their wisdom. Your stories, too, will convey comfort, humor, and yes, wisdom. Start with a simple covered dish dinner party. Reach across generations, ethnic backgrounds, and class distinctions. Your sisters are waiting…let the stories begin!

Dinner Questions

❑ How have you learned to cope with your losses?
❑ How have your alligators brought you gifts in your life?

My friend, Ravonda Dalton-Rann, wrote this poem
after attending the Presbyterian Women's Spiritual Retreat
in Winston-Salem, North Carolina.

A Woman's Place

Take me to a place
Where women gather

Where the air is sharp
And light
Where God and the Madonna
Merge into a Holy union

Take me to a place
Where women gather

Where wars are won
Against poverty
Against abuse
And
Against any storm of life

Take me to a place
Where women gather

Where water is purified
Just because your mother poured
it
In God's name

Take me
To a place
Where women gather

I come from a long line of
God-fearing
Feisty
Maverick
Spiritual
Medicine-making
Child-rearing
Define the family by relationship
Head-strong
Village mentality
Bonded
Savvy
So eccentric that people called
them crazy
Put the family first
Seeing and reading the signs
In nature
Air
Dogs
Worms
Birds
Horses
Chicken
Corn
And
Yes, tobacco

Beautiful
African-American women
who loved many
European-American women

So God
Please
Take
Me
To
A
Place
Where
Women
Gather

Like many of you
I rose early this morning
And walked outside
Looking and listening
For my red bird
To sing my song of the day

It was the birth of morning
Just when the dark
Meets the dawn
Like a razor

When I realized it was still dark
I wondered if this winged angel
Would sing

And to my delight

She did
And many of her sisters joined
her
In a simple song
That was deep in rhythm

Take me to a place where
women are gathering

This poem is supposed to be a
"welcome"

But the birds did that for me
Like all our ancestors
Who came flowing like the tide
Voluntarily
And
Involuntarily

We
Are
Here

On the same ark

Beginning
Again

We have come here
At this point
In time
Answering one call
With one purpose

To do something that comes so
natural to us
Whether we have done it
physically
Or not

We have gathered
To give birth
To nurture
To read and to raise

Our knowledge of God
And learn more about His and
Her
Purpose in our lives

And because we are women
We will take those lessons home
with us
And teach
Others

Welcome
Sisters

To this place where
women have gathered
In name of the Mother/Father
God

AMEN

For information about Ana's uplifting, fun programs, contact:

Ana Tampanna
Ph. 336-765-2886
Fax: 336-765-9799
Email: Tampanna@mindspring.com
2670 Belwick Dr.
Winston-Salem, NC 27106

"Ana had her finger on the pulse of the audience; she got through to them, she reached their soul, and also made them laugh."

—BOB MORRIS, TECHNICAL SPECIALIST
WAKE FOREST UNIVERSITY

SUGGESTED READING

A Course in Miracles, Foundation for Inner Peace, Library of Congress Catalog Number 76-20363, 1975.

Angelou, Maya. *I Know Why the Caged Bird Sings*. New York: Oxford University Press, 1970.

_____. *The Heart of a Woman*. New York: Random House, 1997.

Breathnach, Sarah Ban. *Something More: Excavating Your Authentic Self*. New York: Warner Books, 1998.

Cameron, Julie. *The Artist's Way*. Los Angeles, CA: Jeremy P. Tarcher/Perigee, 1992.

Chideya, Farai. *The Color of Our Future:Race for the 21st Century*. New York: William Morrow, 1999.

Coey, Nancy. *Finding Gifts in Everyday Life*. Raleigh, NC: Sweetwater Press, 1995.

Cohen, Alan. *The Dragon Doesn't Live Here Anymore: Loving Fully, Living Freely*. Somerset, NJ: Alan Cohen Publications, 1981.

Diamant, Anita. *The Red Tent*. New York: Picador USA, 1998.

Duerk, Judith. *Circle of Stones: Woman's Journey to Herself*. Philadelphia: Innisfree Press, 1999.

Fulghum, Robert. *From Beginning to End: The Rituals of Our Lives*. New York: Villard Books, 1997.

Gotsch, Gwen and Torgus, Judy, eds. *The Womanly Art of Breast Feeding*. Franklin Park, IL: La Leche League International, 1991.

Hopson, Darlene Powell and Derek S. *Raising the Rainbow Generation*. New York: Simon and Schuster Publishers, 1993.

Jones, Laurie Beth. *The Path: Creating Your Mission Statement for Work and Life*. New York: Hyperion, 1996.

Kensington Ladies' Erotica Society. *The Ladies Own Erotica: Tales, Recipes, and Other Mischiefs by Older Women*. Berkely, CA: 10 Speed Press, 1984.

Kübler-Ross, Elisabeth. *On Death and Dying*. New York: MacMillan Publishing Co., 1969.

Louden, Jennifer. *The Woman's Retreat Book*. San Francisco: Harper, 1997.

Lunardini, Christine and Adams, Bob. *What Every American Should Know about Women's History*. Holbrook, Ma: Bob Adams, Inc., 1994.

Maine, Margo, Ph.D. *Body Wars: Making Peace with Women's Bodies*. Carlsbad, Ca.: Gürze Books, 2000.

Marotta, Priscilla V., Ph.D. *Power and Wisdom: The New Path for Women*. Plantation, Fl: Women of Wisdom (wwwwomenofwisdom.com,), 1999.

McWilliams, John-Roger and Peter. *You Can't Afford the Luxury of a Negative Thought*. Los Angeles: Prelude Press, 1991.

Perry, Joan. *A Girl Needs Cash: Banish the White Knight Myth and Take Charge of Your Financial Life*. New York: Times Business, 1997.

Pipher, Mary. *Reviving Ophelia: Saving the Selves of Adolescent Girls*. New York: Ballantine Books, 1994.

Rosemergy, Jim. *A Daily Guide to Spiritual Living*. Unity Village, MO: Unity Books, 1991.

Sadker, Myra and David. *Failing at Fairness: How America's Schools Cheat Girls*. New York: MacMillan Publishing Co., 1993.

SARK. *Succulent Wild Woman, Dancing with Your Wonder-full Self*. New York: Fireside Books, 1997.

Schaef, Anne Wilson. *Women's Reality*. Minneapolis, MN: Winston Press, 1981.

Vanzant, Iyanla. *Faith in the Valley: Lessons for Women on the Journey to Peace*. New York: Fireside, 1996.

Recommended for Daily Journaling:

Master Mind Journal. Church of Today, PO Box 280, Warren, MI, 48090-0280.

Give the gift of inspiration, connection, and laughter to women you care about

Order on-line at: www.alligatorqueen.com

CHECK YOUR LEADING BOOKSTORE OR ORDER HERE

❏ **YES**, I want _____ copies of *The Womanly Art of Alligator Wrestling* at $16.95 each, plus $4 shipping per book (North Carolina residents please add $1.10 sales tax per book). Canadian orders must be accompanied by a postal money order in U.S. funds. Allow 15 days for delivery.

❏ **YES**, I am interested in having Ana Tampanna speak or give a seminar to my company, association, or organization. Please send information.

My check or money order for $_____ is enclosed.

Please charge my ❏ Visa ❏ MasterCard
                   ❏ Discover ❏ American Express

Name_____

Organization _____

Address _____

City/State/Zip _____

Phone_____ E-mail _____

Card # _____

Exp. Date_____ Signature _____

Please make your check payable and return to:
Silsby Publishing Company
2670 Belwick Drive
Winston-Salem, NC 27106

Call your credit card order to: 888-412-0065
Fax: 336-765-9799